PIONEERS IN EARLY CHILDHOOD EDUCATION

D1236075

Rachel and Margaret McMillan, Maria Montessori and Susan Isaacs have had a major impact on contemporary early years curriculum theory and practice. This new book introduces students and practitioners to the ideas, philosophies and writings of these key thinkers in early childhood education and shows how they relate to quality early years provision today.

The book explores the influences that shaped the ideas, values and beliefs of each pioneer and clearly demonstrates how they have each contributed to our knowledge of young children's learning and development. It then examines these in the context of current policy to highlight the key ideas that practitioners should consider when reflecting on their own practice.

Features include:

- Summaries of each pioneer's ideas and their influence on contemporary practice
- Practical examples to illustrate key principles
- Reflective questions to encourage practitioners to develop and improve their own practice.

Written to support the work of all those in the field of early childhood education, this book will be invaluable to students and practitioners who wish to fully understand the lasting legacies of these four influential women.

Patricia Giardiello is Senior Lecturer in Early Childhood Education at Liverpool Hope University, UK.

PIONEERS IN EARLY CHILDHOOD EDUCATION

The roots and legacies of Rachel
and Margaret McMillan,
Maria Montessori
and Susan Isaacs

Patricia Giardiello

Routledge
Taylor & Francis Group

LONDON AND NEW YORK

First published 2014
by Routledge
2 Park Square, Milton Park, Abingdon, Oxon OX14 4RN

Simultaneously published in the USA and Canada
by Routledge
711 Third Avenue, New York, NY 10017

Routledge is an imprint of the Taylor & Francis Group, an informa business

British Library Cataloguing in Publication Data
A catalogue record for this book is available from the British Library

Library of Congress Cataloging-in-Publication Data
Giardiello, Patricia.
Pioneers in early childhood education : the roots and legacies of
Rachel and Margaret McMillan, Maria Montessori and Susan Isaacs /
Patricia Giardiello.
    pages cm
1. Early childhood educators. 2. McMillan, Rachel, 1859–1917.
3. McMillan, Margaret, 1860–1931. 4. Montessori, Maria, 1870–1952.
5. Isaacs, Susan Sutherland Fairhurst, 1885–1948. 6. Education and state—
Great Britain. I. Title.
LB1775.6.G53 2013
372.21–dc23   2013008626

ISBN: 978-0-415-63781-7 (hbk)
ISBN: 978-0-415-63782-4 (pbk)
ISBN: 978-0-203-08430-4 (ebk)

Typeset in Bembo
by Cenveo Publisher Services

MIX
Paper from
responsible sources
FSC
www.fsc.org   FSC® C013604

Printed and bound by CPI Group (UK) Ltd, Croydon, CR0 4YY

To all my family for their love and encouragement

CONTENTS

List of illustrations   *viii*

Introduction   1

PART I
The early influences   **7**

1 From Plato to Froebel   9

PART II
A history of connections in early childhood
education: four key women pioneers – their
roots and legacies   **51**

2 Rachel and Margaret McMillan   53

3 Maria Montessori   78

4 Susan Isaacs   93

5 The pioneers' legacies to UK and international
   policy on early childhood education   122

References   *139*
Index   *156*

ILLUSTRATIONS

Figures

1.1   Wilderspin's galleried infant schoolroom at Spitalfields
      (*Source*: Froebel Archive for Childhood Studies at Archives
      & Special Collections, University of Roehampton)   39
4.1   The full-page advertisement that appeared in the
      New Statesman (as cited in Gardner, 1969)   101

Tables

1.1   The key ideas of Plato, Aristotle, and Quintilian   10
1.2   The key ideas of Luther and Comenius   23
1.3   The key ideas of Locke and Rousseau   29
1.4   The key ideas of Pestalozzi, Owen, and Wilderspin   40
1.5   The key ideas of Froebel   48
5.1   The key ideas of the McMillan sisters, Montessori, and Isaacs   128

INTRODUCTION

> There is no 'history for the sake of history' here, rather a reflection on some lessons which might be learned in order to understand the present state of early childhood education and how it has come to what it is.
>
> *(Nutbrown, Clough, & Selbie, 2008: 17)*

Ensuring that young children have the best start in life is a national and international priority as can be seen in the plethora of research and government policy initiatives and early childhood programme development around the world in recent years. There is a widely held view that providing quality early childhood education can compensate for disadvantage and provide equality of opportunity for all children who access it. As a consequence, early childhood education operates within a climate of intense scrutiny and on-going debates about how best to provide optimum learning opportunities. Nevertheless, there is the risk that while policymakers and practitioners are actively engaged with guiding and implementing current decisions about practice and provision, less and less time is given to reflecting on where ideas and concepts about early childhood education began and how they have been shaped by those in the past. Amidst current preoccupations, it is easy to lose sight of the fact that although at the turn of the twenty-first century in England there was, for the first time, a key stage in state-funded education for the under-fives, it was at the end of the nineteenth and the first half of the twentieth century that education for the under-sevens made the greatest strides. For example: 'The First World War (1914–18) gave considerable impetus to the development of public involvement in day care provision adding over 100 day care centres outside the formal schooling system across the UK' (Bertram & Pascal, 2002: 9). During this period the McMillan sisters in Deptford, London, Susan Isaacs in the Malting House School in Cambridge and Maria Montessori in Rome, Italy, all supported the concept of early childhood education as being a distinct phase and different from schooling. Although these remarkable women were from different professional backgrounds and were consequently motivated by differing interests and approaches, they all had one thing in common: the recognition of the importance of the earliest years in a child's life. The message handed down from Froebel and earlier philosophers is that early childhood education is different from the concept of traditional education with its emphasis on knowledge transmission, instruction and training (MacNaughton, 2003). This book is written with the intention of demonstrating the ways in which this powerful message was re-evaluated and re-shaped within the context of time, values and beliefs resulting in the bedrock principles that underpin current play-based early childhood education.

The continuing influence of the four women pioneers

It was often in the area of early childhood education and care, closely related to the traditional female realm, that women first claimed new roles for themselves. In the years just before and after the start of the twentieth century, when state welfare, structures and bureaucracies were still rudimentary and fluid, women began to exert a powerful influence on state definitions of the needs of mothers and children and the designs of institutions and approaches to address them (Koven & Michel, 1990). The McMillan sisters, Montessori and Isaacs were also part of the first wave of the women's movement and exerted considerable influence and were also part of the progressive movement within the field of early childhood education. They were well-educated women with sufficient financial resources to drive their ambitions for social welfare and educational reform, although Rachel and Margaret McMillan did not always have enough money to support their work. Despite being contemporaries, they never collaborated, operating instead within their own circle of friends and professional associates. The McMillan sisters, who are referred to in this book by their first names to avoid any confusion, carried out most of their pioneering work in London, as did Isaacs. Montessori was an Italian who began her pioneering work in Rome but later travelled extensively, mainly under political duress. Through their work, they shared a history of connections in early childhood education.

Contemporary perspectives

Contemporary early years curriculum theory and practice owes much to these four women who through their deeply held convictions demonstrated the transforming potential of early childhood education in relation to sociocultural reform and the rights and well-being of children. When reflecting on existing principles and patterns of early childhood education, such as those found in the current English Early Years Foundation Stage[1] (EYFS) (Department for Education, 2012b), it is evident that relatively little has changed in the values and beliefs of what constitutes good practice since the contribution of these four remarkable women.

However, the political context of early childhood education has changed significantly in the United Kingdom since the time of these women pioneers.

For example, 1998 saw the launch of the National Childcare Strategy, and, as part of a massive anti-poverty investment, central government began the funding of early childhood education and care. In ensuring young children's entitlement to quality provision, generic curriculum guidelines and a related assessment system, the Foundation Stage Early Learning Goals and Profile were introduced to all settings in receipt of funding, and a system of unified inspections began run by the Office for Standards in Education (Ofsted) (Anning, 2004). At the time of writing this book the current government's commitment to evidence-based policy development in early childhood education has resulted in an independent review of the previous EYFS (Department for Children, Schools and Families, DCSF, 2008) undertaken in 2011 by Dame Clare Tickell. Megan Pacey, Chief Executive of Early Education[2] said:

> the publication of this independent review confirms that across the wide range of early childhood settings in which it is delivered, the Early Years Foundation Stage continues to be embraced as a positive framework with sound principles that enable practitioners to provide education with an emphasis on learning through play, observing the child and planning from and for children's interests in partnership with parents and other professionals.
>
> *(Pacey, 2011)*

Within the modern context of the above statement can be seen the underlying commonalities between each of the women pioneers, which form the bedrock principles of effective early childhood education both in the United Kingdom and beyond.

These are:

- learning through play
- observing the child
- planning from and for children's interests
- partnership with parents and other professionals

What this book has to offer within the current context

The focus of his book is particularly on the way these four women extended the earlier philosophers' and educators' debate about the education and welfare of young children, especially in light of the published Tickell Report on EYFS: *The Early Years: Foundations for Life, Health and Learning* (Tickell, 2011), with its renewed emphasis on personal, social and emotional development, communication and language, and physical development, which featured so strongly in these women's work.

One of the dilemmas posited by Tickell when discussing the EYFS is how to retain what is really good about it but take away some of the bureaucracy (Tickell, 2011). Tickell made 46 recommendations designed to build on and improve the current EYFS statutory framework. Unsurprisingly, but no less alarmingly, one of the most sensitive issues Tickell uncovered through the review was the question of how children's learning and development should be supported in the early years. This stems from the continuing confusion among some early years practitioners on how to interpret the EYFS requirement for planned purposeful play. In supporting learning, Tickell acknowledges the importance of a balance between child-initiated and adult-directed activity but makes a further recommendation:

> that when working with young children, the exchange between adults and children should be fluid, moving interchangeably between activities initiated by children and adult responses which helps build the child's learning and understanding. Throughout the early years, adults should be modelling, demonstrating and questioning.
>
> *(Tickell, 2011: 3.33: 29)*

The dilemma over how to plan for purposeful play mandates a re-examination of the insightful contribution the key women pioneers made to the design of effective early childhood education.

> Understanding how play has been interpreted throughout history and how educators and psychologists view play today can help teachers of young children better understand the nature of play and how to use it in early childhood programs.
>
> *(Saracho & Spodek, 1995: 129)*

The structure of the book

The book consists of five chapters, divided into two parts. In part I, chapter 1 focuses on the four women pioneers' early influences from Plato to Froebel. Part II, which comprises the four remaining chapters, explores the roots and legacies of the pioneers. Each chapter begins with a brief summary of the ideas discussed. The text is punctuated with tables that summarise the main ideas of the early key thinkers discussed and identify their major writings. Below the tables are 'Questions for reflection' that ask the reader to pause and engage in an activity or debate that reinforces the notion of early childhood educators as being reflective practitioners. At the end of each chapter there are ideas for further reading.

The contents of the book

The book adopts a historical stance and, in Part I, explores the development of early childhood education as a discrete field through critically reflecting upon the early philosophers of the past whose ideas, values and beliefs were so influential in shaping the women pioneers' thinking. All four women had broad national and international experience and were well read in philosophy, classical and pedagogical theories and politics. Each of the women's approaches to early childhood education clearly embraced many of the key ideas and concepts identified as effective by the earlier philosophers and educators such as Plato, Aristotle, Quintilian, Comenius, Rousseau, Pestalozzi, Froebel and others as discussed in chapter 1. It is important to recognise the relationship between the women pioneers' own ideas and concepts and those of their predecessors in order to trace the emergence of particular trends and visions for early childhood education. By exploring the historical, philosophical, sociocultural and political contexts that have influenced the ideas of the early philosophers and subsequently those of the four women pioneers, early years practitioners are able to adopt a knowledgeable stance in conceptualising the direction of early childhood education.

Part II continues with the historical stance and explores the roots and legacies of the four women and the contribution they each made to early childhood education today. Presented in chronological order of date of birth, each of the pioneers' significant events and key moments at particular times of their lives are introduced and carefully examined, thus providing a clear insight into the way they developed their ideas on how best to provide young children with the best start in life.

The concluding chapter summarises each of the women's most significant contributions to early childhood education in the United Kingdom as discussed in earlier chapters of this book. The chapter then moves on to discuss the pioneers' impact on policy and provision in other countries and also considers their contribution to early childhood education from the post-modernist perspective provided by Foucault's 'regimes of truth'.

The central aim of this book is to provide an opportunity for early childhood students and existing practitioners to critically reflect on the perceptions and understandings about the purpose of early childhood education and its contribution to children, family and society: past, present and future.

As Foucault reminds us:

> There are times in life when the question of knowing if one can think differently than one thinks, and perceive differently than one sees, is absolutely necessary if one is to go on looking and reflecting at all.
>
> *(Foucault, 1985: 8)*

Notes

1 The EYFS specifies learning and development requirements that early years providers must deliver by law. The requirements include Early Learning Goals and educational programmes, organised into seven areas of learning: communication and language; physical development; personal, social and emotional; literacy; mathematics; understanding of the world and expressive arts and design.

2 Founded in 1923, the British Association for Early Childhood Education (Early Education) is the leading independent national charity for early years practitioners and parents, campaigning for the right of all children to early education of the highest quality (source: www.early-education.org.uk).

PART I

The early influences

1
FROM PLATO TO FROEBEL

Introduction

> Only by building on the past, and understanding the past, can we come to understand the practices of the present and seek better ways of working with young children.
>
> *(Spodek & Saracho, 2003: 3)*

In this chapter the imagination, ideas, values and beliefs of the early philosophers and educators from Plato to Froebel are considered in terms of how they influenced each of the women pioneers' approaches to early childhood education. It is important to recognise the relationship between the women pioneers' own ideas and concepts and those of their predecessors in order to trace the emergence of particular trends and visions for early childhood education. Through presenting previously unexamined connections, derived in the main from the early philosophers' own published writings, the intention is that students and practitioners will be able to situate key philosophical ideas and concepts, much in the same way as the women pioneers did in their time, within the context of current early years practice and provision.

The following discussions explore the key ideas of Plato, Aristotle and Quintilian in relation to children's learning, development and education. These are summarised for a quick reference in Table 1.1.

Ancient Greek and Roman philosophers: Plato, Aristotle and Quintilian

To begin to examine, within the European context, the earliest records of early childhood education, the following discussions start with the ideas of two ancient

TABLE 1.1 The key ideas of Plato, Aristotle, and Quintilian

Key thinker	Key ideas	Key writing
Plato (c. 428–347 BC)	• from birth the welfare of a child was the responsibility of the entire community • playful activity was the best way to educate young children and should begin early because of the importance of initial impressions on the formation of a child's character • made a clear distinction between frivolous and serious play and viewed it as an anticipatory socialisation process • links purposeful play to learning through effective pedagogical approaches – play and work were not opposed to each other • believed in a state-controlled curriculum to ensure appropriate skills were developed for both citizenship and leadership in later life	*Republic* (360 BC): devoted to explaining what kind of education is required for a just society
Aristotle (384–322 BC)	• divided a system of continuing education into periods of seven years: the first period is that of early childhood education • avoid formal study until the child is seven • learning should not be limited to youth but should continue throughout life • viewed early childhood education as a parental responsibility, particularly of fathers, for ensuring that play and physical exercise takes place • placed importance on early learning experiences in identifying children's individual talents, skills and abilities, which should be nurtured and enhanced • recognised the importance of nurturing good moral and social values essential for later lifelong learning	*The Nicomachean Ethics* (c. 334): an influential text on ethics in which he also explored the idea of lifelong learning
Quintilian (AD 35–100)	• a strong foundation in early childhood education is essential for later success • young children should experience the joy of learning so as to remain motivated to learn throughout their schooling and beyond • emphasised the value of observing children and recognising individual strengths • the very best teachers were needed at the start of a child's education • held high standards for teachers and the importance of careful training • saw dangers in the way children were brought up by parents, believing that if parents themselves were uneducated, this would have a lasting detrimental effect on their children	*De Institutio Oratori* (c. AD 93): about the value and purpose of education

Greek philosophers – Plato and Aristotle – followed by those of the Roman teacher of rhetoric, Quintilian. The ideas of these ancient Greek and Roman philosophers may seem very distant, but on closer examination their views on the potential of each young individual and the way in which society can foster it are not too dissimilar from those presented in the twenty-first century. R. Smith (2010) writes:

> since all of philosophy can be described as 'a matter of footnotes to Plato' (A. N. Whitehead, 1929) there can be no grounds for wondering if it is relevant to go back to the work of a philosopher who lived and taught in Athens in the fourth century BC.
>
> *(Smith, 2010: 159)*

Although there are many other ancient civilisations that flourished in the near East and North Africa, the first known discussions of children at play and its relation to early education made their appearance in the fourth century BC in ancient Greece (Frost, 2010). This period in history saw the rise of the Greek city state (*polis*), which was the world's first political and social community (Morris 1989). Although built upon the first true slave society, within the *polis* was the concept of the freedom of the citizen.

Plato (c. 428–347 BC)

Plato, who first debated issues of socialisation and morality, wrote that from birth onward the welfare of a child was the responsibility of the entire community, and since nothing learnt under compulsion is well remembered, learning through playful activity was the best way to educate young children. At the time there was great concern about the decline of moral standards in children, and therefore wisdom, courage, temperance and justice were seen as paramount virtues to be acquired through purposeful education (Dobrin, 2001). Then, just as now, education was seen as the solution to all ills in society.

Most of Plato's views on education appear in his best-known work, *Republic* (360 BC), which is devoted to explaining what kind of education is required for a just society. Socrates (c. 469–399 BC), Plato's mentor and teacher, was the formative influence on thinking at the time, and although he chose to write nothing down himself, believing that once the word was removed from the orator it assumed a new status of authority and objectivity, many of his ideas were recorded by Plato and other contemporaries in the form of *Socratic Dialogues* (Nutbrown et al., 2008). In the *Republic* Plato emphasises the importance of learning and knowledge and uses the allegory of the cave dweller's ascent into the sunlight to illustrate the journey towards enlightenment. According to Krentz (1998), to understand Plato's philosophical messages in the *Republic* necessitates close attention to the connections between education and culture (*paideia*) and the pedagogical approach (*paidagogia*) to teaching and learning. Interestingly, the ancient Greek words for education/culture (*paideia*), play (*paidia*) and children (*paides*) all have the same root. The central aim of pedagogy was to encourage learning as a form of play, which Plato viewed as anticipatory (or proactive) socialisation, in which children would develop the skills necessary to become future leaders in a just society (Krentz, 1998). Plato also demonstrates through his dialogues that education and the love of learning should begin early because of the importance of initial impressions on the formation of a child's character:

> You know also that the beginning is the most important part of any work, especially in the case of a young and tender thing; for that is the time at which the character is being formed and the desired impression is more readily taken.
>
> *(Plato, 360 BC/2008: 49)*

In relation to Plato's suggested design for early childhood education, from birth to aged 6, he makes the distinction between frivolous play, which is playful amusement and serves only to divert attention away from the intended educational goal, and the more serious form of play experienced through music, storytelling and physical games. For Plato, play and work are not opposed to each other – sentiments that are reflected in Montessori's approach to early childhood education. The way in which Plato links purposeful play to learning through effective pedagogical approaches also resonates well with those involved with early childhood education today, and his writings would not look out of place in the Early Years Foundation Stage (EYFS) (Department for Education, 2012b), with its emphasis on promoting children's welfare and learning through play. Jean Jacques Rousseau (1712–1778), who adopted many of Plato's ideas in his own works, called the *Republic* the greatest treatise on education ever written and urged those interested in state education to read it (Frost, 2010). However, Plato was not without his critics. Karl Popper, an Austrian philosopher of the twentieth century, argued that 'Plato recognises only one ultimate standard, the interest of the state . . .' (Popper, 1952: 107).

The state as educator

Censorship of the curriculum is explicitly recommended in Plato's *Republic,* and it is no exaggeration to assume, with Plato, that the welfare of the whole community depends on the education that the state provides for its citizens and potential leaders (R. Harris, 2009). The idea that an education system should fundamentally serve the purpose of allocating individuals to future roles in society has a compelling logic. On the other hand, this control over curriculum content could be construed as grandiose state planning and consequently an anathema by advocates, such as Popper, of a free and open society in which individuals can pursue their own goals for learning. The political question of who should control the curriculum has been settled in England and elsewhere through the introduction of the National Curriculum (1989). In the late 1980s in the United Kingdom teachers lived through the Conservative government's reforms of the education system driven by a desire for what Pollard (1989: 367) refers to as 'cultural homogeneity' and 'industrial efficiency'. The subsequent introduction of the 1986 Education Act and the Education Reform Act 1988, which provided the legislative framework for the introduction of the National Curriculum (1989) in England and Wales, heralded the beginning of the end of autonomy for the teaching profession. Following the introduction of the National Curriculum, there was widespread concern among early years teachers that play, as a vehicle for learning, would be marginalised and that early childhood education would be would be subject to 'top-down influences'. This was a time of great determination within the academic field of early childhood education and the community of practitioners who continued 'to lobby for play as an integral part of a broad, balanced and relevant early childhood curriculum' (Wood & Attfield, 2005: 18). Eventually, after over 12 years of applying constant pressure and the re-modelling of previous curriculum documents, there is now the Early Years Foundation Stage (EYFS) (Department for Education, 2012b), which enshrines a statutory commitment to play-based provision and clearly reflects the bedrock principles of the four women pioneers' vision for early childhood education.

Plato devoted a great deal of time in his writings in regards to education of the child. On the basis of his view that the state should take responsibility for the child's future role as a leader and citizen, he most probably would have approved of the EYFS, as it serves the youngest children well, mandates specific learning and development goals under the guidance of specially trained practitioners and recognises the central contribution parents make to the child's development.

Aristotle (384–322 BC)

Possibly more than anyone, it was Aristotle who influenced the fundamental characteristics of Western culture and society. He was extremely well-educated and considered to be a polymath. By analysing, defining and classifying the various branches of knowledge, he laid down the foundations for modern science and philosophy, dominating thinking until as late as the seventeenth century (Robb 1943).

Aristotle, initially a student of Plato, was very much a Platonist. However, unlike Plato, he did not write a specific text on education but discussed the subject in other works. He shared Plato's ideas regarding the importance of early childhood education but went further in arguing that children possessed differing talents and skills that should be nurtured and enhanced. For all his great learning, Aristotle was a very human person and, according to Robb (1943), was not oblivious to the social forces that shape a growing child. One of the fundamental principles of Aristotle's pedagogy is that education – particularly moral education – is largely to be attained through personal associations. In this way young children could experience learning that was of great social value and, when coupled with the learning of good habits, was the key to being a worthy citizen. In view of the central role education played in the development of the individual within society, Aristotle devoted a great deal of thought to perfecting an ideal system of continuing education.

Seven-year cycle

Aristotle believed that learning should not be limited to youth but should continue throughout life, dividing his system of continuing education into periods of seven years. The first period is that of early childhood education. This was the responsibility of the parents, particularly the father, and should allow for a great deal of play and physical exercise (Aristotle, c.334 BC/2009). Up until the age of five there should be no demands for study, but toys were seen as useful and even when older, children would be given ivory figures and letters to help with reading. There is some discrepancy in the literature about schooling between the ages of five to seven, mainly due to fragmented information available (Frost, 2010, Hummel, 1993). However, what is clear in Aristotle's writings is that at seven years of age children entered formal schooling until the age of 21, but at that point education was not completed. This is similar to the UK system (although the compulsory starting age for formal schooling is age five) where, if students remain in full time education, they can complete a first degree at the age of 21.

Lifelong learning

As can be seen from the following statement, taken from his writings: *The Nicomachean Ethics*, Aristotle was the first advocate of lifelong learning:

> But it is surely not enough that when they are young they should get the right nurture and attention: since they must even when they are grown up, practise and be habituated to them, we shall need laws for this as well, and generally speaking to cover the 'Whole of Life'.
>
> *(Aristotle, Book X/, c.334 BC/2009: 200)*

Aristotle's philosophy of education and lifelong learning has lost none of its relevance in today's global community. According to Hinchliffe (2006: 93), 'the current dominant concept of lifelong learning has arisen from the pressures of globalisation, economic change and the needs of the "knowledge economy"'. However, this is clearly distinct from Aristotle's notion of lifelong learning, which is not just about the acquisition of operational knowledge but more about the pedagogy of self-improvement. Aristotle recognised the importance of early experiences in identifying children's individual talents and abilities and the importance of nurturing good moral and social values essential for later lifelong learning. These ideals resonate well with the values and beliefs of the four key women pioneers and lie at the heart of effective early childhood education today.

Quintilian (c. AD 35–100)

Although Plato suggested a design for early childhood education, it was not until two and half centuries after Plato's treatise on education that Quintilian, a teacher of rhetoric in imperial Rome, wrote his seminal work, *De Institutio Oratori* (The Education of the Orator), published c. AD 95. He holds the accolade of being the first state-funded teacher in Western civilisation, and he promoted virtue through specific curricular aims and methods. Although building on Plato's dialogues regarding early childhood education, which were later expounded on in Rome by Cicero (106 BC–43 BC), Quintilian drew on his own experience as a teacher when formulating ideas about the value and purpose of education. He believed that a strong foundation in early childhood education was essential for later success and that young children should experience the joy of learning so as to remain motivated to learn throughout their schooling and beyond. In order for this to take place, the very best teachers were needed at the start of a child's education (Kasper, 2005). Quintilian emphasised the value of observing children and recognising individual strengths, thus providing a strong connection to Montessori (1912/1964), Isaacs (1930) and current early years practice. Quintilian maintained high standards for teachers who must be wise, speak well and be accomplished in all branches of learning. The importance of careful training, particularly in the initial stages, was the overriding factor in ensuring that children received the very best teaching, leaving a lasting legacy to initial teacher training today (Bennett, 1909; Pascal, 1984).

The effects of poor parenting

Quintilian saw dangers in the way that children were brought up by parents, believing that if parents themselves were uneducated, this would have a lasting detrimental effect on their children. These concerns, handed down through the ages, are echoed in current educational research projects such as 'the social evils' debate, a public consultation conducted by the Joseph Rowntree Foundation (Watts, 2008). A summary of the findings revealed that family breakdown and poor parenting were said to underlie many other social problems and to leave children without sufficient guidance or support (Watts, 2008). Today, just as in first-century Rome, parenting skills are seen as the key to children's achievements and further successful learning.

As can be seen, Plato, Aristotle and Quintilian, as regards the education of young children, have greatly influenced educational thought up to this day and their writings have become the basis of many educational policies.

Table 1.1 shows the key ideas of Plato, Aristotle and Quintilian in relation to children's learning, development and education.

QUESTIONS FOR REFLECTION

Reflect on your own childhood in relation to *play* and compare this to the childhood experiences of a young child that you know, as well as someone older than yourself. Are they similar or different? Share your findings with others in your group including what you learnt from playing.

Do you agree with Plato that nothing is learnt under compulsion? If you do, consider what factors may affect a young child's motivation.

Reflecting on Popper's criticism of Plato's ideas on state controlled education, compare the possible advantages or disadvantages of having a statutory framework, such as the English Early Years Foundation Stage, which sets out welfare and developmental goals for children five years and under.

In relation to Aristotle's views, consider what sort of experiences you would provide in promoting young children's spiritual, moral, social and cultural development.

Considering Quintilian's strongly held views regarding the teaching of young children, what are the skills, characteristics and qualities needed to work with very young children and their families?

Debate whether free parenting programmes, such as those offered by the government, support or stigmatise parents. Visit www.foundationyears.org.uk/ and critique the services on offer for parents.

Further reading

Else, P. (2009). *The value of play.* London, UK: Continuum.
Layard, R., & Dunn, J. (2009). *A good childhood: Searching for values in a competitive age.* London, UK: Penguin Books.

Having discussed the thoughts and ideas of Plato, Aristotle and Quintilian, the chapter moves on to discuss the contributions to early childhood education of Martin Luther and Jan Amos Comenius.

Two key philosophers and educators of the Reformation and Renaissance: Luther and Comenius

Up until the middle of the fourth century AD, the aim of Greek and Roman education had been to prepare children to become good and useful citizens of the state (Cuberley, 2005). From around the eighth century onward, the church gained control of education, and the salvation of souls took the place of social welfare (Thorndike 1940). In most provinces in France and Italy, education can be traced back to the time of Charlemagne (c. 742–814), King of the Franks and Emperor of Rome (Thorndike 1940). Evidence of church schooling for the poor children of the community is provided by the decree of the Third Lateran Council in 1179, which reads, in part:

> Since the Church of God is bound to provide for the needy, . . . in order that the opportunity of reading and making progress may not be taken away from poor children, who cannot be aided by the resources of their parents, let some sufficient benefice be assigned in every cathedral church for a master who shall teach gratis the clerks of the same church and poor scholars.
>
> *(as cited in Thorndike 1940: 401)*

The focus in this section of the chapter is on the development of early childhood education in Europe, following the fall of the Roman Empire in the West around 476 AD, and the emergence of the Renaissance, an essentially cultural movement emanating from Italy in the fifteenth century and spreading to the rest of Europe by the seventeenth century. Therefore, as a result of the political changes in Europe in the fourteenth century, changes took place in the spiritual and cultural environment, as well as in the views of its people.

In the rapidly developing towns of Northern Italy such as Genoa, Milan and Venice in the North and Florence in the centre, an early capitalist urban society flourished; the idea of a free and educated person held sway, and humanistic thought (human values and concerns) spread throughout Europe. The sixteenth century witnessed the rapid development of the natural sciences, and the invention of the printing press (c. 1440) widened opportunities for education and scientific study (Zufiaurre, 2007).

The Ancient Greek and Roman philosophies and ideas concerning education discussed earlier fell by the wayside following the collapse of Rome in AD 476, the period the early Italian scholar Francesco Petrarca (1304–1370) referred to as the 'Dark Ages' because very little was known about it (Poskoff, 1952). According to Poskoff (1952), because of a reawakened emphasis on classical scholarship, the fourteenth century marks an increasing interest in the works of Quintilian, many of which were dispersed around various monasteries in France and Italy. Petrarca, who spent a great deal of his life translating Latin manuscripts as he travelled around Europe came to own a copy of Quintilian's text (Poskoff, 1952). Petrarca's enthusiasm for this find ignited renewed interest among other scholars for a humanistic philosophy of education. Known as one of the great humanists of the Renaissance, Martin Luther stated that he preferred Quintilian to almost all other authorities on education 'for he gives a model of eloquence and teaches by the happiest combination of theory and practice' (as cited in Frost 2010: 13).

Martin Luther (1436–1546)

Martin Luther was an Augustinian monk and theologian in sixteenth-century Germany who brought about reformation in education as well as religion following a disagreement with the Roman Catholic Church. Hewes (2005) believes that the greatest influence on early childhood education today began in 1517 with Martin Luther, with his radical proposal of universal compulsory education and state support for schools (Hewes, 2005). After breaking away from the Roman Catholic

Church in the early 1500s, Luther had advanced the radical idea of state schools for both boys and girls. Consequently, although Luther did not work out an educational theory, he did work very hard to encourage an education for all (Sandsmark 2002). Luther's ideas also contributed to current pedagogical practices as he was a careful observer of children and proposed that methods of teaching be adapted to meet children's individual differences and stages of development (Frost 2010). The widespread developmental perspectives in early childhood settings today stem from Luther's ideas that children go through predictable sequential stages. To illustrate his conviction, Martin Luther wrote 'My [son] Hans is about to enter upon his seventh year, which is always climacteric, that is, a time of change. People always change every seventh year' (Luther, 1532/1889: 98).

To Luther, the right training of children was a divine requirement, and he believed that children's education should be liberal and pleasant and not subjected to the cruel discipline in existence in many institutions during this period. In his *Letters to the Mayors and Aldermen*, Luther suggests ways of utilising young children's natural activity and inquisitiveness in their education:

> Now since the young must leap and jump, or have something to do, because they have a natural desire for it that should not be restrained, (for it is not well to check them in everything,) why should we not provide such schools, and lay before them such studies?
>
> *(Luther, 1532/1889: 160)*

Furthermore, through these letters Luther advised public officials to take educational responsibility and emphasised schooling's political, economic and spiritual benefits.

Well-regulated schooling

Luther insisted that schools should be organised and inspected by state officials to ensure that teachers, many of them pastors, were educating children in correct religious doctrines and training them to become literate, orderly and productive citizens. In 1527, at the instigation of Luther, all the churches and schools in the Saxony region were inspected by Melanchthon[1] and two colleagues, who were entrusted with the task (Orstein & Levine, 2008). In this respect Luther planted the first seeds of what has become an increasing culture of accountability in which state-controlled organisational disciplinary mechanisms are now widely used. For example, in England, Ofsted, which was introduced as part of the Education Act in September 1992, holds not only schools to account but also a wide range of statutory children's services through regular inspections.

The printing press revolution

The early history of printing is another important factor in the spread of Luther's educational reforms and subsequent changes in the collective social consciousness

(Luke, 1989). What distinguished the sixteenth-century discourse on childhood education from that of previous times was the systemisation of those ideas into print (Luke, 1989). In Foucault's (1975) view, the way in which ideas are organised or systemised is as important as the content of those ideas. The mere fact that ideas are conceptually or materially ordered often provides a better understanding of the 'conditions of possibility' (Foucault, 1975: xix).

One type of printed literature to emerge from the Reformation was, in 1520, the catechism, a form of instruction that is still used today in Christian religious instruction in the form of questions and answers (Hampson-Patterson 2007). At the time Luther was shocked that many pastors and just about every lay person he encountered knew very little about Christian teachings. He decided to put in place measures to remedy this situation and, believing that the family had a key role in forming children's character and spiritual and moral behaviour, encouraged families to read and pray. To facilitate this he wrote and published in 1529 the *Lesser Catechism – Luther's Little Instruction Book* (McGrath, 2001). Luther avoided the use of Latin for this endeavour, preferring to use the vernacular, which was German in this case, thereby recognising the importance of attracting a wide readership. Luther's views on women's education still maintained traditional restrictions as domestic duties and child-rearing were still very much in the female domain, but Luther's desire for everyone to read in their own language meant that girls as well as boys had the opportunity to attend primary schools. The instruction book was a success and much appreciated for its ease of communication and was widely adopted within schools and homes of the Wittenberg region in Germany, raising literacy rates substantially (Orstein & Levine, 2008).

Comenius (1592–1670)

According to Compayre and Payne (2003), in the first half of the seventeenth century Jan Amos Comenius, who was a Czech theologian, carried on the educational thought of Luther. Comenius was a major thinker whose views on education foreshadowed those of Rousseau (Ingall, 1994). Comenius put forward the idea of a more democratic school system, which used the vernacular (language of the people) in the teaching of young children up to the age of 11. Comenius felt that nature establishes the order of development in a child step by step. This is shown in the following statement taken from Comenius's *The Great Didactic* (1628/1967), which also demonstrates his understanding of how young children learn: 'All subjects that are to be learned should be arranged so as to suit the age of the students, that nothing which is beyond their comprehension be given them to learn' (Comenius, 1628/1967: 115–116).

Phases of development

Building on Luther's ideas, Comenius proposed a system of progressive instruction adjusted to the stage of development the child had reached, education for all children of both sexes, rich or poor, and in doing so set the pattern for modern Western education (Peltzman, 1998). Comenius respected the individuality and differences among children, commenting that:

> There is as great a difference between the minds of men as exist between various kinds of plants, of trees, of animals; one must be treated in one way, and another in another, the same method cannot be applied to all alike . . . each one will develop in the direction of his natural inclinations.
>
> *(Comenius, 1628/1967: 115–116)*

Comenius organised his system of education into six phases, with informal education taking place within the family during the first six years of life; collective early childhood education provided for children from aged 5 to 6 years; formal education would begin with schooling at the elementary level for children aged 6 to 12; secondary schooling to the age of 18. Then there would be further education to age 24, with systematic learning continuing informally through life (Gundem, 1992). Comenius's emphasis on the importance of both pre- and post-compulsory education within his system of learning has most certainly furthered educationalists' understanding of the benefits of lifelong learning to this day (Knapper & Cropley, 2000). Furthermore, Comenius's principle for taking the child by gradual, logical steps from the simple to the complex resonates with the EYFS (Department for Education, 2012b) and its linear approach to learning.

The maternal school

Comenius called the first phase the *maternal school* (Comenius, 1633/1907: 68) as from birth to the age of 6 the child's first teacher was the mother. Interestingly, this terminology was adopted both in France (*l'école maternelle*) and in Italy (*scuola materna*) to describe early childhood education provision for young children. Comenius placed a great deal of importance on the education of very young children, believing that even the preparation of the mother during the child's pre-natal period is the *fundamental stone* upon which to build the whole system of subsequent education, so vital in the universal reform of human society (Capkova, 1970). Most likely the values and beliefs of the Unity of Brethren,[2] a persecuted religious group into which Comenius was born, influenced his thinking. Prevented from establishing formal schools, the Unity of Brethren developed family education, which included the very youngest children.

Importance of starting education early

For Comenius it seemed natural to start education as soon as possible, since he believed that is it easier to educate than to re-educate, and he produced a theory of education for young children entitled the *School of Infancy* to advise parents on the aims and content of education before school formally started at 6 years.

Comenius was far-seeing, and nothing was left to chance, as every aspect of the child's well-being received attention, including the value of play, learning through the senses and the use of first-hand experiences – learning by doing. In fact, Comenius would go as far as stating that children should be allowed to play with anything as long as it was not harmful (Capkova, 1970). For Comenius 'the object of education was the knowledge of things, knowledge of oneself and knowledge of others' (Comenius, 1633/1907: 16–22). It is also clear that Comenius held very young children in high esteem. The following tribute to childhood illustrates this well: 'Whoever has within his house youth exercising themselves in piety, morality and knowledge possesses a garden in which celestial plants are sown, watered, bloom and flower . . . how inexpressibly blessed are such parents' (Comenius, 1633/1907: 16–22).

Education for all

Having experienced the conflicts of the Thirty Years' War (1618–1648) with its destruction of entire regions throughout Europe, Comenius cherished the thought that educational reform, starting from the earliest years, would bring about a reform not only in Europe, but in the entire world (Suchodolski, 1970). Comenius's whole school system was based around what he referred to as *Pansophia* – Universal Wisdom – which became the dominant principle of everything he wrote. He believed fervently that if knowledge could be universalised, it could be taught to anyone irrespective of their social or economic position, religion, gender, race or nationality. Comenius clearly drew on Plato's ideas when developing his system of *Panpaedia* – Universal Education. However, the title of his treatise, *Didactica Magna* (The Great Didactic; published c. 1628) demonstrates Comenius's far-reaching goal of establishing an inclusive system of education which by its very nature differs from Plato's vision of an elitist nation state.

The first illustrated children's picture book

To facilitate the youngest children's language and literacy skills (both in the vernacular and Latin) and to develop their knowledge of the world Comenius produced *Orbis Pictus: The World in Pictures* (1657/1910). It is considered to be the first illustrated book of its kind for children and was in use for over a century from the time it was first published. The book contained 150 chapters and covered topics such as religion, zoology, inert nature, botany and humans. Charlton (1969) argues that the use of pictures to illustrate printed work was already commonplace by the time *Orbis Pictus* appeared in Nuremberg in 1658. But it was Comenius's emphasis on the systematic use of visual aids to link to children's learning and sensorial experiences of the everyday world that was innovative at the time. Through pictures alongside words Comenius wanted to arouse children's interest in learning and to motivate them for further schooling (Gundem, 1992). Young children's scholastic and recreational reading books today, dictionaries and encyclopaedias in particular, follow this approach. At the time, the impact of this book, which was later translated throughout Europe, could be compared to the introduction of audio visual techniques in the classroom today. Both the *School of Infancy* and *Orbis Pictus* were originally part of *The Great Didactic*, but so popular were these two chapters that they became books in their own right (Cuberley, 2005).

The father of modern pedagogy

The influence of Comenius can be clearly seen in the women pioneers' approaches to early childhood education, and his views are as applicable today as they were 400 years ago. He was, on the one hand, an objective idealist with theological and utopian ideals influenced by Bacon's *New Atlantis* (1626) and, on the other hand, a pragmatic educationalist with definite views on how his system of education should be delivered. It is the latter perspective that earned him the name of *The Father of Modern Pedagogy* (Iovan, 2010). Sadly, despite his lifelong work on establishing free education for all, Comenius never quite fulfilled his dream. His attempt to set up universal free schools did not materialise, mostly because of the religious uprisings that were taking place between Protestants and Catholics and his consequent need to keep moving from country to country to escape persecution.

Comenius's legacy

Perhaps Comenius's most significant legacy was the claim that each and every child had a right to free education (Watts, 2008). This right, further endorsed by Montessori in 1937 though the creation of the *Social Party of the Child,* has become enshrined in Article 28 of the UNCRC (United Nations, 1989) some 350 years later. Comenius's ideas are clear to see in the later writings of Rousseau (1762/1979), Pestalozzi (1801/1894) and Froebel (1826/1906), as they further developed early childhood education in the eighteenth and nineteenth centuries. Comenius also pre-dated Dewey (1916) and the four women pioneers through his focus on learning through the senses, first-hand experiences and learning by doing (Comenius, 1628/1967). In describing the path to knowledge and understanding Comenius states:

> The comparison throws remarkable light on the true nature of knowledge. Whatever makes an impression upon my organ of sight, hearing, smell, taste or touch, stands to me in relation of a seal by which the image of an object is impressed upon my brain.
>
> *(Comenius, 1628/1967: 44–45)*

Remarkably, Comenius also compared the brain to pliable wax; this is supported by recent scientific research on brain development, which shows the importance of stimulating experiences in a child's early years (Blakemore & Frith, 2005)

Table 1.2 shows the key ideas of Luther and Comenius, in relation to children's learning, development and education.

TABLE 1.2 The key ideas of Luther and Comenius

Key thinker	Key ideas	Key writing
Martin Luther (1426–1546)	• children go through predictable sequential stages • methods of teaching to be adapted to meet children's individual differences and stages of development • proposal of universal compulsory education and state support of schools • primary school education for both boys and girls • children's education should be liberal and pleasant and not subjected to cruel discipline • family have key role in forming children's character and spiritual and moral behaviour • encouraged families to read and pray together by providing printed religious books with text in the vernacular (language of the people)	*Letter to the Mayors and Aldermen* (1532): advising public officials to take educational responsibility while emphasising schooling's political, economic and spiritual benefits
Jan Amos Comenius (1592–1670)	• placed emphasis on the importance of both pre- and post-compulsory education within the school system of learning • children's learning to be led by gradual, logical steps from the simple to the complex • saw the preparation of the mother during the child's prenatal period as fundamental to subsequent education • from birth to the age of six the child's first teacher is the mother in the home • children should be allowed to play with anything as long as it was not harmful • believed in the educational potential of a universal language • produced *Orbis Pictus,* considered to be the first illustrated book of its kind for children • emphasised the systematic use of visual aids to link to children's learning and sensorial experiences of the everyday world	*The Great Didactic* (1628–1632): puts forward the idea of a democratic school system, which used the vernacular. *The School of Infancy* (1633): advising parents on the aims and content of education before school formally starts at 6 years of age

QUESTIONS FOR REFLECTION

Consider in what way Luther's methods of teaching were a precursor of developmentally appropriate practice (DAP). Read the DAP position statement on http://www.naeyc.org/positionstatements/dap/ and compare with the key principles of the EYFS framework.

What was your favourite book as a child? Did you have a regular bedtime story? Given Luther's emphasis on families reading together, what are, in your view, the benefits or otherwise of shared book-reading?

Do you agree with Comenius's sentiment that children should be allowed to play with anything as long it is not harmful? If so, within the confines of UK health and safety regulations, what would be the challenges and barriers for early childhood practitioners in providing children with risk-taking opportunities?

Reflecting on Comenius's idea of a child's right to a free education, consider the purpose of education to children and society. Either working on your own or with others, compare and contrast the schooling of young children from around the world. The Bernard Van Leer Foundation is a good source of information. Visit http://www.bernardvanleer.org/

Further reading

Bredekamp, S., & Copple, C. (2010). *Developmentally appropriate practice in early childhood programs form birth through to age 8*. Washington, DC: Naeyc Publications.

Guldberg, H. (2009). *Reclaiming childhood freedom and play in an age of fear.* London, UK: Routledge.

McBride-Chang, C. (2012). Shared book-reading: there is no downside for parents. In S. Suggate & E. Reese (eds.), *Contemporary debates in childhood education and development*. Abingdon, UK: Routledge.

Having discussed Martin Luther and Jan Amos Comenius, the chapter now moves on to discuss the contributions to early childhood education of John Locke and Jean Jacques Rousseau.

Key thinkers of the Enlightenment: Locke and Rousseau

The period in European history that is referred to as the Enlightenment or the Age of Reason (circa late seventeenth century to mid-eighteenth century) marked the beginning of new ways to understand the world, which later became known as 'scientific inquiry'.

Locke (1632–1704)

One of the key thinkers of the mid-seventeenth century was John Locke (1632–1704), an Englishman who was both a philosopher and physician and enormously influential in the progression of the European Enlightenment. Locke was deeply dissatisfied with education as practised in his own day, and his writings throw light on the aims and methods of the late seventeenth century.

Importance of the child's environment

The most general charge against schooling in the seventeenth century was that it failed to adapt its ideals to the profound changes taking place both socially and culturally, maintaining instead the system of instruction aligned to the medieval church (Adamson, 1922). Locke's critique of the status quo certainly shaped the theory and practice of his immediate successors, particularly in France and Germany, through the philosophies of Rousseau and Froebel. At the root of most of Locke's thinking was an inquiry into the origins and extent of human knowledge. In attempting to counteract Descartes' (1627) theory of *'innate ideas'* (the theory that certain knowledge exists within us either before or at birth), Locke took the opposite extreme position in his philosophy and held that knowledge is entirely the product of lived experiences (Hatfield, 2003). Locke's view was that at the time of birth a child's mind was a *tabula rasa* (blank slate) upon which experiences would make their mark. In his pursuit of truth, Locke believed that the child's mind was malleable and that, rather than being corrected from birth, it should be shaped or moulded. In *An Essay Concerning Human Understanding* (1690) Locke subscribed to ideas such as the importance of the child's environment and the significance of experience in influencing children's thoughts and behaviour, as can be seen in this statement:

> Let us suppose the mind to be, as we say, white paper void of all characters, without any ideas. How comes it to be furnished? Whence comes it by that vast store which the busy and boundless fancy of man has painted on it with an almost endless variety? Whence has it all the materials of reason and knowledge. To this I answer, in one word, from EXPERIENCE.
>
> *(Locke, 1690/1959: 311)*

Locke believed that first-hand experiences obtained through the senses – which he referred to as *Sensations* – triggered internal workings of the mind, which he called *Reflections* (Locke, 1690/1959). Locke explains that because children enter this 'world of new things' with 'minds disposed to wander', the first few years of life are usually used in looking 'abroad', by which he means that:

> Men's Business [in childhood] is to acquaint themselves with what is to be found without; and so growing up in constant attention to outward sensations, seldom make any considerable reflection on what passes within them, till they come to be of riper years; and some scarce ever at all.
>
> *(Locke, 1690/1959, Book 2: 8)*

A sound mind in a sound body

This attention to the mental thought processes of children from birth onwards led to a new field of study in the late eighteenth century, called developmental psychology, which had a major impact on the study of child development in later years (Sobe, 2010). Locke's theories on childhood and education appeared in a guide called *Some Thoughts Concerning Education,* published in 1692. The guide, which evolved from a series of published letters to his cousin Edward Clarke, also places strong emphasis on physical activity and begins with the now familiar adage 'a sound mind in a sound body is a short but full description of a happy state in this world' (Locke, 1692/1910, Section 1: 6). Influenced by the perceived robustness of children living in rural communities, Locke recommended that children from privileged backgrounds should be exposed to a regime of cold foot baths, few and loose-fitting clothes and a simple diet to counteract their pampered lives. Locke also provided guidance regarding the benefits of being in the open air, which resonate well with the McMillan sisters' Open Air Nursery Schools discussed in chapter 2.

Locke commented:

> Another thing, that is of great advantage to every one's health but especially children's, is, to be much in the open air, and very little, as may be, by the fire, even in winter. By this he will accustom himself also to heat and cold, shine and rain; all which if a man's body will not endure, it will serve him to very little purpose in this world: and when he is grown up, it is too late to begin to use him to it: it must be got early and by degrees.
>
> *(Locke, 1692/1910, Section 10: 9)*

Locke's writings were essentially aimed at upper- and middle-class families, but some of the lower classes took his writings and applied them to their children (Gay, 1998). In many respects Locke's ideas were not complex and could be readily applied, regardless of financial circumstances. In Locke's guide (1692/1910) can be found the sources of the four women pioneers' principles of early childhood education, such as health and well-being, freely chosen activities, learning through the senses and first-hand experiences as opposed to rote learning from textbooks. Montessori was clearly informed by many of Locke's key ideas in developing her own revolutionary method of education.

Views on discipline

He did not agree with physical punishment when it came to disciplining children, preferring instead the approach he called *pain or pleasure.* This took the form of intrinsic rewards such as verbal praise or stern looks on the part of the adult to show disapproval (Sobe, 2010). Capturing and maintaining individual children's attention without the use of physical coercion was central to Locke's philosophy; however, he also believed that children should conform to culture rather than make culture conform to children's nature. It is this belief that sets him apart from the French philosopher Jean-Jacques Rousseau, who is credited with being committed to the child's nature (MacNaughton, 2003).

Rousseau (1712–1778)

Rousseau proposed that children were born innocent with natural goodness and should be educated in a non-restrictive environment to encourage independence and freedom (Gutek, 2003). Although influenced by Plato's writings, Rousseau saw education as a liberating force rather than training for a specific occupational role (Oelkers, 2002). Rousseau asserts:

> What is to be thought, therefore, of that cruel education which sacrifices the present to an uncertain future, that burdens a child with all sorts of restrictions and begins by making him miserable, in order to prepare him for some far off happiness which he may never enjoy?
>
> *(Rousseau, 1762/1979: 50)*

The importance of exercising one's own 'free will' was a central political and educational concept in Rousseau's thoughts (Riley, 1991). For Rousseau, the first task of the educator was not to make lasting impressions on the young children's mind, as Locke proposed, but instead to allow children to be shaped through their own senses and inner voice (Gutek, 2003).

> Oh, wise man, take time to observe nature; watch your scholar well before you say a word to him; first leave the germ of his character free to show itself, do not constrain him in anything, the better to see him as he really is.
>
> *(Rousseau, 1762/1979: 58)*

Although in tune with Locke's ideas, this was a marked shift towards a more child-centric approach to education, later to be reinforced through the theories of Freud (1907) and Piaget (1954).

According to Compayre (1907), Rousseau was the initiator of what later became known as the 'modern movement'; he became the leader of most of the educators who came after him, including Pestalozzi, Froebel and Dewey. The term 'modern' in this sense refers to the constant and progressive movement that has to be considered as Oelkers (2002) states as an 'open horizon' for change, such as taking educational changes towards a meritocratic and socially mobile society.

Natural interests

Rousseau's novel ideas on education were presented in the form of a work of fiction called *Emile: or on Education,* which was published in 1762 and subsequently studied widely throughout Europe and America, even becoming a form of gospel in some quarters, much to the displeasure of the Catholic Church, which viewed it as heretical doctrine and ordered its destruction (Dent, 2005). Put simply, it gives an account of how Rousseau would educate an imaginary student from infancy to adulthood. However, the person who expected to be given a straightforward principle for education or a method to go by would have been disappointed. Instead, Rousseau proposed an idea that encourages educators to stand back with the minimum of interference rather than teach to definite aims of disciplines, ability and knowledge. In considering the role and aim of Rousseau's thinking, the concept of nature forms the transcendental starting point to Rousseau's system of education (Kontio, 2003). In other words, education should take its cues from nature, structuring itself around the natural stages of development all children go through. Like Luther and Comenius, he, too, identified individual differences in children and believed that educators should address children's natural interests and curiosity by favouring activities that foster judgement and reasoning and that play should be a central component of their lives (Frost, 2010).

Time and space

Time was another important consideration in Rousseau's *Emile*. He stated that the greatest, most important and useful rule is simply 'not to gain time, but to lose it' (Rousseau, 1762/1979: 93). What Rousseau meant by this was that children from the age of 2 until as late as 11 should be allowed time to develop and learn though self-discovery in the environment and the natural unfolding of the child's abilities without the pressures of formal schooling. However, as Løvlie and Standish (2002: 335) comment: 'in the ears of neo-liberal educationists, who strive for efficiency and excellence in schools, such a precept sounds utterly irrelevant and even irresponsible'. Rousseau did not see education as conforming to the dictates of society but, rather, as the medium through which to reform society. From a contemporary perspective, education that is based upon a 'conforming to society' position prepares children for the adult world through organising learning that is considered to be the most valuable and significant in their society However, a 'reforming society position', which stems from the ideas not just of Rousseau and Comenius before him but of others, such as Pestalozzi and Froebel in the late eighteenth and early nineteenth centuries, rests on the belief that education should produce an autonomous, self-governing and morally rational being ready to participate fully in society on reaching adulthood (MacNaughton, 2003).

Rousseau's three principles

Rousseau's lasting legacy is that three principles of contemporary education were established: natural growth and development, the child's active involvement in education and individuality (Hewes, 2005). He also advocated sensory training and using objects to study instead of symbols. Although at the time these principles were not implemented by many teachers, they did arouse discussion and they have influenced early childhood education ever since (Hewes, 2005).

Although at the time they were unaware of what was to come, both Locke's and Rousseau's ideas instigated the initial rumblings of the French Revolution, a period of great social and political unrest, which began in 1789.

Table 1.3 shows the key ideas of Locke and Rousseau in relation to children's learning, development and education.

TABLE 1.3 The key ideas of Locke and Rousseau

Key thinker	Key ideas	Key writing
John Locke (1632–1704)	• a child's mind is a *tabula rasa* (blank slate) upon which experiences make their mark • importance of the child's environment and experiences in influencing their thoughts and behaviour • placed emphasis on physical activity and popularised the phrase 'a sound mind in a sound body . . .' first coined by the poet Juvenal in Ancient Rome • learning through the senses, and first-hand experiences as opposed to rote learning from books • gave attention to the mental thought processes of children from birth onwards, which led to the later field of developmental psychology • disagreed with physical punishment, preferring the use of intrinsic motivation • believed that children should conform to culture rather than make culture conform to children's nature (Rousseau took opposing view)	*Some Thoughts Concerning Education* (1692): included education principles such as health and well-being, freely chosen activities, learning through the senses and first-hand experiences as opposed to rote learning from textbooks
Jean Jacques Rousseau (1712–1778)	• children are born innocent with natural goodness • education should take its cues from nature and allow time for children to develop and learn through self-discovery and natural unfolding of their abilities • play being a central component of children's lives • child-centric approach to education in which the educator should allow children to be shaped through their own senses and inner voice • advocated sensory training and using objects to study instead of symbols • education as a medium with which to reform society	*'Emile: or on Education'* (1762): presented profound ideas on education as a liberating force based on a fictitious child's experiences

QUESTIONS FOR REFLECTION

In relation to the opposing views of Locke and Rousseau regarding the purpose of education in society, whose ideas do you favour? Provide reasons and share with a colleague or peer.

What research evidence is now available to dispute Locke's view of the child's mind as a *tabula rasa*?

What are your views on children being allowed to shape their own learning? Are you able to draw on any examples from practice to illustrate the points you make?

Reflect on your own experience in early childhood settings and consider whether or not children are able to complete an activity or task in their own time. How do routines within settings impact on children's use of time and space?

In relation to Locke's emphasis on a sound body and mind, consider what impact health and well-being has on children's lives in developed and developing nations. Visit http://www.unicef.org.uk/Latest/Publications/child-wellbeing-progress/ to read the latest reports

Further reading

Bradshaw, J., & Mayhew, E. (2011). *The well-being of children in the UK*. The University of Bristol, UK: The Policy Press.
McDowell Clark, R. (2010). *Childhood in society for early childhood studies*. Exeter, UK: Learning Matters.
MacNaughton, G. (2003). *Shaping early childhood*. Maidenhead, UK: Open University Press.

Having discussed the thoughts of Locke and Rousseau on early childhood and their views on education, this chapter now moves on to discuss the contributions of Pestalozzi, Owen and Wilderspin to early childhood education.

Pestalozzi (1746–1827)

Johann Heinrich Pestalozzi, a Swiss–Italian educator, was greatly influenced by Rousseau's ideas and set about putting them into practice by designing an educational method that took him a lifetime to implement effectively. *Émile* was to remain his bedside book throughout his life, and a year before his death he was still praising its author as the educational key player of the old world and the new (Soëtard, 1994).

Pestalozzi presented his own ideas on education in *Leonard and Gertrude,* published in 1780, in which he discusses education as being central to the 'regeneration of a community' (Nutbrown et al., 2008: 9). During Pestalozzi's time Switzerland was the centre for many progressive and innovative cultural and literary ideas 'as well as the focal point of progressive educational thought' (Barlow, 1977: 2). Thus began a new era in education when the ideas of earlier reformers were actually tried out and tested, which is now commonly referred to as putting theory into practice.

Education as social justice

Hewes (1992: 3) refers to Pestalozzi as the 'foster father of early childhood education' because of the way he gathered together previously excluded children of the poor and improved their appalling living conditions. Long before universal schooling, Pestalozzi and his colleagues set about overcoming the humanistic problems of educating large groups of poor and orphaned children who were considered even by social reformers to be uneducable, both cognitively and morally (Adelman, 2000). As Nutbrown et al. (2008) point out, this was a clear example of education as a matter of social justice, and the idea that children should have rights is nothing new. In Pestalozzi's pedagogy social reform was the prime motive of his work.

The Pestalozzi method

In the running of previous educational establishments, Pestalozzi experienced a series of unfortunate administrative failures, which were not helped by the political upheaval taking place in Switzerland in 1803 (Chernin, 1986). However, fortunes changed for Pestalozzi when he received a favourable report from the Swiss authorities regarding his pedagogical endeavours. Pestalozzi was then able to move to Yverdon in 1805 to open an educational establishment, which expanded rapidly and was named the Pestalozzi Institute (Chernin, 1986). The institute included an 'infant childcare centre (mainly for orphans), a boarding school for boys, a school for young men, and a pedagogical seminary for teachers' (Chernin, 1986: 61). This huge undertaking attracted many interested parties from all over Europe eager to learn from Pestalozzi's innovative teaching, which later became known as the Pestalozzi Method (Soëtard, 1994). In the early nineteenth century there was a great desire to experiment with ground-breaking approaches to educating young children, particularly those who were previously excluded because of their low social status (Chartier & Geneix, 2006). At Yverdon, Pestalozzi put into practice what were seen as 'innovations in pedagogy: self-activity through apperception, simultaneous teaching, group discussion, peer tutoring and the object lesson' (Adelman, 2000: 106). Pestalozzi was adamant that children must be given opportunities to be actively involved in their own learning through apperception, which is, put simply, the capacity to assimilate new ideas through ideas already acquired. He favoured unhurried teacher-led group discussions in which children could mull over newly acquired concepts and ideas about the world in which they lived (Smith, Smith, & Pergo, 1994).

The object lesson was a pedagogic means to put into practice Pestalozzi's principle of experience before words, which meant learning through activity and through the handling and use of material objects rather than simply through words or definitions – an approach that is closely related to contemporary constructivism (Gutek, 2000).

International interest

In the years following the Napoleonic Wars (1799–1815), Yverdon was visited by hundreds of curious inquirers, including Froebel and Robert Owen (see below). It is possible to draw parallels with the interest shown in Pestalozzi's innovative pedagogy to the interest shown in the Montessori Method (Montessori, 1912/1964), developed by Maria Montessori (1870–1952) in the early twentieth century and still attracting worldwide attention to this day, and the current interest in the Reggio Emilia Approach (Edwards, Gandini, & Forman, 1998). The Reggio Emilia Approach, which has gained international momentum since the 1980s, attracts huge numbers of visitors from all round the world who want to study the results of the work and commitment of Loris Malaguzzi (1920–1994), who left the legacy of seeing young children as competent and capable of co-constructing their own knowledge and theories through self-discovery in a stimulating environment (Malaguzzi, 1996). Both Montessori and Malaguzzi drew on the ideas of key thinkers of the past, as did Pestalozzi. What set Pestalozzi apart from others at the time was the way he researched his own practice with children – although Soëtard (1994) argues that this could also be a weakness, as he never detached his work entirely from himself, his life and his experiences. But on the other hand, as it is nearly impossible for anyone to fully detach themselves from their own values and beliefs, this is actually a strength, as Pestalozzi drew on his own pedagogic knowledge and understanding, beliefs and experiences to create a new way of educating for children's freedom and autonomous learning.

Fostering reflective learning and practice

Adelman (2000) declares that Pestalozzi made one of the most remarkable contributions to education through the pedagogic means of fostering reflective learning in children. Pestalozzi observed that each child learnt in his or her own way, drawing on direct experience, through reflection fostered by the teacher, and through discussion and reconstruction and problems based on children's developing interests (Adelman, 2000). Pestalozzi also tried to keep children's hands, hearts and heads in equilibrium and felt that there was definite danger in attending to just one of these elements (Soëtard, 1994). However, according to Brühlmeier (2010: 47), 'the precise sequence "head, heart and hand" occurs only once in the forty-five volumes of his writings'.

In October 1801, Pestalozzi wrote *How Gertrude Teaches Her Children*, a guide for mothers in which he refers to this trinity of words in many different ways in order to express his thoughts in a wider context:

> It is incomprehensible that mankind, does not begin to bring to bring out a perfect gradation of methods for developing the mind and feeling. . . as my [the child's] physical powers increase, by virtue of the laws of my [the child's] development. . . the first instruction of the child should always be the business of the senses of the heart.
>
> *(Pestalozzi, 1801/1894: 190)*

In the above quote Pestalozzi places greater importance on feelings and emotions than on the cognitive domain in supporting the child's development. Pestalozzi recognised that the path of development was dependent on social and emotional maturity.

Social pedagogy

Pestalozzi's principles of head, heart and hand remain central to current notions of social pedagogy. Furthermore, the social dimension to his work is nowadays closely aligned to the roles of developmental aid worker, teacher and community worker (Petrie, 2004; Smith & Whyte, 2007).

Pestalozzi believed that education can influence both social circumstances and social change, and it was these beliefs that attracted interest from all over Europe. Two such interested people were James Pierrepont Greaves (1777–1842) and Charles Mayo (1792–1846), both important English educators who, according to Lathom (2002), worked with Pestalozzi in Yverdon for three years and on their return to England were instrumental in spreading his ideas and techniques. (While at Yverdon, as well as teaching, Greaves interpreted Pestalozzi's works for English visitors.) In his writings, Pestalozzi recognised the importance of the mother in a child's life and the impact the mother–child relationship had on the child's development. In a series of letters addressed to Greaves in England during the period October 1818 to March 1819, Pestalozzi expressed his ideas on early education. Through the medium of these letters, which were published in 1827, he drew attention to the vital role of the mother in supporting the earliest stages of education and appealed to her sense of maternal responsibility. Pestalozzi also reinforced the importance of acquiring the necessary skills in the task of early education. In his last letter, Pestalozzi wrote:

> For an example, I might refer to one of the numerous instances. . . which a mother has devoted much of her time, and best abilities, to the acquirement of some branches of knowledge. . . that she should qualify herself for the most perfect education of those nearest and dearest to the heart. . . have here supposed the most powerful motive, that of maternal love; but it will be the task of early education to supply motives which at a tender age may excite an interest in mental exertion, and yet be allied to the best feeling of human nature.
>
> *(Pestalozzi, Letter XXIV, 20 March 1827)*

He also recognised the importance of a close relationship between the home and school to help ensure the child's success (Bowers & Gehring, 2004). With his emphasis on experiential learning, reflection and practitioner action research Pestalozzi led the way for proponents of his ideas to build on and refine further his pedagogical approaches.

Owen (1771–1858)

Among the most influential proponents and visitors to Yverdon was Robert Owen, a Welshman who took over the management of New Lanark cotton mills in January 1800 and ran them until December 1824. It was a large-scale development of the water-powered technology of the industrial revolution, boasting four huge mills and employing more than 2,000 workers, including women and children (Davis & O'Hagan, 2010). During the reorganisation of the facilities, Owen established the first British community nursery and infant school of its kind in New Lanark, where care, health and education were provided for his workforce and their children. Owen, often referred to as the father of English Socialism (Gorb, 1951; Miliband, 1954) – which is paradoxical, considering he was also a wealthy capitalist – recognised that caring for his workforce and their families led to increased productivity, and he saw how important early childhood education and care was in the new social order of the time.

Working together to reform society

Because of shared ideals, Owen was keen to visit Yverdon to see at first-hand how Pestalozzi managed to combine child-centred education with social enterprise, which was intended for both rich and poor children but particularly for the working-class children who would together socially reform society. According to LeBlanc (2000), Owen would have found the older children attending classes for up to ten hours a day, six days a week, with no exams or marks given out; children becoming proficient in handling carpentry tools, operating lathes, a printing press and book binding, far removed from the risk-averse society children live in today in the United Kingdom (King & Howard, 2010). Weekends were set aside for hiking through the countryside, swimming and ice skating, which the children would have prepared for in advance by reading maps and planning the journey, the older children guiding the younger ones, with the core subjects being mathematics, chemistry, physics, zoology and botany.

It was clear where Owen got many of his ideas from, and following his visit to Yverdon and other Pestalozzian schools in the region he was convinced that an educational system that contained representatives of all social classes had the potential to create not just a model village, but a new social system throughout the world (McLaren, 1996). Owen argued that the existing social order in Britain, which was a result of three major factors – rapid technological development, increased industrial employment and the growth of the factory system – was responsible for the physical and social deterioration of the working-class families, and that it was the manufacturing and business classes that had it in their power to change it through the provision of well-rounded education (Gorb, 1951). Greaves was critical of Owen's materialism but did acknowledge the British infant school movement's debt to Owen, 'the lever that was moved to move this immense machine', who 'stirr'd up others to fill up and finish the work' (as cited in Lathom, 2002: 61).

The first ever workplace nursery

For Owen, although education was crucial, its main purpose was the creation of citizens for a new society (Smith & Whyte, 2007). Clear parallels can be drawn to the current resurgence of citizens for a new society, which is once again, in the twenty-first century, a major issue for educators, governments and policymakers throughout the world.

Owen grasped the opportunity to test out his theories of social reform when he took over the ownership and management of the New Lanark Mill. Resisted at first by the community, Owen prevented children under 10 from working in the mills, and he accepted them at school from the age of two, effectively establishing the first ever workplace nursery, which enabled mothers to retake their place in the factory earlier and keep up the family income more efficiently. Seeing education as the main agent of change – reflected in the name of his school, *The Institute of the Formation of Character* – maximum use was made of the two-storied school building, with children using it by day and adults during the evening. Some 300 children were educated at the school, with boys and girls in the same classes (Gordon, 1994). The teaching methods and curriculum reflected the influences of earlier educational reformers such as Rousseau and Pestalozzi; however, it was also the influence of his own experiences that were to form the basis for Owen's own theories of education (Gorb, 1951). Owen had written about his ideas on social reform in a series of essays, 'A New View of Society, or Essays on The Principle of the Formation of the Human Character', and 'The Application of the Principle to Practice' in 1813–1817.[3] In his first essay, Owen, with a certain degree of self-confidence, prepares the way for the introduction of his guiding principles, offering an insight into the possibilities of bringing about social change on a national scale.

> The present essays therefore are not brought forward as mere matters of speculation, to amuse the idle visionary who thinks in his closet and never acts in the world: but to create universal activity, pervade society with a knowledge of its true interests and direct the public mind to the most important object to where it can be direct to a national proceeding.
>
> *(Owen, 1813: 17)*

Owens's experiment in New Lanark was of particular significance at this time in British history for of three main reasons: 'urban population growth: a growing interest in the purpose of education and the issue of social control' (O'Hagan, 2007: 3).

Owen's 'experiment', as he saw it, was successful in proving the truth of the principle that the character is formed for, and not by, the individual. Furthermore, Owen believed strongly that early influences were very important in the formation of the character of the child. In his third essay, which was a written record of the applications of his principles in the New Lanark community school, Owen stated that 'much of temper or disposition is correctly or incorrectly formed before he [the child] attains his second year; and many durable impressions are made at the termination of the first twelve or even six months of his existence' (Owen, 1813: 81).

Purpose-built learning environment

When Owen proposed to build an infants' school at a cost of £5,000, some of his business partners grumbled at the expenditure and foreseeable annual drain on profits and urged him to re consider. But Owen got his own way, seeing it as money well spent, and the school was built and opened to every child who had learnt to walk, at a cost of £2 per head per annum (Pike, 1963).

Owen set out specific guidelines and carried out regular inspections of the nursery and infant school. He believed that in order for the development of a well-balanced child, formal schooling should not begin too early, and when it did begin, there should be a large element of recreation and amusement. It was for this reason that children at New Lanark did not leave the nursery to attend the infant school below the age of five (Gordon, 1994). The physical layout of the nursery and infant school was revolutionary, with spacious, airy rooms and playgrounds introduced for the first time. Robert Owen's eldest son, Robert Dale Owen, provides a useful description of the New Lanark schools:

> Two large airy rooms were set apart, one for those [children] under four years and one for those from four to six. The last room was furnished with paintings, chiefly of animals, with maps, and often supplied with natural objects from the garden, fields and woods. . . the examination and explanation of which always excited their curiosity and created an animated conversation between the children and their instructors, now themselves acquiring new knowledge.
>
> *(Owen, 1874: 114)*

The design of the curriculum

Much of the curriculum consisted of singing, dancing, music and – uniquely for British schools at the time – playing. He discouraged the use of books but was keen to provide interesting and useful resources. These resources would not look out of place in any nursery setting today, and the idea of co-constructing knowledge together, which was to form part of Susan Isaacs's pedagogical approach at the Malting House School (Isaacs, 1930), can now be seen in the Reggio Emilia approach to early childhood education (Rinaldi, 2006).

Owen disapproved of extrinsic incentives, and there were no rewards or punishments; he believed that 'the children are governed, not by severity but by kindness; and excited, not by distinctions, but by creating in them a wish to learn what they are taught' (Owen, 1813: 9). The role of parents, particularly the mother in the early years, was stressed and they were encouraged to display kindness and affection and be good role models with regard to displays of kindness in manners and feelings (Gorb, 1951).

Parenting classes

Parent classes were held on a regular basis, and experts in the field of health and education were called upon to provide informative lectures and instruction. The school was free, and although attendance was not compulsory, most of the children attended, including those from neighbouring villages (Gorb, 1951). Social inclusion and early intervention, which are key aspects of current social policy in the United Kingdom, were clearly part of Owen's plans for social reform.

Indoor and outdoor learning

Owen, supporting the idea of free enquiry and rationality, based his opinions and beliefs on reason and knowledge rather than on religious or emotional belief (Owen, 1874). Owen also believed all children should be equipped to make rational judgments and be furnished with the facts, and he stressed the importance of informal learning 'which should not be solely confined to the four walls of a classroom but in the play-ground, fields, gardens and museums' (Owen, 1842: 10). In this way children would avoid knowing without understanding and be able to understand what they read (Hamilton, 1989).

Owen's significant contribution to early childhood education and community care is clearly acknowledged now; however, his methods were far too advanced for his times and aroused opposition because of a lack of understanding of his educational theories and principles and how to put them into practice (Gorb, 1951). What is now referred to as good early-years pedagogy (Moyles, Adams, & Musgrove, 2001; Siraj-Blatchford, Sylva, Muttock, Gildewn, & Bell, 2002) was not obvious to those teachers more accustomed to rote learning from books (McCann, 1966). However, Owen, eager to popularise his educational ideas, invited a stream of distinguished visitors and gave them all copies of his publication, *A New View of Society* (Owen, 1813). Most of the visitors had a professional interest, as entries in the visitors' book between 1795 and 1825 reveal a large number of lawyers, merchants, clergy, naval and army officers, doctors and teachers, including those from colleges and universities (Donnachie, 2000). This led to two further schools opening in London in 1819 and 1820, managed by Owen's teaching protégé, James Buchanan, and Samuel Wilderspin, who had taught for a short while at New Lanark (Turner, 1970).

Although Owen was the founder of the nursery school in the United Kingdom, it was Wilderspin who established the British Infant School System and in so doing shaped the development of infant schools for working-class children (Read, 2006).

Wilderspin (1791–1866)

Wilderspin set out his ideas for the establishment of infant schools in the guide *On the Importance of Educating the Infant Poor from the Ages of Eighteen Months to Seven Years,* first published in 1824. In the introduction, Wilderspin makes a reference to nature, but, rather than placing emphasis on early education as the facilitator of the natural unfolding of the child's mind, he presents it predominately as a corrective process: 'It is an old proverb – 'bend the twig while it is young' and it is the duty both in civil, moral and religious point of view to take particular care of the infant mind' (Wilderspin, 1824/1993: 14).

Wilderspin's influence spread rapidly: before 1819 there had been no infant schools as such in England, but by 1836 there were almost 3,000, catering for 90,000 children (Turner, 1970). Although the idea was well intentioned, children as young as two, attending these schools, would be subjected to long periods of passive instruction in arithmetic, reading, science, religious education and singing and marching sessions.

Efficiency, first and foremost

Wilderspin's galleried schoolroom, capable of containing up to 100 children, ensured that all focus was on the central authoritative figure of the teacher, which facilitated the delivery of his teaching method, incorporating simultaneous instruction and a considerable body of rote-learning – a far cry from the airy, spacious classroom and the key features of the curriculum devised by Owen, influenced by Rousseau and Pestalozzi (Read, 2006). The teaching staff was usually male, as women were considered too frail for the job of disciplining such large groups and standing before them to deliver lessons (Bruce, 2010). Note in Figure 1.1 how some children are standing up and holding their hands out in response to questions being asked about, for instance, an object being passed around, a place on the map or a picture from the scriptures. Asking children to put up their hands as part of a question-and-answer session is still part of the teacher's repertoire in schools today.

Compared by his contemporaries to Pestalozzi, Wilderspin adapted the 'Object Lessons' to a whole-group question-and-answer session to accommodate the large groups of pupils. However, Wilderspin disputed any comparisons, stating that any similarities were purely coincidental:

> Pestalozzi, I have understood, was led to the use of them [geometric shapes] by observing the wants of young minds, in a similar manner that I was myself. . . if two men look at the moon, both would see it round, bright and mottled. . . the probability is that views will coincide.
>
> *(Wilderspin, 1840: 44)*

The creation of such large galleried schoolrooms reflected the mechanisation of the factories and cotton mills, with their emphasis on efficiency and productivity. Wilderspin, adopting similar methods to schooling, was able to instruct huge groups or 'batches' of children at a time while exercising power and discipline.

FIGURE 1.1   Wilderspin's galleried infant schoolroom at Spitalfields (*Source*: Froebel Archive for Childhood Studies at Archives & Special Collections, University of Roehampton)

To some extent these influences still remain during school assemblies, whole-class teaching and even 'circle time' (Mosley & Murray, 1998), when I have observed children as young as four years of age sitting crossed-legged for almost an hour (Giardiello, 2006). However, in fairness to Wilderspin and his supporters, during the British industrial revolution schooling in itself had been a response to the need to manage a growing population, and within the discriminating space of the schoolroom the productive regulation of large numbers of pupils also required new methodologies (Deacon, 2006). The later introduction of easel-style blackboards and the use of teaching posts where children, grouped according to age range, gathered around a teaching assistant eventually led to separate classrooms leading off from the large schoolroom (Read, 2006).

School playground

Although it was first introduced by Owen, it was the school playground that was to become Wilderspin's lasting legacy in the architectural design of infant schools. However, rather than a place for playful activities and discoveries as realised in New Lanark, Wilderspin's provision of playgrounds was merely an extension of his firm religious and moral principles. The moral management of children's free-time periods was part of this, and the playground' was seen as a place designed for promenades in the fresh air, regimented physical drill and other 'useful' outdoor pursuits rather than as a place to play' (Armitage, 2005: 540).

A time of innovation

There was at the time a good deal of innovative and often improvised teaching practice, particularly in the management or otherwise of the youngest children. Arising from this was a new-found pedagogic force that claimed that children and young people could acquire both intellectual and moral rationality through the medium of class-based instruction and directed outdoor pursuits (Hamilton, 1989). This combination of a managerial and a utilitarian approach attracted a great deal of ideological capital that eventually brought the full-scale classroom system into being with the main aim of producing children competent enough in reading, writing and arithmetic to become useful members of the workforce (Hamilton, 1989).

In the sphere of children's services in the United Kingdom, it was Owen who provided a lasting legacy in the way he recognised the importance of combining education, health and social care for young children and their families. Owen did much to advance the notion of different disciplines working together, often referred to by professionals in the field as 'joined-up thinking', demonstrated in the development of UK Sure Start Children's Centres (Department for Education, DfE, 2010), which provide early education as well as care, health and family-support services for families with young children, including teenage mothers. At the last count in 2010 there are 3,500 Children's Centres, enabling over 2.7 million children under five and their families to access a range of integrated services (Fifth Report, 2009–2010; House of Commons Children, Schools and Families Committee, CSFC, 2009).

Table 1.4 shows the key ideas of Pestalozzi, Owen and Wilderspin in relation to their practical approaches to children's learning, development and education.

TABLE 1.4 The key ideas of Pestalozzi, Owen, and Wilderspin

Key figure	Key ideas	Key writing
Johann Pestalozzi (1746–1827)	• instigated a new era in education when the ideas of earlier reformers were tried out and tested – now often referred to as theory into practice • saw education as a matter of social justice and believed that education can influence both social circumstances and social change • believed that no undue pressures or influences should warp the development intended by nature, thereby preventing the child from growing to fulfil their inherent potential • fostered reflective learning in children through pedagogic means • introduced innovative pedagogy such as the promotion of self-driven activity through *apperception* – i.e. building on previously assimilated ideas; simultaneous teaching through unhurried group discussion; peer tutoring and the object lesson	*Leonard and Gertrude* (1780): sets out his vision for education as a means of regenerating a community *How Gertrude Teaches Her Children* (1801): sets out a method of teaching that was both playful and practical rather than didactic and authoritarian

TABLE 1.4 (Cont'd)

Key figure	Key ideas	Key writing
	• endeavoured to keep children's hands, heart, and head in equilibrium and felt the dangers of attending to just one of these elements • recognised the impact the mother–child relationship had on the child's development and the importance of a close relationship between home and school to help ensure the child's success • introduced the notion of being a reflective practitioner through researching own practice	
Robert Owen (1771–1858)	• strongly believed that early influences were important in character formation • recognised importance of combining, education, health and social care for young children and their families, establishing the first community nursery and infant school of its kind in Britain • stressed importance of parents, particularly the mother, and regularly held parenting classes to develop their child-rearing skills • believed that in order for the development of a well-balanced child, formal schooling should not begin too early; when it did begin, there should be a large element of recreation and amusement • revolutionised the physical layout of the school by providing spacious, airy rooms and introduced playgrounds for the first time • discouraged the use of books and learning by rote but keen to provide interesting resources for the young children and their teachers to discover, examine and explain together	*A New View of Society*(1813): sets out guiding principles on the possibilities of bringing about social change on a national scale
Samuel Wilderspin (1791–1866)	• created large galleried classrooms to enable the instruction of huge groups of children as young as two years of age and introduced the practice of instructing children to hold up their hand before answering a question • adapted Pestalozzi's 'Object Lessons' to a whole group question-and-answer session to accommodate the large groups of pupils in the galleried classrooms • aimed to produce children competent enough in reading, writing and arithmetic to become useful members of the work force • considered women too frail for the job of disciplining such large groups of children • incorporated the school playground into the architectural design of infant schools • used the school playground for regimented physical drills rather than as a space for play	*On the Importance of Educating the Infant Poor from the Ages of 18 Months to 7 Years* (1824): predominately an account of a corrective process in managing very large numbers of children from 18 months to seven years of age

QUESTIONS FOR REFLECTION

Reflect on Pestalozzi's trinity of head, heart and hand and consider the relevance in today's provision for young children.

What does it mean to be a reflective practitioner? Take some time to consider this and then share your thoughts with another person in your setting or group.

How would you go about encouraging reflective learning in young children? Identify opportunities and experiences that you could provide to help children make sense of their learning?

If you were given an opportunity to reorganise the layout of an early childhood setting, both indoors and outdoors, how would you go about it?

Consider ways of supporting young children in developing a sense of right and wrong so they understand why it is important to act thoughtfully towards one another.

Further reading

Ghaye, T. (2011). *Teaching and learning through reflective practice* (2nd ed.). Abingdon, UK: Routledge.

Porter, L. (2008). *Young children's behaviour: Practical approaches for caregivers and teachers* (3rd ed.). Baltimore, MD: Paul H Brookes Publishing.

Having discussed the ideas of Pestalozzi, Owen and Wilderspin and shown how they applied their ideas of education and social reform, the chapter now moves on to discuss the contribution of Froebel to early childhood education.

Froebel and the kindergarten movement

While Owen and Wilderspin were developing their theories on education for social and moral reform in the United Kingdom, early childhood education also began to establish itself in Europe. For a short while Hungary became the centre of early childhood education in Europe with the founding of the first nursery school in Budapest by Countess Theresa Brunswick, a student of Pestalozzi (Vag, 1975). However, it was when Froebel introduced the 'German Kindergarten' that the modern era of early childhood education began, with the concept of structured guided play as the cornerstone of children's learning (Manning, 2005: 372). To many experienced early years educators, 'Froebelianism is connected with the discourse on 'child-centredness', on the richness that 'play' affords the child in the construction of world knowledge, on the conception of unity in and through nature'

(Lee, Evans, & Jackson, 1994: 1). This can be seen in Froebel's *The Education of Man* first published in 1826): 'By this, in the period of childhood, man is placed in the centre of all things, and all things are seen only in relation to himself, to his life' (Froebel, 1826/1906: 97).

Froebel (1782–1852)

Friedrich Froebel was born in the village of Oberweissbach in the forests of Thuringia, Central Germany. Froebel's mother died before he reached the age of one, and his father, a strict Lutheran Pastor, more preoccupied with his duties in the parish, neglected the upbringing of his own son. Consequently, Froebel's early surroundings brought him into contact with nature, and he learned to love being alone in the woods with the streams, plants and animals and his own thoughts and contemplations (Frost, 2010). These experiences, together with a firm Christian faith, had a profound influence on his ideas of an early childhood education, which should be provided within a specially created environment where children could grow and develop in unity with nature and the inner connectedness of all life. However, it took many years of varied experiences before Froebel became involved in early childhood education.

Forester to educator

At the age of 15, having been judged an unlikely candidate for university study by both his father and his stepmother, Froebel became a forester's apprentice and began a lifelong 'religious' relationship with nature, discovering in nature the harmony lacking between people (Walsh, Chung, & Tufekci, 2001). Eventually, in 1805, following a period of study at the University of Jena studying maths and science and work in various jobs in the forestry department, Froebel moved to Frankfurt to study architecture (Walsh et al., 2001). The final career turning point in Froebel's life was when he met and was befriended by Dr Gruener, the headmaster of Pestalozzi's new Model School in Frankfurt. Froebel was offered a teaching position, and he knew at once that he had found his life's work; after five years in the classroom he was eventually to become one of the many scholars to study with Pestalozzi (Armytage, 1952; Manning, 2005). He was enthusiastic about what he had learnt at Pestalozzi's school at Yverdon and respected and valued Pestalozzi's ideas, even though in the formulation of his own educational ideas Froebel was to eventually take a different path (Read, 2003). Whereas Pestalozzi was instinctive and inspirational, Froebel was philosophical and investigative.

The Helba plan

According to Manning (2005), Froebel was driven by the question, 'What is the purpose of education?' To help him arrive at answers, he eventually returned to his homeland and opened his first school in Keilhau in 1817. In the early 1820s the growing popularity of the school necessitated the addition of new buildings. Despite setbacks that were not too dissimilar to those of Pestalozzi in respect of lack of funds and insubordination, Froebel pressed forward with his educational ideas on the reorganisation of his school system, which became known as the *Helba Plan*. Froebel envisaged a three-tier system, starting with a 'Development Institute' for three–seven year olds (Liebschener, 1991). Like Comenius, Froebel (1826/1906: 28) believed in an educational system that would provide learning opportunities lifelong – from 'cradle to the grave'.

In 1835, as Froebel's reputation grew, he was asked to take charge of a new orphanage in Burgdorf, Switzerland. He carried out careful and detailed observations of the many orphaned infants in his care, which served to foster a growing realisation that young children require a distinctive period of schooling that would match their developmental characteristics (Liebschener, 1991). From then on the care of young children became his life's goal, and he dedicated all his efforts to perfecting the education of young children (Liebschener, 1991). Inspired by the writings of Comenius, Rousseau and Pestalozzi, Froebel was concerned about education as the development and extension of natural human activities, and he searched for a word that would reflect this sentiment to describe his environment for young children, which he compared to a nursery where the gardener tended his young plants (Eichhoff, 1988). What became known as Froebel's educational innovation was ultimately named a *kindergarten*, literally meaning a child's garden in German, which was soon to enter the lexicon of languages around the world to represent a particular form of early childhood education (Eichhoff, 1988). Froebel opened his first kindergarten in Blankenburg in 1839; this included self-activity, exploration and imitation activities undertaken by groups of young children guided by a specially trained female teacher (Nawrotski, 2007). Froebel's decisive move towards the introduction of female rather than male teachers is discussed further on in this section.

The potential of play

The creating of the self through play and the 'self-activity' of the child, first termed by Pestalozzi, and now referred to by early educators as children's own interests, was central to Froebel's philosophy (Adelman, 2000).

As Froebel wrote in his treatise, *The Education of Man* (1826):

> Play is the highest stage of a child's development. . . and it is at once the pre-figuration and imitation of the total human life. . . It produces therefore, joy, freedom, satisfaction, repose within and without, peace with the world. . . Is not the most beautiful expression of child life at this time a playing child? – a child wholly absorbed in his play? – a child that has fallen asleep while so absorbed?
> *(Froebel, 1826/1906: 80–81)*

This was in stark contrast to the pedagogical concerns of schools such as those established or influenced by Wilderspin, with their emphasis on moral education, the fostering of early academic skills and traditional rote learning.

Gifts and occupations

Building on Pestalozzi's ideas on experiential learning and the use of first-hand activities, Froebel developed specifically designed materials that he referred to as *gifts* and *occupations* (Taylor Allen, 1988). Froebel used the three tenets of *unity, respect* and *play* to create these gifts and occupations, ensuring that they were familiar and comfortable for the young child to use, thus accelerating and enhancing their learning experience (Manning, 2005). The gifts were small wooden manipulative block-play materials that children used in prescribed ways, and the carefully elaborated instructions for their use signified Froebel's intentions to guide the child towards 'an understanding of the symbiotic interconnectivity between all persons, regardless of social status, with the world, the universe and ultimately with God' (Read, 2006: 306). A far cry from the intricate and highly decorated toys that children from affluent families were given to play with, Froebel designed unadorned gifts, each within their own little wooden box. To use the gift, the lidded box was turned upside down, so that the child began with the perception of the whole (Clements, 1981). Showing his respect for children in the way materials were presented to them, Froebel wrote that 'It is well for him to receive his plaything in an orderly manner, not to have them tossed to him as fodder is tossed to animals' (Froebel, 1826/1906: 205).

The first gift was a series of six woollen balls, each ball a different colour of the rainbow, to symbolise the unity and wholeness of the universe. The second gift included a wooden sphere, a cylinder, and a cube that symbolised unity, diversity and the mediation of opposites. The third to sixth gifts are known as the 'Building Gifts', used to develop the constructive powers of the child, which forms part of continuous provision in most early years settings today (Taylor Allen, 1988).

Through his detailed observations Froebel recognised that young children have a natural building instinct, and to 'make a house' is a universal form of unguided play (Froebel, 1826/1906). From these gifts the children would gradually progress towards building precise forms, each with a philosophical meaning, finally progressing towards abstract symbolism.

Construction, which forms part of continuous provision in early childhood settings today, owes much to Froebel's recognition of the value of block play in early childhood education. However, contrasted to today's often large sets of over 200 pieces or more – which, I have noted during numerous visits to pre-school settings, are frequently provided unsystematically on a carpeted area – Froebel stressed each time employing every single one of the pieces in the set using a ruled grid surface so that children learned flexibility, reflection and elaboration (Froebel, 1826/1906).

Froebel's initial studies in architecture and love of geometrical shapes led him to use the blocks to convey both structure and aesthetics (Clements, 1981). Frank Lloyd Wright (1867–1959), the famous American architect, remarked in his autobiography that his interest in architecture began when he played with the *Gifts* as a child. In the formation of the principles of modern architecture, Wright was a pioneer and a leader who readily acknowledged the debt he owed to Froebel (Clements, 1981):

> Presented by my teacher mother with the Froebel gifts then actually as a child I began to be an architect. For several years I sat at the little kindergarten table ruled by lines about four inches wide. The smooth cardboard triangles and Maplewood blocks were important. All are in my fingers to this day.
>
> *(Wright, 1957: 19)*

The *Occupations* designed for the older children included such activities as paper weaving, paper folding, paper cutting, sewing, drawing, painting and clay modelling (Saracho & Spodek, 2009). Froebel spared the children from having to formally learn to read, write and use numbers (often referred to as the 3Rs in the United Kingdom), but he believed that they would acquire mathematical knowledge and literacy skills by observing real-life forms, specific visual material, from play and by participating in social activities (Valkanova & Brehony, 2006). Although Froebel is primarily remembered for advocating the educational value of unstructured play based on self-activity, the means of regulating children's play through his *Gifts* and *Occupations* was key to the children's intellectual development (Valkanova & Brehony, 2006).

By adopting this methodology, children's creative imagination would be fostered through alternating between convergent and divergent thinking. Recent research studies, such as the *EPPE project* (Sylva et al., 2003), would corroborate the effectiveness of a balanced curriculum between child-initiated and adult-supported activities.

Gardening, music and actions songs

Froebel also linked his concept of self-activity to self-fulfilment acquired through gardening activities, which brought young children into contact with the soil, weather, plants and animals. Froebel also saw the importance of music, recognising that during early childhood music was not so much about nurturing talent but more about exploring the world in musical ways. Froebel's study of music in the home became the basis for his publication, in 1846, of *Mother's Songs, Games and Stories* (Froebel, 1846/1920). Just as the title suggests, it included action songs and finger rhymes, together with their musical notation, woodcut illustrations and guidance on how to present the songs as well as the meanings that could be derived from them. Froebel also incorporated didactic songs into the kindergarten that were often based on his *Gifts* and *Occupations,* which also mirrored everyday family life and relationships, such as sewing, baking and carpentry (Manning, 2005).

Home from home

For Froebel, the kindergarten was an extension of the home with the purpose of cultivating rather than coercing the child's nature. Accordingly, this necessitated a shift away from the idea of the teacher as a figure of paternal authority but, rather, towards the nurturing qualities more associated with women at the time:

Tending to children lay instinctively in the female spirit, argued Froebel, and also served the role of rescuing 'the female sex from its hitherto passive and instinctive situation, and through its nurturing mission to raise it to the same level as the male sex.

(Winterer, 1992: 301)

The time Froebel spent at Pestalozzi's school at Yverdon had deeply influenced his view of the significant role played by mothers in the early education of their children; however, in contrast to Pestalozzi, Froebel advocated a role for women beyond the home environment, which was revolutionary at the time. Furthermore, Froebel was convinced that women needed specific education and training in the raising of young children (Hewes, 1990). But this perceived role for women was ridiculed by the overwhelmingly male educational establishment, which served to reinforce the gendered politics of power at the time (Read, 2003). Nevertheless times were changing, and those people – mainly women – who cared about children and wanted to move away from an education system that prioritised information-giving and punishment as its chief objectives, openly welcomed Froebel's ideology (Woodham-Smith, 1952). One of the most influential women in convincing a sceptical community was Baroness Bertha von Marenholtz-Bulow, who, following Froebel's death in 1852, travelled extensively with Froebel's wife as an advocate for kindergarten education. It was through the patronage of the Baroness that Froebel was invited to speak to the Weimar court and to the Women's Union regarding kindergartens and the higher education of women for the purpose of teaching young children.

Kindergarten as a call to action

Froebel's kindergarten was not just a philosophy but a call to action and a political and social vision, which arrived just at the historical moment when progressive ideas with regard to young children were becoming more widely accepted (Hilton, 2001). Inherent in Froebel's ideas was a potentially subversive force, both in the education system it proposed and in the role it assigned to women, which blurred the boundaries between the public and private domain and led to their ultimate acceptance as paid professional workers in the field of early childhood education (Read, 2003). The call to action would eventually be taken up by Rachel and Margaret McMillan, Montessori and Isaacs in their development of early years pedagogical practices and provision. In 1904, Margaret McMillan would become an elected member on the council of the National Froebel Society (Steedman, 1990).

Froebel's educational philosophy, as laid down in *The Education of Man* (1826/1907), was very complicated and difficult to understand, but by paying attention to the early years as a special period of life with its own characteristics, Froebel was to lay down the foundation for future early childhood education (Vaughan & Estola, 2007).

Table 1.5 shows the Froebel's key ideas in relation to young children's learning, development and education.

TABLE 1.5 The key ideas of Froebel

Key figure	Key ideas	Key writing
Friedrich Froebel (1782–1852)	• believing that early childhood education should be provided within a specially created environment, thought up the term 'kindergarten' to describe a place where children could grow and develop in harmony with their natural surroundings • also introduced the concept of structured guided play through the specially devised *Gifts* and *Occupations*, which were seen as key to the children's intellectual development • observed that young children have a natural building instinct and recognised the value of block play in early childhood education • linked the concept of self-activity to self-fulfilment acquired through gardening activities, which brought young children into contact with the soil, weather, plants and animals • the study of music in the home formed the basis of the publication *Mother's Songs, Games and Stories* (1846); music was incorporated into the kindergarten's daily routine • aware of the significant role played by mothers in early education, advocated a role for women beyond the home environment • concerned to ensure that women, with their abilities in raising children, received specific education and training to enable a child-centred approach to learning and teaching	*The Education of Man* (1826): focused on the concept of child-centred education and advocated the educational value of unstructured play based on self-directed activity

QUESTIONS FOR REFLECTION

Reflecting on Froebel's view, what distinguishes early childhood education from other phases of schooling? Discuss this with others in your group.

What value do you or your setting place on block play? Can you identify the developmental aspects of playing with blocks?

What does a child-centred approach look like in practice, including the role of the adult?

Have the ideas of the early key thinkers, as discussed in this chapter, influenced the way you work with children and their families? Can you provide any examples from your experience?

Further reading

Gura, P. (1992). *Exploring learning: Young children and blockplay*. London: Paul Chapman Publishing.
Rose, J., & Rogers, S. (2012). *The role of the adult in early years settings*. Maidenhead, UK: Open University Press.

This chapter has shown that the importance of the earliest years in a child's life have been recognised throughout history. From Plato to Froebel, each of the influential early thinkers directed the product of their thoughts to parents, teachers and practitioners, leaving a lasting record in their published works. The overriding motivation behind each of their ideas on children, childhood and early childhood education stemmed from the desire to provide the most favourable circumstances in which children could flourish and develop. Despite their often differing stances, the key thinkers shared similar values and beliefs about the potential of each child and in doing so laid down the foundations for later understanding about children's learning and development.

Part II discusses the roots and legacies of the four key women pioneers in early childhood education, whose ideas, values and beliefs were clearly influenced by the works of these early key thinkers and educators.

Notes

1 Phillipe Melanchthon studied theology under Dr Martin Luther, and they became lifelong friends.
2 The Unity of Brethren is a religious group tracing back to the Hussites, a group of followers of John Huss, who was a predecessor of the Protestant movement of the sixteenth century and was burned at the stake for what the civil authorities considered to be his heretical views of the Catholic Church.
3 These essays reached five volumes and were also translated into French and German, turning him into a figure of national significance and giving him a firm foundation on which to build his theories of education further, which he did in New Lanark (Gordon, 1994).

PART II

A history of connections in early childhood education

Four key woman pioneers – their roots and legacies

Having discussed in Part I the influences of the early philosophers on early childhood education, culminating in Froebel's widespread kindergarten movement, Part II now explores the four key women pioneers' contribution to early childhood education in relation to children, society and culture. Exploring the contribution that these women made to early childhood education is imperative to a complete understanding of the practice of the past, in the context of time and place, to provide a fuller comprehension of the present. There is legitimacy in interrogating and critiquing long-held systems of values and beliefs that underpin current emergent pedagogies in order to avoid a stagnant orthodoxy in early childhood education (Moss, 2006, Penn, 2007). Critical engagement with historical ideas and developments forms the starting points for considering where early childhood education has come from and 'where present policies fit' – or do not fit – 'with the lessons of history' (Nutbrown et al., 2008: 4).

2
RACHEL AND MARGARET MCMILLAN

Introduction

Educate every child as if he were your own.

(Rachel McMillan, cited in McMillan, 1919/1930: 8)

This chapter tells the story of the McMillan sisters' early experiences, endeavours and gradual involvement in socialist activities, which then led to their pioneering work in alleviating the plight of inner-city children and their families both in Bradford and in London. The discussions will reveal that as the McMillan sisters set about the reclamation of working-class childhood they eventually established the idea of early childhood education and care as an interventionist approach.

The sisters' early experiences

Rachel (1859–1917) and Margaret (1860–1931) were born in New York, but they returned to Inverness, Scotland, with their mother following the sad deaths of, first, their younger sister Elizabeth from scarlet fever and then of their father in 1865. Rachel and Margaret attended Inverness High School and Academy, and their education according to Steedman (1990) was almost certainly designed to prepare them for the genteel labour market. When their mother died in 1877, it was decided that Rachel, who had spent the previous three years teaching at a Ladies' College in Coventry run by two distant female relatives, should take on the duties of nursing their sick grandmother. During this time Rachel, an avid reader, came across a series of articles on child prostitution in London written in *The Maiden Tribute* by W.T. Stead. These graphic accounts of child sexual abuse were to have a profound effect on Rachel, who from then became interested in social politics.

In 1887, visiting cousins in Edinburgh, Rachel was to encounter an even wider range of socialist ideas, which changed the course of her life. At the age of 29, following the death of the sisters' grandmother, Rachel travelled to Bloomsbury in London to take up paid work as a junior superintendent in a working girls' home, where the occupants were either out of work or in low-paid jobs (Bradburn, 1989). In 1878 Margaret had gone to Germany and Switzerland to complete her education, eventually taking up a position as governess in Edinburgh. Following the break-up of a seemingly tempestuous love affair,[1] Margaret returned to Geneva to continue her education. It was during this period that Margaret would inevitably be exposed to new philosophical, political and economic theories, including those of Karl Marx. This experience extended her intellectually and socially (Bradburn, 1989). After finishing her studies in Geneva, Margaret eventually took up a post as governess with a young family in Ludlow. There she tutored the children of the rector, living in the rectory, which was also a welfare centre with a dispensary and cottage hospital. It was here that Margaret was able to see a wealthy, privileged family taking responsibility for the local community, and this experience provided her with a strong urge to find her own true calling, which was to help those less fortunate (Bradburn, 1989).

It is clear that, while apart, each experienced a profound spiritual awakening that shaped the future direction of the sisters' lives. Once reunited in London, they both became committed to the socialist philosophy, and education and welfare became central to their lives (Bradburn, 1989). Through attending socialist meetings, they got to know and work with the key figures of the socialist party: James Keir Hardie, who became the first leader of the Labour Party, and George Lansbury, elected as Labour MP for Bow, who also became leader (Shepherd, 2004). The sisters also joined the intellectual wing of the socialist party, known as the Fabian Society, a group of well-educated men and women of the time with high ideals and a strongly developed social conscience, including Irish dramatist George Bernard Shaw, who was later to visit the McMillans' open-air nursery in Deptford (Bradburn, 1989). It was through these encounters that the sisters, and Margaret in particular, found their true calling to improve the lives of the working classes on socialist lines. Margaret began by volunteering to teach singing to factory girls in the evenings, but she soon found herself out of her depth. The factory girls were now so deeply engrained in their working-class culture that any attempt to change their ways was greeted with derision and a certain pride (Bradburn, 1989). Taken aback by her initial failure, Margaret McMillan later wrote: 'I had failed in my first attempt to step outside my own life and its cares. The East End did not want me. It had no use for my feeble powers and vain offerings' (McMillan, 1927: 41–42).

Following this experience, Margaret, in search of employment, retreated to the world she was more accustomed to and took a position as governess to the adopted child of Lady Meux at 41, Park Avenue, London (Bradburn, 1989). Surrounded by the trappings of wealth, which also included access to Sir Henry Meux's various country estates around England and in France, Margaret would later draw on this lifestyle and environment in the design of the open-air nursery garden discussed in detail later in the chapter (Bradburn, 1989).

Margaret continued with her Christian socialist activities in her free time and left Lady Meux's employment, perhaps because of strained relationships. She once again joined Rachel and continued to earn money from writing articles for socialist papers and giving impassioned lectures on the reform of society (Steedman, 1990).

By all accounts Margaret was a formidable woman who held audiences spellbound; she was described by Robert Blatchford[2] as a blend between Joan of Arc, as she spoke of being guided by voices in her head, and Florence Nightingale, because of her feminist stance in fighting for the common well-being of those less fortunate (Bradburn, 1989). However, Margaret was by no means a radical feminist, developing her own brand of socialism and feminism, which was less about the emancipation of women and more about providing a platform in which socialist ideals could be given a voice. This is far removed from the theoretical approach of socialist feminism, which seeks to extend the Marxist concept of the reproduction of labour to include household labour and child care in theorising feminism (Levine, 1987). It would be Montessori who responded to this particular theoretical stance.

Child poverty: a century apart

Together with her sister, Margaret campaigned tirelessly to ameliorate the physical and intellectual welfare of socially and economically deprived children living in overcrowded inner-city dwellings. Margaret recollected in *The Nursery School,* published in 1919, that

> the life of children is so inert and so unwholesome that they do not digest well. This is true of many well-cared-for children. . . as well as of the poor and neglected. They sit about. They are often over clothed. They do not bathe often or regularly. They do not run and shout in the open. They sleep in faint air.
>
> *(McMillan, 1919: 43)*

Margaret is described as the *children's champion* in the biography written by Lowndes (1960), an accolade not too dissimilar to the one given to Gordon Brown, the Labour Prime Minister from 2007 to 2010, as they both placed an emphasis on the benefits of childcare provision in the struggle against poverty. This analogy will be explored further in the concluding part of this chapter.

A short history of working-class housing conditions in the late nineteenth and early twentieth centuries in London

In order to understand what lay behind the McMillan sisters' concern for the children of poor and working-class families, it is useful to provide a brief overview of the emerging perception of the plight of the inner-city child.

During the 1800s, a great many families in Britain lived in terrible poverty, and many parts of Victorian cities were overcrowded, dismal and bleak. London itself became characterised by increasing 'social polarisation' and 'special segregation' represented in the contrast between London's East and West Ends (Brehony, 2003: 89). The result was that the middle and upper classes had little contact with or knowledge of the urban poor and the way they lived. This lack of knowledge also meant that in educational discourse at the time, discussion of children in the city was frequently accompanied by fears and anxieties of a social class nature (Brehony, 2003).

Poverty in London became the subject of various ethnographic studies carried out by Henry Mayhew, which he later collected and published in four volumes, titled *London Labour and the London Poor* (1861). However, these studies did little to dispel anxieties as they employed the genre of travel literature and were written in the style of intrepid explorers making exciting discoveries of the previously unknown (Wohl, 1990, as cited in Brehony, 2003). According to Champkin (2007), Mayhew is often referred to as the statistical Charles Dickens as he attempted to calculate the state of the London poor, although he was clearly not a statistician.

Adding to the emerging discursive construction of working-class childhoods was John Thomson's[3] use of photographic images to illustrate lengthy written accounts of life as experienced on the streets of the East End of London (Smith, 1996). The following quote is an excerpt from the preface of the publication, which he co-authored with socialist Adolph Smith, called *Street Life in London* (1877):

> We have sought to portray these harder phases of life, bringing to bear the precision of photography in illustration of our subjects. The unquestionable accuracy of this testimony will enable us to present true types of the London poor and shield us from the accusation of either underrating or exaggerating individual peculiarities of appearance.
>
> *(Thomson & Smith, 1877)*

These images would have added further credence to many of the Victorian elite's perception of poor children as dangerous threats to the social order while at the same time as sentimental objects of unspoilt and innocent humanity (Koven, 2004).

The Reverend Andrew Mearns's booklet, *The Bitter Cry of Outcast London: An Inquiry into the Conditions of the Abject Poor,* published by the Congregational Union in 1883, also attracted widespread attention, particularly in the middle-class magazines of the time (Glennerster, Hills, Piachaud, & Webb, 2004). Mearns's description of poor peoples' living conditions was viewed as an emotional portrayal of the horrors of day-to-day existence in the 'slum' areas of London. At this point it is worth considering the word 'slum'. At the time it was used to describe the overcrowded dwellings of the urban poor, leading to the expression 'slumming it'. Leading up to the Second World War, Britons from a great many walks of life went 'slumming' to see for themselves how the poor lived, some out of curiosity, some for amusement or voyeurism, and some from a sense of 'altruism' (Koven, 2004: 203).

Drawing on literary meanings, the word 'slum' also became both a powerful and a dangerous metaphor as it serves as a conduit for filth, low morals standards and low intelligence, confusing the physical problems of the poor-quality housing with the characteristics of the people living there (Gilbert, 2007; Read, 2010).

Issues around the living conditions of the poor in London came to a head with the violent demonstrations of the mid-1880s. Most of the press of the day presented these demonstrations as Britain teetering on the brink of a social revolution, when they were actually about hunger and lack of work (Bales, 1999). Although there was little or no possibility of these outbursts of frustration and demand becoming an actual threat to the stability of London's social system, the working class was feared and perceived as a threat by much of the rest of London and the policymakers. Consequently, during this period politicians con-centrated on suppression rather than understanding (Bales, 1999). In February 1886, six months after the major riots, Charles Booth (1814–1916), philanthropist and social researcher who is seen as the father of modern poverty study, put the validity of Mearns's previous account of immense deprivation to the test. With a team of researchers, Booth set about systematically mapping the extent of poverty in East London. This was carried out by means of a painstaking house-by-house survey in the attempt to answer three relatively straightforward questions about poverty in London: 'How many people are living in poverty? What brought them to poverty or keeps them impoverished? And what might be done to alleviate this poverty? (Bales, 1999: 155). Given the recent figures of child poverty in the United Kingdom,[4] it may not come as a surprise that Booth's findings identified that a third of London's population lived below or on his level of abso-lute poverty, and that this poverty was likely to have been caused by unemploy-ment or casual employment. Booth also cautiously suggested re-locating the very poorest to 'industrial colonies', where they might be 'well housed, well fed and well warmed and taught and trained and employed from morning to night (Booth, 1889: 167).

Needless to say, these relatively simple findings caused much political debate. Booth's main aim was to show things as they really were rather than offer viable solutions, but what resulted was an emergence of a new social science of poverty measurement, which played a part in shaping people's understanding and eventu-ally policy decisions (Glennerster et al., 2004). Booth's survey was published as *Life and Labour of the People* in 1989 and was recommended as essential reading by the *Christian Socialist* newspaper (Bales, 1999).

The McMillan sisters also went into the slums of Victorian London to bear witness to the hardships of the poor, and Margaret's own contributions to episodes of history was when from the 1890s onwards she started to publish her written depictions of working-class childhood (Steedman, 1990). Against this social milieu of extreme poverty and abetted by the rapid growth of the science of social statistics and sanitation, the McMillan sisters set about the reclamation of working-class childhood and in doing so eventually established the idea of early childhood education and care as an interventionist approach.

The Bradford years 1893–1902

The London Dock Strike of 1889 was the turning point in the McMillan sisters' lives, and it also prompted Margaret's first piece of published writing, which was a sympathetic piece about the wretched lives of family men subjected to casual labour (Steedman, 1990). The McMillan sisters, along with other educators, supporters of the cause and political activists provided by the socialist movement, supported the grossly exploited dockers' demand for a six-pence-per-hour wage, which they achieved after five weeks of highly organised strike action (Steedman, 1990).

The sisters continued to be involved in spreading the word of Christian Socialism, but in a renewed effort to revive the socialist movement, at the invitation of Fred Jowett, a fellow socialist, Margaret and Rachel eventually left London for Bradford in 1893. At the time Bradford was one of the foremost mid-Victorian towns and had a thriving textile industry. That year saw the birth of the Independent Labour Party (ILP) in Bradford, where the work of securing the support of the Trade Unions was more advanced than in London. Developing a reputation as a powerful public speaker, Margaret was asked to stand as one of the Party's candidates at the Bradford School Board Election and, having gained her seat by a narrow majority, took her place on the Board (Bradburn, 1976).

The youngest and only female member on the Board, Margaret McMillan began her work by concentrating primarily on leading political agitation against the half-time system, whereby children could leave school for half-time employment at the age of 11. Following her first visits to the elementary schools, Margaret later wrote that in the 1890s conditions 'were worse than anything described or painted. . . the half timers slept, exhausted at their desk' (McMillan, 1927: 87–88). Following a deputation to the then Liberal Home Secretary, Henry Asquith, the school-leaving age was eventually raised to 12 in 1899. Within this new-found political initiative for socialism and welfare reform, the McMillan sisters, like countless other educated middle-class women who were free from domestic drudgery, were carving a niche for themselves as part of the socialist movement. 'It was there in Bradford that she [Margaret] first saw children from back to back houses, who were sewn into their clothes, who arrived at school hungry and dirty and whose bodies were indescribably disease ridden' (Bradburn, 1976: 19).

Furthermore, as social reformers and in the interests of the health of the family and the education of their children, the McMillan sisters claimed the right to instruct and regulate the conduct of working-class women in establishing the right for all disadvantaged children to full and free development (Koven & Michel, 1990).

Election to the School Board enabled Margaret to break new ground and further the cause of education to include improvements for the under-fives.[5] Margaret had found her true role, and during the eight years she remained in Bradford she worked tirelessly for her cause, often spending time away speaking and lecturing incessantly around the country and producing a plethora of articles about theories of child development, physiology and hygiene. Rachel supported her sister before returning to London at the end of 1883 to embark on the Sanitary Institute's two-year training course in order to become a qualified sanitary inspector (Steedman, 1990). Separation was not an attractive proposition for either of them, but, following her inner convictions and conscious of their precarious financial situation, Rachel first took up paid employment as organising secretary to the Women's Industrial Council in Liverpool, simultaneously gaining experience in social work before moving to London to take up her studies. After qualifying she became a peripatetic teacher of hygiene for Kent County Council (Bradburn, 1989).

The work that Rachel undertook in rural Kent between 1896 and 1913 as a teacher of hygiene clearly influenced Margaret's advancement of the theory of childcare provision and child development. An avid reader, the theories of Charles Darwin and the works of Plato, Locke, Rousseau, Pestalozzi and Owen also informed Margaret's writings, and she studied Froebel's ideas on child-centred learning and play with great attention (Bradburn, 1976). Like Montessori, she was also drawn to the ideas of Seguin (1812–1880), who gave great impetus to the emergent sciences of the child and child development stemming from an essentially Darwinian, biological and evolutionary episteme (Brehony, 2009). Despite the fact that Montessori is best remembered for her sensorial materials using Seguin's ideas as a guide, it was Margaret, in 1896, with the approval of the head teacher, who first carried out experiments founded on his principles in Belle Vue School, Bradford, before Montessori began her work. These included the use of tactile materials varying from the smoothest satin to the roughest fretted wood for children to touch with their eyes closed; writing on wet sand, drawing and painting on canvas and easels, colour wheels and scales of coloured paper for the children to grade and name. Furthermore, desks and benches were replaced with child-sized chairs with rounded backs and small lightweight tables providing more room for the children to wander freely. Initially this was not well received by the School Board or parents, who complained that it would be difficult to attract grants and scholarships to run the schools. However, after a time, these innovations would become recognised as valuable contributions to the children's education (Bradburn, 1989: 58–59). It was only after the success of her first two campaigns for free school meals and school medical inspections that Margaret, together with Rachel, started her third campaign for a nursery education framework, which gave prominence to sensory training within a natural environment (Blackstone, 1974).

Medical inspections first began in 1894 in Bradford, but in October 1899 Dr James Kerr, together with Margaret, launched a campaign that eventually led to the establishment of school clinics. School nurses were appointed to visit schools and examine children. There was thus in the Bradford experiments a potential model for subsequent activities (Petrina, 2006). Being present at these first medical inspections, Margaret saw the urgent need for medical reform and began a long campaign to improve the health of children by arguing that local authorities should install bathrooms, improve ventilation and supply free school meals (Bradburn, 1976, 1989).

Margaret was also concerned that children under the age of five,[6] pushed into the schools by harassed mothers, could not learn, given the crowded infant classes, the inappropriate curricula and teaching methods that still operated the 'monitorial' system so favoured by Wilderspin in maintaining discipline. These factors were in turn affected by 'the iniquitous system of payment by results' (Bradburn, 1976: 27). With the passing of the 1870 Elementary Education Act, which legislated for the provision of partially public-funded education aimed specifically for working-class children, the salary of schoolteachers was based on the system of payment by results, which was tied to the criterion of a restricted curriculum with the emphasis almost exclusively on the 3Rs. Public funding for the schools required a minimum standard of being able to 'read a short passage from a newspaper; writing similar matter from dictation; working sums in practice and fractions' (R. Williams, 1961: 137). Margaret clearly saw the need for a certain kind of nursery education but she was also aware that this would require joint action from a number of different bodies if the problems arising from the social, political, economic and cultural factors were to be eradicated (Bradburn, 1976). Like Pestalozzi before her, Margaret's thoughts were primarily ethical and arose from a sense of social justice. Encouragingly, in 1905 the Board of Education published a report entitled *Children Under Five Years of Age* compiled by five women inspectors who were asked to inquire into the suitability of the curriculum for very young children, The inspectors, led by Katherine Bathurst, the first woman inspector of infant schools, were well qualified and experienced for their posts (Goodman & Harrop, 2000). They were highly critical of the practice they had observed and considered that children under five were receiving too much formal training in the 3Rs. They found needlework an inappropriate activity and thought that the discipline was too rigid. Furthermore, sleeping arrangements were inadequate, and the classrooms were ill ventilated and unhealthy; it was clear that health care was not considered an essential part of the curriculum (Straw, 1990).

As a result the Board permitted local authorities to exclude from their schools children under five years of age, if they so wished. The report concluded that for young children from imperfect homes it was necessary that some public authority should provide opportunities in the form of nursery schools. It would take another thirteen years for the recommendations of the report to be acted upon (Brehony, 2009).

Bradford to London

When the work initiated in Bradford faced the possibility of being implemented on a broader scale nationwide, Kerr and Margaret both moved back to London in 1902 to continue their campaign for the establishment of school clinics and nursery education (Blackstone, 1974). Following their successful campaign in Bradford, the Education (Provision of Meals) Act was passed in 1906, which allowed local authorities to provide school meals. Now no longer a question of party politics, the introduction of school meals marked a broader ethical shift in which people across the political spectrum recognised that hunger now had to be governed socially (Vernon, 2005). Furthermore, the 1907 Education (Administrative Provision) Act saw the introduction of medical inspections of children in elementary school, which eventually led to women gaining new opportunities as social workers, health visitors and school nurses (Koven & Michel, 1990). The range of child welfare initiatives implemented in this period eventually led to the welfare state (Read, 2010). However, these measures should not be looked upon as purely altruistic, as recruitment for the Boer War had shown that Britain's working classes were in poor health, and these two Acts of Parliament were also an attempt at reform from the bottom up. At the time of the Boer War, about half of the 7,000 candidates for recruitment were found to be unfit for military service, and many were rejected because of poor physique, including dental reasons (Gelbier & Randall, 1982).

Hendrick (1997) points out that in saving the child, the nation state had other motives, such as population levels, the civilisation of the masses and a desire to breed a race capable of competing in the twentieth century. Furthermore, those subscribing to eugenic ideals (Erichsen, 1993; Hendrick, 1997), prevalent at the time, saw the problem as primarily concerning the quality of future generations and believed that social engineering would do away with, or weaken, the effect of nature's shaping forces.

The physiological approach, which was adopted in the medical inspections of working-class children at the time, did hold imperative the collection of data about bodily processes of growth and development. In this respect it did imply a form of stocktaking of the future workforce and therefore the suggestion of an element of social control as feasible (Erichsen, 1993). However, the McMillans would not have subscribed to this form of categorising, as their concerns were on the transformation of working-class childhoods and more aligned to the Rousseau-esque ideal of the child as a romantic free spirit. Nevertheless, underpinning their concerns was an overriding moral stance that socially and economically disadvantaged children needed to be rescued from the depravities of working-class culture.

QUESTIONS FOR REFLECTION

In light of what has been discussed so far in this chapter, consider whether or not current early years policy and provision continue to support the idea that economically disadvantaged children and their families are in need of 'rescue'.

To what extent has the interventionist approach to early childhood education and care shaped the evolution of education and childcare policy and provision?

The Deptford years

In London, Margaret's administrative involvement in education expanded, and in 1903 she became manager of three Board Schools in Deptford. Kerr, in his role as Chief Medical Officer to the London School Board, reinforced the belief that health, growth and diet were the main priorities in supporting working-class children and their families. Soon realising that preventative measures and long-term solutions were needed in order to make any educative impact of the lives of these children, Margaret regularly visited Rachel in Bromley to discuss her concerns (Steedman, 1990). In debates with her sister, Margaret finally 'located the genesis of the health centre' (Steedman, 1990: 30). As a consequence, Margaret's first venture was the opening, in 1910, of a medical treatment centre on behalf of Deptford's children. With the opening of the clinic, Margaret's interest in early childhood education increased.

Margaret turned to the Froebelian movement for inspiration on how to go about establishing her own particular design of nursery practice and provision and was elected to its Council of the National Froebel Society in 1904 (Steedman, 1990). At its peak in 1914 the London-based Froebel Society and its regional branches enjoyed a membership of approximately 3,000 people, of whom 90 per cent were Froebel-trained teachers providing a structure of professionalism in the field of early childhood education (Brehony, 1994). The domination of the Froebel Society was later to give way to the various empiricist and pseudo sciences, such as phrenology, which proliferated in the wake of Darwinian Theory (Brehony, 2009).

The open-air camp

At the turn of the twentieth century, a great deal of attention in Europe and Britain was focused on the *Open Air School Movement* in combating not only the spread of tuberculosis,[7] but also other socially constructed risk factors such as truancy and delinquency.

> it seems not improbable that the open-air school will be recognised by future historians of education not merely as a therapeutic agent but rather as marking one long step towards that school of the future where the child will not have to be either feeble-minded or delinquent or tuberculosis or truant to enjoy the best and fullest sort of educational opportunity.
>
> *(Ayres, 1910: 8)*

The open-air school, originated in Germany, was essentially a compromise between the educator and the medical doctor – the former insisting on intellectual development and the latter on curative treatment (Connolly, 2004) Ever since the time of the ancient Greeks and Romans, the advancement of education moved more and more indoors, despite the efforts of early philosophers such as Comenius, Locke, Rousseau and Pestalozzi (Broughton, 1914). No doubt influenced by the early philosophers and Froebel's ideas of children being in touch with nature, a certain impetus to the open-air school movement in the United Kingdom had been given by prior investigations, carried out by Margaret McMillan, into the reasons for 'the unusually high preponderance of men and women of university rank who came from the Western Isles and Highlands of Scotland' (Broughton, 1914: 12). The explanation provided was that as children they had taken an active part in the outdoor pursuits of their parents, becoming both physically fit and mentally active.

Hence, when at school, they learned rapidly and with ease, outstripping the achievements of their peers (1914: 12). Margaret also makes reference to the productive outdoor lifestyle in her publication: *Education through the Imagination* (McMillan, 1904)

> The Hebridean child does not live in a bare playground or crowded house. He goes out in a small boat with his playmates on the great ocean. He climbs the rocks to find the wild birds' eggs, and goes out with the fishing fleet to do his share of work.
>
> *(McMillan, 1904: 146)*

In order to counteract the stultifying effects of the system of elementary education that working-class children experienced in the London Board schools, and reinforced with the medical knowledge of the therapeutic benefits of being out in the open air as much as possible, the McMillan sisters opened their first open-air camp in 1911. Initially attended by children aged 6 to 12 who quite literally camped outside overnight, younger children were not catered for until 1914, with the opening of the first open-air nursery school in Church Street, Deptford (Bradburn, 1976). The children attended the open-air camp after school to have a bath, a meal and then to sleep outside, the girls in the garden and the boys sleeping in the nearby graveyard. Each morning the children breakfasted on porridge obtained from Inverness in Scotland before attending the Board school. The McMillans were practising preventative medicine, and the principle behind this experiment was to get the children out of their crowded, poorly ventilated homes and give them a good night's sleep (Steedman, 1990). As a result of this initiative the children's health improved, and they built up resistance to disease.

The medicinal and educational potential of working outside began to be seen, but the McMillans soon came to realise that they were getting to the children too late and needed to work with much younger children (Straw, 1990). Their ambition to establish an open-air nursery garden school drew a step closer

Blueprint for a nursery garden school

Despite drawing on Froebel's influences and pedagogical approach, the McMillans' nursery garden school was very different from the Froebelian kindergarten, being less philosophical and oriented purely and simply to education (White & Buka, 1987). Margaret and Rachel, who had left her full-time post in Kent to join her sister in 1913, planned their nursery garden school to promote all aspects of the child's development alongside the promotion of good health, happiness and respect for others. For the McMillans these were the characteristics, handed down from the philosophies of the enlightenment, that were deemed essential in ensuring children's well-being in adulthood and the production of a just and caring society. The McMillans' campaign for the provision of nurseries with gardens stemmed from a deep desire to reduce the impact poverty had on young children living in overcrowded squalid conditions, with little opportunity to access green spaces. This coincided with long-held 'romantic notions that located the child not in the gutter of a city street but in the natural environment of the field and forest' (Read, 2010: 2). Up until the industrial revolution, '*the city* defined itself and its spatial limits against the surrounding countryside, and so belonged to and situated itself as a central feature within a rural landscape' (Mazzoleni, 1993: 298). Then followed a rapid urban and industrial growth as families moved away from their rural communities and agricultural work enticed by the mass demand for labour to be found in industrialised cities. Thus in the wake of the industrial revolution industrialised cities in England became a sociocultural phenomenon, and romanticised evocations of the countryside provided a sense of security, intimacy and community (Mazzoleni, 1993). Furthermore, since Rousseau's conceptualisation of the child as innocent and connected to nature, childhood has long been associated, in the collective imagination of adults, with images of the rural and the countryside. Consequently, as the childhood play of working-class children moved from the fields to the streets, the McMillan sisters adopted the 'garden', both literally and as a metaphorical trope (Steedman, 1990). The belief in the capacity of natural beauty and the arts to reform the individual was at the heart of socialist activities at the time, and as part of the socialist movement the McMillans strove to incorporate this belief into the design of their nursery garden.

> The garden is essential matter. Not the lessons or the pictures or the talk. The lessons and talk are about things seen in the garden, just as the best of all the paintings in the picture galleries are shadows of originals now available to the children of the open air. Ruskin declares that all the best books are written in the country. . . Little children, as well as great writers, should be, if not in the country, at least in a place that is very like it. . . If not in great space with moorland or forest and lakes, at least in sunny places, not in foul air and grimy congestion.
>
> *(McMillan, 1919: 4)*

The creation of the first open-air nursery garden

As the open-air camp school was only used after the school day had ended, Margaret invited the children's younger brothers and sisters to play in the garden during the day. As the number of children grew in attendance, in March 1914 the sisters moved to a much larger site in Stowage, owned at the time by London County Council, which had been left to go to waste. The rental charge of a shilling per annum was on condition that the agreement could be terminated at a day's notice (Bradburn, 1989).

> It was a big waste of stones, of brick bats and tin cans strewn over an acre of earth all rough and covered with wild growth and half withered grasses.
>
> *(McMillan, 1919: 347)*

The garden developed slowly, but at this stage, according to Margaret, it was the open space that mattered. The children had ample space, approximately an acre of land, to move around the garden freely, which not only ensured that the children were healthy and developing physically, but also that they could learn through this movement, just as much as they could learn through their senses.

> Children want space at all ages. But from the age of one to seven, space, that is ample space, is almost as much as food and air. To move, to run, to find out by new movement, to 'feel one's life in every limb,' that is the life of early childhood. And yet one sees already dim houses, behind whose window and doors thirty to forty little ones spaces are penned in 'Day Nurseries.' Bare sites and open spaces are what we need today.
>
> *(McMillan, 1919: 11)*

There is a direct correlation between external environmental factors and places where children can be defined and valued as responsible citizens (Vecchi, 2005), and the McMillans would have endorsed the view that children have a right to inhabit spaces that are aesthetically pleasing because it promotes both an attentive and an empathetic relationship with their surroundings (Straw, 1990).

The increasing knowledge and skills concerning children's health and well-being they had acquired over the preceding years served the sisters well. Rachel focused mainly on the health of the children in the nursery school, while Margaret considered the children's learning and development. Margaret's own work in the field of child development, while influenced by Froebel and the value of spontaneous play, drew on other specific sets of knowledge that emerged in the late nineteenth century, such as the physiological accounts of physical growth and the psychological notion of stages of development (Steedman, 1990). In planning the open-air nursery, the sisters were conscious that childhood was a time of change and transformation, and following the theories of the early philosophers identified clear stages of development from birth to age seven – 'that great milestone noted by the leaders of all great races and religions, and now by those who tell us that brain growth stops here' (McMillan, 1919: 14). Up until the middle of the twentieth century it was generally believed that the brain was 'hard-wired' and that it was impossible to alter development that was genetically pre-set. This has now been refuted, as recent scientific research has shown that the brain is, from birth, constantly organising and reorganising (Doherty & Hughes, 2009). Recent neurological research with brain-imaging technology has also shown that babies and young children who experience an interactive and stimulating environment develop cognitively faster (Blakemore & Frith, 2005).

Margaret would probably have lent support to this observation as, aware of the importance of experiential learning and influenced by the work of Pestalozzi and Froebel and Owen, they organised the garden into different sections, similar in the way a classroom is organised for different types of play activities. There was a gymnasium, an area for scientific and environmental discovery, a horticulture section which consisted of a kitchen and herb garden and a greenhouse, and a play and building area (Straw, 1990).

Margaret considered play as having a significant place in early childhood education and emphasised using play as a medium for skill development and experimentation, insisting on the importance of outdoor play areas. In this outdoor environment the children could follow their interests without interference, having learned how to use each section accordingly. For Margaret what was important was not the giving of instructions but the preparation of a 'suitably provocative environment. . . as it is not the lack of instruction that impoverishes and arrests the little child of poor streets – it is rather the shrinkage in possibility of any kind of experiment in his narrow surroundings' (McMillan, 1930: 78). The risks of playing in the streets and learning the cultural identity of street life was precisely what the McMillans wished to prevent, and their open-air nursery garden was part of the child-saving response to the situation (Read, 2010). Despite the streets and surrounding open ground being social spaces where children's imagination could flourish and where skills learnt would foster their personal, social and emotional development, the risk of catching germs and diseases far outweighed the benefits. However, the McMillans did provide opportunities for positive risk-taking as their nursery garden was arranged on different levels, with both hard and grassy surfaces, rough stones leading up to the terrace walks, narrow paths that were straight and smooth so that children could run and give chase and graded steps for exercise in jumping. Margaret advised that the garden 'must be planned with an eye to real safety; but fitted with the kind of apparatus that that will provoke children not only to play but to play bravely and adventurously' (McMillan, 1919: 28).

There were walls to jump off and trees to climb, and children were allowed to use real tools such as hammers, saws and hand drills, and large building materials such as bricks, planks, ladders, barrels and ropes. Such activities have been banished from many settings today because of fear of litigation. But, as the McMillans demonstrated, there is a difference between ensuring that the nursery environment is as safe as necessary, and as safe as possible. Complying with safety regulations through the removal of *all* potential hazards can inadvertently result in the elimination of significant opportunities for positive risk-taking (Stephenson, 2003).

Article 31 of the United Nations Convention on the Rights of the Child (UNCRC; United Nations, 1989) recognises children's right to play, and play-related issues emerge as a key theme within research on children's use of space. A study by Fjørtoft and Sageie (2001) in Telemark, Norway, found that nursery children with regular access to the outdoors not only had better motor skills but also greater levels of understanding about the environment. Research carried out by Martensson et al. (2009) shows that different types of natural features within an early years setting's outdoor space impact on children's levels of attention, highlighting the particular importance of elements such as trees, shrubbery and varied terrain, which reinforces the McMillans' understanding of the benefits of a nursery with a garden.

Whether it is children living in overcrowded accommodation or in bleak concrete inner-city estates, the issues that the McMillan sisters raised at the turn of the last century are still as pertinent today, given the high level of social deprivation in our cities (Parekh, MacInnes, & Kenway, 2010). Furthermore, constraints such as increasing traffic and the fears over safety and litigation in an increasingly risk-averse society have greatly reduced the amount of control children have on how, where and who they can play with in their free time (King & Howard, 2010).

Paradoxically, across the United Kingdom, despite increased anxiety about health and safety and the fear of litigation, there is increasing support for learning outside the classroom. Political interest has been stimulated because of the perception that children are increasingly separated from the natural environment (Higgins, 2010). As such, there is currently renewed interest in the use of outdoor environments in early child-hood education, and the English EYFS (Department for Education, 2012b) and the Welsh Foundation Phase (Department for Children, Education, Lifelong Learning and Skills, 2008) both state the need for the provision of regular outdoor experiences. Although written almost a century later, the following statement reflects the McMillans' sentiments regarding children's need for space: 'Appropriate space is essential for phys-ical movement both indoors and outdoors in order that children can use their bodies actively to gain spatial awareness and experiment with movement and without restric-tions' (Department for Children, Education, Lifelong Learning and Skills, 2008: 6).

Notwithstanding romantic notions of the rural idyll discussed earlier, there appears to be an innate desire in human beings, and particularly in young children, to relate to the natural world, which has been theorised as 'biophilia' by Wilson (1984: 1). As summarised by Bird (2007: 28), 'the biophilia hypothesis describes the existence of a genetically based human need and preference to affiliate with nature'. There is also evidence that early significant life experiences – particularly outdoors – are important in environmental orientation as well as to the child's developmental benefits. One of the most reassuring aspects of their open-air nursery garden according to Margaret was that it was a 'home and haunt of living things' (McMillan, 1919: 30). The sisters showed how outdoor spaces could be easily developed for wildlife and plants, which fostered within the children a love of taking care for living things. In today's society with concerns about sustainability, the sense of wonder for the natural world can be the starting point for inspiring action to pro-tect and conserve the natural environment, initiating behaviours and attitudes that young children will carry with them for life. According to Pramling-Samuelsson and Kaga (2008), there is a great deal in the philosophy and traditions of early child-hood education that aligns with education for sustainability – for example, the use of the outdoor space for learning, integration of development, education and care, learning through concrete experiences and real-life projects, and involvement of parents and communities can be traced back through the McMillan sisters to the early philosophers (Pramling-Samuelsson & Kaga, 2008).

The nursery school as an agent of change

The death of Rachel McMillan in March 1917, which according to the lit-erature was on account of the extremely arduous work of managing the

Clinic, the open air camps and the nursery school in Margaret's intermittent absences as she toured the country in the campaign for nursery schools. This left Margaret with extreme feelings of guilt, but with a renewed determination in building for Rachel's memory, she moved steadily towards the goals which they had set together.

(Steedman, 1990)

In a long-awaited response to the *Children Under Five Years of Age* report (Board of Education, 1905), the Education Act of 1918 finally gave powers to Local Education Authorities to open nursery schools and classes, which, in return for inspection, could receive a grant (Brehony, 1994). The subsequent placement of nursery schools under the Board of Education's Medical Branch echoed the McMillans' own emphasis on the importance of children's health as they knew that children could not learn if they were ill, tired and hungry.

It is worth noting, however, that what may have seemed a vindication regarding the status of universal nursery education was, in fact, tempered by the reality that the provision of nursery schools would be restricted to those areas where they could be justified as a necessary intervention (Brehony, 2009). This limitation on the provision of nursery education was fortuitous, as the economic situation in the wake of the First World War deteriorated rapidly in England from 1921, leading to extensive cuts in public expenditure, mirroring the same monetary situation the United Kingdom is facing during the 2000s and 2010s (Brehony, 2009).

Margaret continued to write profusely on a wide range of issues related to the welfare of children, but it was *The Nursery School,* published in 1919, which set out to provide a response to questions about the necessity of nursery schools she was frequently asked by policymakers:

Why, we are asked, do we want Nursery Schools? Should not every mother take entire charge of her little ones till they are of school age? Is it not her duty to remain to remain at home and to devote her time to them?

(McMillan, 1919: 6)

As both a socialist and a pragmatist, one of Margaret's fundamental principles for open-air nursery schools was to bridge the huge divide at the time between rich and poor families. She was keen to replicate the childhood experiences of the privileged classes who lived in spacious houses with fine gardens and servants (Bradburn, 1989). Margaret McMillan (1919: 6) also recognised in the working-class families that they were 'developing new susceptibilities', and though they might not have the income of their wealthy counterparts to do things alone, they could collectively experience some of the same riches in the fullness of time, and nursery schools would play a part in this. Margaret's experiences as a governess gave her an insight into how a well-to-do mother would nurture the development of her young child or children with the assistance of employees in the household, such as a nanny, nursery maid, cook and gardener. Inspired by her socialist ideology, Margaret saw nursery schools as a way of providing similar experiences for financially deprived families, which would rival any of those of wealthier households (Sayle, 1929). The basis on which Margaret designed her nursery school is delineated clearly by A. Sayle, chairman of the Women Sanitary Inspectors' and Health Visitors' Association, who viewed the open-air nursery schools as national assets.

> Perhaps the best standards by which to judge the [McMillans'] nursery school is that of the best private nursery in which several children are growing up together. We must assume that the occupants of the nursery can always play in the garden, that a grown up person with nothing else to do, is always at hand, possessing knowledge and skills in all matters affecting their needs, physical, mental and psychological. We must also assume that a doctor examines the children at regular intervals perhaps monthly and that a trained nurse is on the premises every day.
>
> *(Sayle, 1929: 589)*

Through the establishment of open-air nursery schools, Margaret was both revealing and illuminating the lifestyle of privileged families, with the intention of creating a similar space for economically deprived children to learn and develop and also a space for progressive social change. In recognising the potential of nursery schools as agents of change, Margaret forged close links with the parents, and mothers in particular, who had received little or no education, encouraging them to participate in the activities and learn alongside their children (Steedman, 1990). One of the benefits was the way in which parents were able to make a cognitive leap in understanding that disease and ill health were not a matter of course but were, rather, the result of material circumstances that they themselves could change. For example, witnessing the production of food in the nursery garden would help working-class parents to break the chains of dependence on their employers by growing their own produce (Steedman, 1990). Bourdieu's post-structural concept of social capital is useful when reflecting on Margaret's compensatory education, as he refers to the significance of social relationships or networks in accessing and maintaining resources in order to gain socially desirable ends (cited in Lee & Bowen, 2006).

Margaret's attention not only to disadvantaged children but also to their parents was seen as a great social weapon in the fight against sociocultural deprivation, and she saw it as important that 'The people want – not a great imposing place, miles away – but a familiar place, close by, where the best that is known about treatment and training can be under their eyes and at their service' (McMillan, 1911).

While Margaret McMillan was claiming what was best for the parents whose children attended the open-air nursery schools, she could just as well be describing the Sure Start Local Programme a century later (DfE, 2010). The government-funded Sure Start programmes, introduced in 1999, which were initially aimed at only the most deprived areas in England, have much in common with the McMillans' community-based nursery provision at the time, both providing early childhood education integrated with family health services and training advice for parents.

What is significant is the similarity of conditions and aspirations for disadvantaged children and their families at the turn of the last century to those of today.

QUESTIONS FOR REFLECTION

What links can you identify between the ways of working with children and their families in contemporary early childhood settings with those of the McMillans' open-air nursery school?

Reflecting on your own geographical area, does the range of early childhood services on offer meet the diverse needs of young children and their families?

Do you agree that there is an innate desire in human beings, and particularly in young children, to relate to the natural world?

What would you say to those who see the main purpose of being outdoors as being for children to 'let off steam'?

As we have seen from the ideas of the earlier philosophers discussed in Chapter 1, early childhood education has, from its beginnings, always had differing influences and followed a different path from other spheres of education, including the provision of a completely distinct outdoor area. Wilderspin's use of the outdoor space, which we recognise to this day in the traditional primary-school playground, was markedly different from that of Owen and Froebel, who were both so influential in the initial concept of the McMillans' open-air nursery garden (McCann & Young, 1982).

However, the success of the open-air nursery school lay in the ability of the teacher. Margaret felt challenged by her own approach to teaching and soon came to recognise that 'the type of relationship between teaching and the transmission of knowledge' required careful consideration in the education and care of young children (Steedman,1990: 184). Informed by her own extensive reading, Margaret went to great lengths to close the gap between theory and practice, and a distinct feature of the open-air nursery school was the attached training centre. Margaret expected the provision in her open-air nursery to match local needs and argued that the practitioners, including teachers, should make themselves familiar with the lifestyles of the children and parents, analyse social situations and devise suitable programmes for children while also encouraging parents to accept broader educational responsibilities (Bradburn, 1976). The training that the student teachers undertook both in the open-air nursery and in the neighbourhood was a combination of childcare and education training (Steedman, 1990). Emphasis was placed on training students how to observe and understand the children's behaviour both inside and outside the home, and Margaret urged the students to look beyond the child's present deficits to what he or she could become, given a nurturing environment (Steedman, 1990). This necessitated careful sustained observation of the same child over time within specific domains of physical, cognitive and language development. Although viewing childhood as a time of swift transformation, Margaret also considered changes over time in terms of discrete stages passing over early infancy as a time when 'a little one sleeps much. . . and as a toddler he wants to run and range all over a large place. . . . At three or four he has become another person with new needs and desires and later still he is a schoolboy' (McMillan, 1919: 14). Dividing up the children's stages of development in this way helped Margaret to work more effectively with the children as well as embracing the emerging science of child study, a parallel here with the 'birth to three matters' categorisations of four broad stages (Abbott & Langston, 2004).

Factors influencing the scientific study of children in the wake of Darwinism and traced back to Preyer (1841–1897) in Germany and to Hall (1844–1924) in the United States were identified as: new interests in scientific methods of enquiry; teaching methods and standards of education in the newly established universal schooling; and children's health, including social and emotional development and parenting (Doherty & Hughes, 2009). As the earliest years were seen to be increasingly important in furthering the understanding of human development, nursery schools were seen to be living laboratories in which a great deal of data could be systematically gathered (Singer, 1992). As revealed in her writings, Margaret was interested in research conducted according to hermeneutic methods, which aimed at acquiring an intuitive understanding of how children think and learn through the use of careful observations leading to developmentally appropriate teaching (McMillan, 1904, 1919). Margaret wrote: 'It is, of course, true that any real live undismayed venture in education is research and leads to discovery' (McMillan, 1919: 5). Margaret expected her students to think about what they were doing, mirroring Pestalozzi's emphasis on reflective practice, to question accepted procedures, make new discoveries and to innovate (Bradburn, 1976).

The Rachel McMillan Teacher Training College

As the Deptford open-air schools developed, so did the training provision for teachers, and in 1919, two years after the death of Rachel, the Rachel McMillan Teacher Training College was accorded recognition by the Board of Education as a training centre for all nursery staff (Mansbridge, 1932). Margaret went on to establish various categories of students in her training centre, and alongside student teachers were groups of young girls training to become nursery helpers or assistants,[8] depending on their length of training. These were often young women under 18 years of age whose training consisted largely of the physical care of the children, such as toileting, washing and supervising children during mealtimes, but who also kept records of attendance as well as of their physical and cognitive development (Bradburn, 1976). As a lasting legacy to her sister and spurred on by the belief that she could staff the nursery schools of the future, Margaret set about establishing a teacher-training college. Putting her political affiliation to one side, Margaret elicited support from Nancy Astor (1879–1964), the first woman to be elected to the House of Commons and a Conservative. They had become acquainted through their mutual work for the Nursery School Movement, which transcended party politics. With the financial backing of Lady Astor, the Rachel McMillan Teacher Training College, named in honour of Margaret's sister, was opened on 8 May 1930, and students took a three-year full-time course leading to a Froebel Certificate.[9]

Margaret's vision of having the right combination of appropriately trained staff, each confident in their own role of supporting both the education and the care of young children, was quite radical at the time as she saw the nursery and the Training Centre as places where class-barriers could be broken down (Bradburn, 1976). Not everyone shared Margaret's vision, as officials from the teaching unions and school-teachers accused her of diluting the profession (Bradburn, 1976). Noteworthy is that prior to Margaret's' training innovations, 'Froebel-trained teachers operated in an exclusive world of expensive education' (Kamm, 1971: 48), and there were educators who 'felt that [although] these more cultivated young ladies were precisely what state infant schools needed to lift them above the level of unimaginative drill, the social obstacles were hard to surmount' (Roberts, 1976: 255). But Margaret wanted the Rachel McMillan Teacher Training College to be a centre that drew together people wanting to work in differing child-related professions from all walks of life (Bradburn, 1976). In retrospect, Margaret did acknowledge that this approach had added to the confusion about the fundamental aims of nursery schools (Bradburn, 1976).

Traditionally, England's early childhood education and care system has featured divisions between early childhood education, childcare for the children of employed parents and childcare delivered as part of child welfare services (Lloyd & Hallet, 2010).

Despite the growing nursery-school movement and Margaret's tireless efforts right until her death, the expansion of nursery-school provision in the United Kingdom throughout most of the twentieth century was constrained by their cost and by the view, among some in the academic community and policymakers, that the best place for most children below school age was with their mothers in their homes (Blackstone, 1974; Brehony, 2009; David, 1993). This debate was given renewed momentum in the 1950s, when John Bowlby (1907–1990) first developed his attachment theory, which claimed that there would be serious damage to a

---

QUESTIONS FOR REFLECTION

Reflecting on Margaret McMillan's recognition of the importance of combined education and care, consider the EYFS's role in promoting multi-agency working and the perceived benefits for children and their families.

Consider the skills and expertise you could contribute to a multi-disciplinary team.

Read the Nutbrown Review, available online at www.education.gov.uk/nutbrown and consider how important having qualifications that are of a high standard is in supporting children's learning and development. If possible share your views with other practitioners to gain a broader perspective.

child's emotional development if the attachment between child and mother was severed in the first year of the child's life (Bowlby, 1969). Attachment theory was adopted and popularised in major government reports and used as a justification for providing limited services for young children, or withholding them altogether (Central Advisory Council for Education, 1967; Department for Health and Social Security, 1976; Penn, 2002, 2007).

The McMillans' lasting legacies

As well as campaigning for the introduction of school meals and school medical inspections, Margaret, along with her sister Rachel, provided a blueprint for nursery education in the United Kingdom that grew from an intense dissatisfaction with the elementary system of the late nineteenth century. Instead, they designed and eventually provided an environment of integrated learning (far removed from the subject-by-subject-based learning with its emphasis on memorising and rote learning encountered in the Board Schools), which was naturally appealing to young children and helped both teachers and children to make the connections between home and school (Straw, 1990). In Margaret Mcmillan's own words, 'A Nursery School is, or should be, part of the home life' (McMillan, 1919: 12). The McMillans' open-air nursery schools provided outdoor space for children to move around and play with other children in fresh air for good health and a large variety of first-hand experiences that enabled the children to make scientific and environmental discoveries while developing their language skills (Steedman, 1990). The driving force behind the McMillans' methodology was that children needed to be healthy before learning could take place, in keeping with Locke's (1692) understanding that a healthy body and a healthy mind went hand in hand, and in order for this to happen, learning took place predominantly outdoors. The McMillans reacted strongly to school buildings, which they considered fortress-like, cold and uninviting; instead, they provided shelters in the nursery-school garden to act as cover when the weather was inclement and to provide toilet, washing and cooking facilities (Straw, 1990).

From the hopeful beginnings of the open-air nursery schools, the McMillans' lasting legacy to early childhood education is the paradigmatic shift in interpreting the nature and needs of young children towards concerns about the lasting effects that extreme social deprivation has on children of working-class families, thereby moving away from the purely philosophical paradigm that had underpinned the practices of Froebel (Cunningham, 2006). In a sense, the success of the McMillans' outdoor learning experiment worked against universal nursery education, as it came to be seen not as a new form of education to be provided for all, but a compensatory form of education to promote good health in children from disadvantaged backgrounds (Blackstone, 1974; Woodhead, 1985). This theme would later be reinforced by the Hadow Report, which, although it was supportive in recognising the benefits of early childhood education and made specific reference to the works of Froebel, the McMillans and Montessori, also declared that, 'where home conditions are good, the best place for the child below the age of five is at home with his mother' (Hadow, 1933: 111–112).

This compensatory theme continued to be aligned with early childhood education both in the United Kingdom and United States, with the rise of 'programmes' in the 1960s and 1970s. For example, in 1964 the *Head Start* programme was introduced in the United States to support children from socially and economically disadvantaged backgrounds in achieving school readiness or preparedness. Barnett and Hustedt (as cited in Carpenter, 2005: 177), identified generally positive evidence regarding Head Start's long-term benefits stating that 'every dollar spent in the early years saved the state seven dollars later on by reducing the interventions necessary on crime, welfare, mental health and job prospect'.

This influential programme, which identified early childhood education as an effective tool in eradicating many of the problems associated with disadvantage, became the inspiration behind the Sure Start Programme introduced in 1999 in the United Kingdom as part of the then Labour government's drive to eradicate child poverty and social exclusion by 2020, a date extended from 2010 demonstrating the enormity of the challenge.

Owing to the poor general state of the nation's children at the time, the McMillan sisters occupied a significant place in history as new ideas concerning children and childhood emerged in the late Victorian and Edwardian period. By placing the tackling of child poverty and disadvantage high on the political agenda, they changed preconceived perceptions and achieved much for future generations:

> She [Margaret] realized that poverty, ignorance and disease were not only harming an adult population but mortgaging the growth of the next generation also. She yearned to change the system which created the conditions she abhorred. At the same time she realized that sick children could not wait for political reform. She fought to cure the dirt and disease that she saw every day in the mothers and children round her, and the fight for political reform as well.
>
> *(Bradburn, 1976: 45–46)*

Before moving on from discussing the work of the McMillan sisters to considering Maria Montessori, it is worth pausing to draw attention to Margaret McMillan's political successor in endeavouring to combat the effects of poverty and disadvantage on children and their families.

In March 2004, Gordon Brown as Chancellor, was hailed as a 'childcare champion' by the pressure group and childcare charity the Daycare Trust in response to the 2004 Budget, which directed increased spending of £669 million on early years education (Ball & Vincent, 2005). There are some useful comparisons to be drawn, as both the McMillan sisters and Gordon Brown recognised the need to intervene as early as possible in order to break the circle of disadvantage in a child's life. Not since Margaret McMillan's campaign for nursery schools in the 1920s (Brehony, 2009) has Childcare as a policy issue received so much intense attention as under the

1997–2010 New Labour government (Ball & Vincent, 2005). In Gordon Brown's Spending Review Statement (July 2004) to the House of Commons it is evident that he shared the McMillans' desire for universal nursery provision. Brown said:

> While the nineteenth century was distinguished by the introduction of primary education for all and the twentieth century by the introduction of secondary education for all, so the early part of the twenty-first century should be marked by the introduction of pre-school provision for the under-fives and childcare available to all.
>
> *(Brown, 2004)*

When Chancellor, from 1997 to 2007, Brown's focus on childcare as an anti-poverty strategy resulted in a raft of policies, including the National Childcare Strategy in May 1998. Between 1998 and 2004, about 500,000 children were lifted out of poverty (J. Harris, Treanor, & Sharma, 2009). However, progress since 2004 has faltered and then reversed as spending increases have not continued, despite one in three children currently living in poverty in the United Kingdom (J. Harris et al., 2009). Fiscal measures alone do not provide the solution, as employment, education, training, housing and the environment are all important in breaking the cycle of poverty, which inevitably shapes children's growth and development.

In May 2010 the coalition government's policies and goals in tackling poverty and social exclusion were still unclear according to Parekh et al. (2010), despite the publication of its *State of the Nation Report: Poverty, Worklessness and Welfare Dependency in the UK* (Department for Works and Pensions, 2010). This comprehensive report acknowledges the evidence of the EPPE study, which shows that good-quality childcare as well as good-quality parenting are particularly important for children from disadvantaged backgrounds in narrowing the gap in achievement (Sylva, Melhuish, Sammons, Siraj-Blatchford, & Taggart, 2004).

Frank Field's government-commissioned study, *The Foundation Years: Preventing Poor Children from Becoming Poor Adults* (Field, 2010: 5), reinforces generally held views, concerns and perspectives of those in the field of early childhood education that 'children's life chances are most heavily predicated on their development in the first five years of life'. The report also argues that it is parental education, coupled with good parenting and the opportunities for learning and development in the foundation years, that together matter more to children than money in determining whether their potential is realised in adult life. Despite these acknowledgments, the severity of the recent spending cuts imposed on Local Authorities in England places the future of many Sure Start Children's Centres under threat of closure (Toynbee, 2011).

The Children Act 2004 does place a duty on services to ensure that all children, whatever their background or circumstances, have the support they need to achieve the five outcomes[10] of the *Every Child Matters: Change for Children* (ECM) (Department for Education and Skills, 2004). It remains to be seen whether the well-being of children remains at the forefront of policymakers' decisions.

Unless children's rights and well-being remains a driving force in the inception and implementation of policies that tackle inequalities and social exclusion, society in the United Kingdom runs the risk of a lost generation.

Margaret McMillan would, most probably, be dismayed at the level of poverty in the United Kingdom today, and the sentiments she expressed in *The Nursery School* (1919) are as relevant now as they were at the turn of the last century. However, in the twenty-first century the portrait of child poverty is different from that of the working-class children living in the poor housing conditions of late-nineteenth- and early-twentieth-century Britain. As identified in the previously mentioned studies, poverty for children living in today's Britain is more likely to mean not having adequate winter clothing; not having enough money to go on holidays or school trips; living in poor housing conditions; eating irregularly and consuming cheap food of a poor nutritional standard. The impression of what poverty actually is and how to measure it has changed over the last hundred years or so, although many of the fundamental issues of what it is to be poor remain astonishingly familiar in twenty-first century Britain.

QUESTIONS FOR REFLECTION

In what way have the McMillan sisters played a role in driving and shaping educational and social policy towards recognising the value of parental and professional partnerships in supporting children and their families?

Reflecting on the discussions within this chapter, consider how, in the twenty-first century, poverty impacts on young children's learning and development. Has anything changed since the work of the McMillan sisters? Discuss your views with a fellow student or colleague.

Further reading

Baldock, P., Fitzgerald, D., & Kay, J. (2009). *Understanding early years policy.* London, UK: Sage.

Barker, R. (ed.) (2009). *Making sense of every child matters.* Bristol, UK: Policy Press.

Pratt-Adams, S., Maguire, M., & Burn, E. (2010). *Changing urban education.* London, UK: Continuum.

Notes

1 Albert Mansbridge, who, according to Elizabeth Bradburn, knew Margaret intimately, said that although Margaret was conscious of this tempestuous affair all her life, she very rarely referred to it (Bradburn, 1989).

2 Robert Blatchford (1854–1943) was a socialist campaigner and author. He founded the Manchester branch of the Fabian Society, launching a weekly newspaper, *The Clarion,* in 1891.

3 John Thomson (1837–1921), born in Edinburgh, became a photographer and experimented with microphotography (early style of documentary). His most famous work, *Street Life in London,* is regarded as a classic social documentary. Source: http://www.vam.ac.uk/ Victoria and Albert Museum.

4 In 2008/09, two very different patterns were apparent among children in low-income households. The number of children in low-income, working households ('in-work poverty') has never been higher. The rise from 2007/08 was slight but meant that 2.1m children – 57 per cent of all children in poverty – lived in a household with at least one working adult. Conversely, the number of children in low-income, workless households was, at 1.6m, the lowest since 1984. This figure has fallen consistently since 1995/96. A likely explanation for this fall in out-of-work child poverty is the increase (of nearly £5 per child per week) in Child Benefit and Child Tax Credit in April 2008. Source: *Households Below Average Income,* Department for Work and Pensions (based on analysis by IFS); data for Great Britain.

5 In those days infant mortality in Bradford was one in five. Source: 'A Fighter for the Children', *The Times,* Monday, 4 July 1960, p. 13.

6 Since the Education Act of 1870, five has been the statutory school starting age. However, the Act did not set a lower age limit, as school was considered less a place for learning and more a place to spend time before children reached the age of paid work.

7 It was estimated that in the first decade of the twentieth century one in eight deaths was attributed to TB (Source: Bryder (1992).

8 When the Second World War ended in 1945, many women who had worked in day care centres during the war stayed on in their jobs. The Government recognised that professional child care was a priority, and the National Nursery Examination Board (NNEB) was founded. Many of the principles that Margaret McMillan established in her training centres were reflected in the NNEB syllabus with its emphasis on childcare, health and hygiene.

9 In 1961 the College was taken over by London County Council, and courses became focused on nursery, infant or junior teaching, leading to a London University Certificate in Education. Source: The Margaret McMillan Collection compiled by the Librarian at Goldsmiths' College [Online], accessed at www.aim25.ac.uk/cats/61/6071.htm on 21 March 2011.

10 The five outcomes are: be healthy, stay safe, enjoy and achieve through learning, make a positive contribution to society and achieve economic well-being.

3

MARIA MONTESSORI

Introduction

> The most important period of life is not the age of university studies, but the first one, the period from birth to six.
>
> *(Montessori, 1967: 22)*

There are many parallels to be drawn between Maria Montessori and the McMillan sisters. The three women worked as contemporaries in Italy and England, but, although Margaret clearly knew of Montessori (Bradburn, 1976; Lowndes, 1960), there is no reliable evidence in the literature that the two ever met. Nevertheless, according to Steedman(1990: 227) 'McMillan's jealousy of her own position as educational innovator surfaced publicly in her pronouncements against Maria Montessori.'

It may well have been that Montessori was first brought to Margaret's attention when the former spoke three times at the 1899 International Council of Women in London (Babini, 2000, Kean & Oram, 1990). Montessori spoke of the very poor conditions of the Italian women teachers and denounced the working conditions of minors in Italy. Clearly well-educated, Maria Montessori possessed the same tenacious personality as Margaret and, like her, held strong political convictions and a sense of social justice, which not only strongly conditioned their professional careers but eventually led to the improvement of the lives of young children and their families living in the deprived conditions of the newly industrialised cities.

Montessori's early years

Maria Montessori (1870–1952) was born in the town of Chiaravalle, Province of Ancona, Italy. The year of Montessori's birth was also the year when Italy became a unified kingdom, in which Rome was adopted as the capital city.[1] Soon afterward, when Montessori was a young child, the family moved to Rome, where her father, a public clerk, took up a position in a newly established ministry. When Montessori was six years old, a left-wing government, under the leadership of Agostino Depretis, came to power and was responsible for inaugurating social and educational reform (Chisnall, 2008). This had a direct impact on Montessori's own educational journey, as in 1883 she began secondary school in the first year that this option became available to Italian girls. Montessori excelled in mathematics, and, in order to fulfil her desire to be an engineer, enrolled at the Reale Scuola Technica Michelangelo Buonarroti in 1883, which was coincidently also the same year that technical institutes first opened their doors to women students. However, these were times when medicine, rather than other disciplines, provided a platform on which to speak out across a broad agenda, including the physical, moral and social regeneration of the recently created Italian nation. Furthermore, in Italy, as in most other European countries at the time, the medical degree provided an early point of access for women to enter universities (Babini, 2000). Consequently, in a complete *volte face*, in 1889 Montessori enrolled in the Faculty of Medicine of La Sapienza the University of Rome, and although she was not, as is generally claimed, the first female medical graduate in Italy, she was the only female during her time at La Sapienza to graduate with a degree in medicine.[2] In 1896, after completing her medical degree, in which she chose to specialise in psychiatry rather than in paediatrics or gynaecology, which were the more accepted routes for Italian women doctors in the late nineteenth century, Montessori began her work in the public medical clinics in Rome.

At the same time she also entered the political arena as a proponent of socialist policies, arising from the Italian feminist movement becoming involved in many national and international initiatives, helping to found female associations, participating in conferences and publishing in the female periodical press (Foschi, 2008). For Montessori, feminism, politics and social medicine were inextricably intertwined, and in the public eye she increasingly became the 'face' of her causes (Babini, 2000: 50). Her contributions to the women's movement were eventually to become overshadowed by her world-renowned achievements in education, but nevertheless Montessori's early political commitment strongly conditioned and shaped her future vocation as an educationist in much the same way as it had Margaret McMillan's. Thus, alongside her political life, Montessori's professional career continued to develop, and she entered the debate on how best to care for the 'feeble-minded' children who were either overcrowding the already hard-pressed provincial 'asylums' or being kept back in elementary schools and weighing heavily on municipal finances (Babini, 2000). Drawing on her experience while working in psychiatric clinics, Montessori took part in the first two Italian conferences on pedagogy, held in Turin, 1898 and in Naples in 1901.[3] Montessori regarded herself as somewhat of an interloper when attending the conference in Turin, because 'the subsequent felicitous union between medicine and pedagogy still remained a thing undreamed of in the thoughts of that period' (Montessori, 1912/1964: 35).

Her papers – one on classification of types and the other on special pedagogy – were very well received by the academic community of scholars and led to her involvement in the newly founded *Lega Nazionale per la Protezione dei Deficienti* (National League for Care and Education of Mentally Deficient Children) (Catarsi, 1995). The League opened the first *Scuola Magistrale Ortofrenica* for 'mentally deficient' children (similar to what would be referred to today in the United Kingdom as a school for children with special educational needs) and invited Montessori to be the director. In the following two years Montessori began, in her own words:

> a genuine and thorough study of what is known as remedial pedagogy and then wishing to undertake the study of normal pedagogy and the principles upon which it is based, I registered as a student of Philosophy at the University.
>
> *(Montessori, 1912/1964: 33)*

It was during this period, between 1898 and 1901, that Montessori's son, Mario, was born (Kramer, 1976). Montessori and the child's father, Giuseppe Ferruccio Montesano, a medical colleague at the above-mentioned institute, never married, so the child was kept secret and was nursed in the Roman countryside; he was legally recognised by his father, but not by his mother. Mario Montessori eventually came to live with Montessori as an adolescent, contributing significantly to the spread of the Montessori 'method'. Both of them together would eventually establish the Association Montessori Internationale as a parent body to oversee the activities of schools and societies all over the world and supervise the training of teachers (Burnett, 1962)

Education for a new society

Returning to the University of Rome as a student of philosophy in 1902, Montessori embarked on a new stage in her career, eventually teaching anthropology at the pedagogical school for the training of teachers, which had been instituted at the Faculty of Education (Facoltà di Magistero) (Foschi, 2008). During that period Montessori produced her first major work, *Pedagogical Anthropology,* which was translated into English in 1913. In this text Montessori explains that, in contrast to general anthropology, which starts from a basis of positive data founded on observation alone, pedagogical anthropology starts from an analogous basis of observation and research. Furthermore, although sharing a theoretical kinship with Rousseau, Pestalozzi and Froebel, Montessori believed that the existing pedagogy, handed down from these three philosophers, was incomplete and vague, as it failed to embrace the importance of studying the child before educating him. Montessori argued that merely deducing what it was like to be a child had resulted in a philosophical rather than a scientific view of the child (Montessori, 1912/1964).

It is worth noting at this point that the world of educational theory that Montessori entered into in Italy was undergoing a fundamental review, mainly brought about by the protracted intellectual crisis that beset post-Risorgimento Italy. New ideas, predominantly within the realms of positivism, were challenging Italian philosophers and demanding explanations such as those of personality, freedom and individual autonomy. Knowing something of the nature of both the intellectual and the political crisis that troubled Italy at the turn of the twentieth century contributes to an understanding of the flux in which education found itself (Gregor, 2005). In the attempt to digest such complex issues emerging at the time, Montessori also entered the debate on education for a new society. For example, by referring to Marxist theory on the image of the labourer as a producer of wealth and well-being accorded the means and conditions needed for his work as a matter of right, Montessori was able to draw a comparison with the child's place in society (Montessori, 1967). In Montessori's view the child, too, is a toiler, and the aim of his work is to 'make a man...fashioning humanity itself'; seen in this way, 'society must heed the child, recognise his rights and provide for his needs' (Montessori, 1967: 17). Montessori believed that if mankind was going to create a new order of society, with morality and social values rather than conquest, power and profit at its core (Duckworth, 2006), then adults, including educators, should have faith in the fresh vitality and uncluttered 'vision of the child as a messiah' (Montessori, 1948/1972: 14). It may have seemed daunting at the time for teachers to consider young children as rights-bearing citizens, but the components of a learning environment that would free children to realise their innate human potential were the essential ingredient in Montessori's vision of education for a new world.

The Children's House and a revolutionary new pedagogy

By 1906 Montessori had become well known in the liberal and radical circles of the Roman elite as a pedagogical expert (Foschi, 2008). It was in this role that Eduardo Talamo (1858–1916), a civil engineer as well as the general manager of the Roman Institute of Real Estate (IRBS), called her to direct the educational activities of the Casa dei bambini, – Children's Houses of the IRBS (Foschi, 2008) in the working-class area of San Lorenzo, Rome. The establishment of the Children's Houses, which were part of a large-scale restructuring of the existing overcrowded tenements with their terrible living conditions, provided Montessori with an opportunity to create a 'real experimental laboratory' in which to observe children closely and develop what she referred to as a revolutionary new pedagogy (Babini, 2000: 63) – revolutionary, as Montessori held the belief that her new pedagogy would also be the source of a more radical transformation of society (Babini, 2000). Sharing the same utopian ideals as Comenius with regard to the purpose of education, Montessori viewed the education of young children as both a socialising and a liberating force; with the establishment of Children's Houses, women would be liberated, and children would no longer prevent women from working and reaching their full potential. Montessori's vision was that the Children's Houses would form the core of a broader project of homes for the future, where public state intervention would ensure that working mothers were supported in their new role by innovations such as the communal kitchen, where the food was ordered in the morning and sent at the proper time, house infirmaries, where the mothers could leave their sick children to be cared for by doctors and nurses, and before- and after-school clubs and reading rooms to add comfort to the adults in the communities:

> the new woman. . . shall be liberated. . . she shall be, like man, an individual, a free human being, a social worker; and like man, she shall seek blessing and repose within the house, the house which has been reformed and communised.
>
> *(Montessori, 1912/1964: 69)*

Montessori's transposition of the mother into someone with a social function stemmed from her practical feminism, grounded in the centrality of the Italian modern era (Stewart-Steinberg, 2007). In January 1907, at the time of the opening of the first Children's House, Via dei Marsi 58, the Italian feminist movement was at its height, and pressure was mounting in the campaign for women's suffrage (Stewart-Steinberg, 2007). It was during this period that Italy also experienced a period of significant growth and modernisation, and it was the image of the 'professional woman' that Montessori wished to promote (Babini, 2000: 54).

In the years following the opening of the first Children's House, Montessori began formulating her ideas concerning a pedagogic reconstruction of early childhood education, which eventually became known as the Montessori Method (Chisnall, 2008). It was with the order of the Franciscan Missionaries of Mary (FMM), located in Rome at Via Giusti 12, that the most influential Children's House was founded in 1910; this was where the first international courses on the Montessori Method were held, and which brought her international acclaim (Foschi, 2008).

Brief overview of the Montessori Method

One of Montessori's contributions towards the vision for a revolutionary pedagogy lay in the way she advocated applying the fundamental principles of the experimental sciences to pedagogy, with the central aim of providing the discipline of teaching with a scientific basis.

> Educators are still very far from having a real knowledge of that collective body of school-children, on whom a uniformity of method, of encouragement and punishment is blindly inflicted; if, instead of this, the child could be brought before the teacher's eyes as a living individuality, he [the teacher] would be forced to adopt very different standards of judgment, and would be shaken to the very depths of conscience by the revelation of a responsibility hitherto unsuspected.
>
> *(Montessori, 1912/1964: 38)*

It is clear that Montessori had a deep respect for the distinct individuality of the child, whose unique identity should be recognised through close observation.

By observation, Montessori meant that teachers should observe children with clinical precision, in order to know exactly what their spontaneous activity was. Furthermore, she believed that each child, although working collectively, should have freedom of movement and independence to choose when and what to learn and not be directed by the teacher.

However, there was a certain dualism in her writing as, while paying attention to science, there was evidence of philosophical reflections in her ideas:

> Many have looked upon materialistic and mechanistic science with excessive hopes. It is precisely because of this that we have entered upon a false and narrow way which must be surmounted if we are to revitalise the art of educating future generations. . . I personally believe that we should give more attention to imparting a spirit to teachers than scientific techniques, that is our aim should be towards what is intellectual rather than material.
>
> *(Montessori, 1948: 4)*

As part of this retreat from positivism, Montessori (1965: 14–15) objected vehemently to the use of measurements to design desks and benches, which forced children to become 'like butterflies mounted on pins. . . fastened each to his place'. Consequently, having criticised traditional school classrooms for their enslaving 'stationary desks and chairs', Montessori's classroom was a child-friendly environment that included small tables and chairs, light enough for a child to carry, low washstands and low cupboards for the children to access materials (Montessori, 1965: 16).

Montessori argued for the liberty of the child, not one of pure abandonment, as advocated by Rousseau, but a freedom that should 'permit a development of individual, spontaneous manifestations of the child's nature' (Montessori, 1965: 28). Furthermore, embedded in this notion of liberty was Montessori's discovery, based on countless hours of observation, that children were not motivated by extrinsic rewards, but, rather, their motivation and persistence at a task were driven by their desire to work at the task itself. For this reason Montessori placed great emphasis on a prepared environment in which freedom was more akin to self-discipline, and not under the direction of the teacher but, rather, a self-correcting pedagogy through the use of didactic material – a practice that Montessori describes as 'auto education' and which is at the core of her scientific pedagogy (Montessori, 1912/1964: 370). Montessori was critically disposed towards Froebel's gifts and occupations, but she found inspiration for her didactic equipment in the theories of French physicians, Jean Itard (1775–1838) and Eduard Seguin (1812–1880), who believed in educating children through their senses. With her scientific training and constructivist leanings, Montessori was to produce equipment that was methodically designed to exploit the progressive order in which young children develop. Montessori wrote: 'The hands are the instruments of man's intelligence. . . He constructs his mind step by step till it becomes possessed by memory, the power to understand, the power to think' (Montessori, 1967: 27).

Materials for sensory learning included sandpaper shapes, rods of beads, graded wooden blocks and insets of geometric forms. Adaptations of Montessori's great array of sensory and sensory-motor didactic materials can be found in most early childhood settings today.

However, the mere presence of the materials would not be enough for Montessori, who believed that only under proper guidance would they be educationally effective. This rested on the principles of recognising children's growth at crucial developmental moments, which Montessori referred to as *sensitive periods*.[4] Montessori proposed that if these periods are given proper consideration, they can be exploited to promote episodes of intense and efficient learning, but if they are not taken advantage of, then the opportunities are irretrievably lost. This developmental sequence of children's mental growth attracted the attention of Jean Piaget, who would eventually move beyond Montessori's concepts to formulate his own developmental psychology (Kramer, 1976). Her pedagogic approach also included *practical life exercises,* which involved both care of self, for example, washing, dressing, tying of shoelaces, and of the immediate environment, such as polishing brass objects, washing up and watering the plants as well as 'grace and courtesy', for example, learning to move gracefully, to greet each other, to lift objects carefully and to receive various objects from each other politely (Montessori, 1912/1964). It was these elements in her approach that caught the attention of Lombardo-Radice, discussed later in this chapter.

QUESTIONS FOR REFLECTION

Do you agree with Montessori that early childhood education is both a liberating and a socialising force for children and their mothers? If so, what links can you make between feminist theory, social justice and early childhood education? Share ideas with your tutor and/or a small group of fellow students.

What aspects of Montessori's *revolutionary pedagogy* can you recognize in early childhood education frameworks such as the EYFS?

In creating an enabling environment what opportunities would you provide for children to independently make choices and decisions?

The teacher as facilitator

Montessori's conception of the role of the teacher differed from that found in the traditional school, where teachers were the focal point of the children's attention. Montessori preferred the term *direttrice* – a directress who would demonstrate procedures and show the correct use of didactic materials. After this introduction, self-corrective learning would take place. The environment would be meticulously prepared before the children arrived, with careful use of space and separate work areas. The directress would remain in the background, directing the flow of routine classroom living, observing and keeping records of the children's activities.

The idea that children could learn for themselves – referred to today as child-initiated learning (David, 1999) – was quite startling at the time for those teachers who considered it their 'bounden duty' to plan for whole-group learning (Burnett, 1962: 73). In contrast to Froebel, who suggested that his teachers should live and play with the children, leading and directing them, Montessori believed that her teachers should remain in the background, watching and facilitating but leaving the initiative entirely to the children. In this respect Montessori's sense of democratic values and social justice influenced her thinking, as she believed that through the development of self-discipline children would be able to act ethically and handle conflict with maturity. In terms of the valorisation of play, although not viewed as a creative force in itself, Montessori did acknowledge it as a tool through which young children might learn about how to become human. Her view of play was in terms of allowing children to express their inner needs, desires and conflicts, but it was not the dominant form of activity (Montessori, 1948).

In April 1912, Montessori published the first of many editions of *The Montessori Method* (Montessori, 1912/1964), in which she describes in great detail her insights regarding the education of these young children in her schools. Reading about the progress of these socially disadvantaged children brought visitors from many parts of the world, and in the United States interest in the Montessori Method reached a peak just before the First World War (Burnett, 1962). In December 1913, Montessori visited the United States with a determined ambition to communicate to the world a new pedagogy that had the ideals of autonomy, independence, freedom and peace in common with the feminist movement. Interestingly, these ideals were better received in the United States than in Italy, as the progressive education of Parker and Dewey was attracting interest (Chistolini, 2009).

QUESTIONS FOR REFLECTION

Think of an early years teacher or practitioner that you have worked with whose teaching style you admire. Can you describe or note down those qualities that you liked? Share your notes with others in your group.

Look at a range of different job descriptions that relate to early childhood education. Compare and contrast these roles with Montessori's idea of an effective early childhood teacher. How would you account for any differences?

Critique of the Montessori Method

In Italy the Montessori Method was evaluated with only a certain degree of approval by Giuseppe Lombardo Radice (1879–1938), a revered Italian educator, who had visited numerous infant and nursery schools across parts of the Italian peninsula and Switzerland, gathering first-hand experience of what he referred to as *critical didactics*. Radice disapproved of the excessive amount of medical and scientific methodology in the lexicon of Montessori's approach (Lombardo-Radice, 1934). He did, however, agree that the Montessori Method was a liberating process for the child. But he also identified, much to his astonishment, that what he considered to be the good elements of the approach – the practical life exercises – came from the ideas of sisters Rosa (1866–1951) and Carolina (1870–1945) Agazzi, which he had witnessed during his visit to Mompiano Nursery in Trieste.

> For years I have preserved the memory of my delightful visit to the Trieste school... and as I had just read the *Method of Scientific Pedagogy,* I defined what I saw as 'Montessori.' Today I realise my inaccuracy, and I know that it ought to have been the other way round; these same characteristics as seen in the Children's Houses should properly be called 'Agazzi'.
>
> *(Lombardo-Radice, 1934: 24)*

This unsurprisingly ignited much debate in the educational and political arena; however, the original nature of Montessori's approach can only in fact be fully grasped by comparing it with the method developed by the Agazzi sisters (Röhrs, 1994). In the years following the turn of the twentieth century, Italian educators and ministers alike were increasingly concerned with the national implications of early childhood education and called for an investigation into the conditions and quality of pre-school institutions (Catarsi, 1985). The findings in 1908 of the lengthy investigations led by Corradini on behalf of the government showed a great variation of distribution according to geographical areas, with some staff having few or no qualifications and most institutions largely managed by private or religious organisations, with only a few actually run by the municipalities (Catarsi, 1985).

Later, in 1914, a royal commission was charged with examining and evaluating the most utilised pedagogic methods in Italy, during which the pedagogic methodologies of Froebel, Agazzi and Montessori were discussed (Catarsi, 1985) The final report[5] that emerged called for a new didactic orientation essentially in line with the pedagogy of the Agazzi sisters (Moretti, 2011). The principal criticism of the Montessori Method was that it favoured an urban child of a certain class and environment, who was not considered to be representative of the national context as a whole. In this respect the Montessorian child – a progressive child – was oriented towards an industrialised society aimed at surpassing the traditional agriculture society (Moretti, 2011). Therefore the motivation for choosing the Agazzi Method as appropriate for the reorganisation of the Italian system was that it was deemed ethically and culturally suitable for the Italian child, even though there were no specific attributes of *italianità* [the true Italian] within the pedagogic approach.

The Agazzi sisters' approach was founded upon a desire to imbue the traditional school environment with elements of family life in order to establish continuity between home and school, thus stimulating the child's creativity in continuous dialogue with the adult. It was this emphasis on dialogue, coupled with certain elements of Froebelism, such as the spontaneous concept of education and the importance attributed to play, that was the deciding factor in selecting the pedagogic approach (Franzé, 2000). It is worth noting that Froebel's kindergartens had been viewed with a certain amount of suspicion when they first arrived in Italy around 1869. Catholic opposition was particularly vigorous, as the Church authorities feared that the introduction of kindergartens into Italy would involve the importation not only of a foreign institution, but of significant numbers of Jews and Protestants (Albisetti, 2009). Taking a different stance, other critics, such as Pietro Pasquali, a member of the royal commission, pronounced in 1898 the metaphysical and mystical spirit of Froebel's pedagogy to be 'dead', although he still praised the ideas of play, activity and liberty for children (Albisetti, 2009).

Montessori and Mussolini

The commission's highly influential criticisms contributed to the relegation of the Montessori Method to a position outside the Italian academic mainstream. They were clearly not ready to embrace Montessori's attempt to liberate the child through the process of self-education and growth. At the time, after years of political upheaval since the *Risorgimento,* the preservation of a national identity took precedence over the values and aims inherent in Montessori's pedagogical approach, founded upon a differentiated path that highlighted the talents of the individual child. However, with the passage of time, which brought about social, economic and political change, the continued relevance of the commission's initial educational aims diminished as Italy increasingly took its place on the world stage. Montessori had moved to Barcelona, Spain, in 1916 and was gaining international recognition for her pedagogical approach. She made numerous attempts to reinstate her standing with the Italian government. Eventually, in the early 1920s, fully endorsed by Mussolini, leader of the newly created fascist government, a strong campaign promoting the method began. By the mid-1920s, the number of Montessori schools had increased notably throughout Italy (Moretti, 2011). In a remarkable turnabout Montessori who, a few years before, had been indirectly accused by the royal commission of having created a method that had little to do with the characteristics of the Italian child, now became a symbol of *italianità* abroad (Moretti, 2011).

According to Kramer (1976), Mussolini's main goal was to promote the modernisation of the Italian state utilising a pedagogical method that promised surprising results in the 3Rs, and that consequently should be incorporated into the fascist scholastic system. Montessori clearly benefitted from this renewed attention and collaborated with the fascists in order to implement her method throughout Italy while endeavouring to maintain political neutrality. But these were turbulent times and, by 1934, unable because of constant fascist surveillance on her schools to continue her exclusive interest on the child as a constructor of society, Montessori finally broke all ties with the fascist government. Mussolini was keen 'to impose a new discipline in education – a discipline to which everyone must submit, the teachers themselves first of all!' (Mussolini, 1933: 262). For Mussolini, fascism would change what he viewed as the old and typically liberal and democratic origin of humanistic education policy, which he believed furnished teachers 'with a good pretext for performing their duties indifferently and for abandoning themselves to subversive thought, even against the state itself' (Mussolini, 1933: 262). As had Popper with regard to Plato's political position, Montessori rejected Mussolini's totalitarian ideology, preferring to move education further towards more democratic ideals and a greater respect for the individual in pursuing their own goals for learning.

Montessori's affinity for the democratic ideal stems from the influences of earlier philosophers such as Locke and Rousseau, who both thought that education should take into account the individual nature of the child and be a liberating force. Initially finding a temporary safe haven in the Netherlands, she continued writing and delivering lectures on education for world peace in a range of settings throughout Europe[6] before moving to India in 1939 to continue her work (Duckworth, 2006).

It is worth noting that Montessori was 69 years old when she first went to India, but, despite her age, she was eager to plan the teacher training course which she had been invited to establish by the international president of the Theosophical Society, George Arundale. He had made the invitation to Montessori while he and his wife, Rukmini Devi, were visiting her in the Netherlands (Wylie, 2008). It was fortuitous that Montessori accepted the invitation and left Europe, accompanied by her son Mario, as later that year the Second World War broke out. However, as Italian citizens, as soon as the war broke out, Montessori and her son were put under house arrest separately (in India), to be reunited only on her 70th birthday following protests to the authorities by her supporters (Wylie, 2008). Finally returning to Italy in 1947, Montessori reflected on aspects she had learned from the Indian families she had lived with and published *The Absorbent Mind* in 1949 (Montessori, 1967), in which she discusses the influences on the child's earliest stages of growth and development including the embryonic stage.

QUESTIONS FOR REFLECTION

Reflecting Montessori's ideological stance, Rogoff (1990) maintains that, in societies where children are integrated in adult activities, children are situated within the community as central to the action. With this in mind, consider how society's culture is reflected in its early childhood education. Share your view with other students or colleagues in your group.

Consider the role of early childhood education in creating a democratic society. What does this mean in practice? Compare your ideas with other students or colleagues in your group and then read: Moss, P (2011) *Democracy as first practice in early childhood education and care* available online at: http://www.child-encyclopedia.com/documents/MossANGxp1.pdf. Compare your shared ideas with those presented in the article and note down the similarities and/or differences.

Montessori's lasting legacies

Although she is best remembered for her 'Method', Montessori's educational approach exemplified the values of progressive education, a movement that emerged from the United States in the twentieth century and sought to free children from oppressive teaching practices and to democratise the schools (Cremin, 1961). When reviewing the emergence of progressive education from a European perspective, Brehony (1997: 429) stated that much of what was identified with Dewey 'might equally have been derived from Froebel or Montessori or any other writer in the child-centred tradition'. Furthermore, as identified in Part I of this text, in the European tradition child-centred and humane approaches to the education of children, as exemplified by Montessori's approach, can be traced back to the earlier works of Aristotle, Quintilian and Comenius.

Part of this progressive movement in the twentieth century meant applying the pedagogical principles derived from new scientific research in the classroom. Developing a pedagogical approach that was founded on methodical scientific observation, Montessori contributed to the growth in scientific study of children at the time. However, although trained in the scientific approach, Montessori did not pursue her study of children in the necessarily restricted environment of a clinical laboratory but focused instead on the humanity of the children and what they were able to do and achieve within the conducive environment of the Children's Houses.

Montessori lived through turbulent times, living in exile and travelling extensively, becoming a global figure with an enduring international influence as her theories and ideas were translated into practice through a proliferation of training colleges and schools worldwide. Montessori's approach can be summed up in two words: *freedom* and *structure*. Seeing education as a process in setting children free, Montessori demonstrated that within a carefully structured environment children could be free to teach themselves, first through the senses and then through the intellect (Duckworth, 2006). Montessori respected the unique individuality of each child, recognising the potential that they possessed within themselves, seeing the role of the teacher not as one who constantly directs, instructs and corrects but as one who observes closely and carefully manages the environment in order for the child to learn, both independently and spontaneously (Montessori, 1912/1964).

Montessori had a great reverence for creation, which is clearly demonstrated in the following statement: 'children must be cared for right from birth, giving attention above all to the fact that they are beings with a mental life of their own' (Montessori, 1967: 61). For her, the child was a promise and a starting-point for the education of the 'new man'. Montessori was keen to demonstrate in her writings the dangers of authoritarian teaching methods:

> The child is like a soul in a dark dungeon striving to come into the light, to be born, to grow... And all the while, there is standing by a gigantic being of enormous power waiting to pounce on it and crush it.
>
> *(Montessori, 1965: 34)*

But it was this interpretation of the traditional role of the teacher that drew criticism and concerned some in the education field – not least Susan Isaacs, who, in her introduction to Guiseppe Lombardo-Radice's text *Nursery Schools in Italy,* stated emphatically:

> A teacher need not become afraid of herself, of her own interest and convictions in learning to respect the personality and the interests of the children. She can leave them free to develop their pursuits and their understanding, without having to maintain dead and colourless neutrality.
>
> *(Isaacs, as cited in Lombardo-Radice, 1934: 19)*

By reassuring teachers in this way, it is clear that Isaacs is admonishing Montessori's pedagogical approach, stating further that 'it is an odd notion to banish the teacher out of respect for the liberties of the taught' (Isaacs as cited in Lombardo-Radice, 1934: 19). Isaacs would have been aware of the major influence Montessori had at the turn of the century, as her ideas on the education of the young child were readily accessible by means of the English translation in 1912 of *The Montessori Method* (Graham, 2009). Furthermore, between 1919 and 1938, a six-month training course for Montessori teachers was held every other year in London and was reported on widely in the national press at the time (Smith, 1985).

Montessori's philosophy of freedom, respect and independence clearly led her to draw on the ideas of Froebel, Rousseau and Pestalozzi in the design of her revolutionary new pedagogy. The Agazzi sisters were also an inspiration with regard to the development of the whole child through their child-initiated practical life experiences, which Montessori re-shaped and adapted using a more methodical and scientific approach (Röhrs, 1994).

Montessori, like her contemporary Margaret McMillan, began her professional career with a social agenda that focused primarily on disadvantaged children. She saw education as the formation of the human personality – hence her eventual total rejection of Mussolini's totalitarian ideology – and she was strong in her belief that social change and world peace would only come about through an educational approach that paid attention to social justice. This required adults and policymakers across all boundaries to change their views on how children were regarded and treated. Rinaldi (2006) comments that Montessori's ideas on education for peace and social justice have been re-worked in the Reggio Emilia Approach to early childhood education. Ideas about participatory democracy and civic responsibilities for the benefit of the community are fundamental to what the protagonists of the Reggio Emilia Approach feel are at the centre of their educational vision (Rinaldi, 2006).

In collaboration with the New Education Fellowship (NEF),[7] Montessori proposed a *Social Party of the Child* to ensure the welfare of childhood and the recognition of children's rights. Although the war intervened in her work, Montessori was able to continue with this theme when she participated in the founding meetings of the United Nations Educational, Scientific and Cultural Organisation

(UNESCO) in 1950 (Barres, 2007). One task was to create the International Institute of Education to promote international peace through education (Barres, 2007). During the discussions linked to educating the '*new man*', Montessori reminded members of UNESCO that this is what she and many others had been doing for the past decades. It would take another fifty years before early childhood education became a priority item on the world's agenda (Barres, 2007).

Although never awarded the prize, Montessori was nominated for the Nobel Prize for Peace in 1949 by Professor Helena Stellway at Utrecht University[8] for furthering international understanding through her educational work. For Montessori, inherent in the very meaning of the word 'peace' is the positive notion of constructive social reform (Montessori, 1948/1972). Maria Montessori died in Noordwijk, Holland, in 1952, but her work lives on through the Association Montessori Internationale (AMI), the organisation she founded in Amsterdam, Netherlands, in 1929 to carry on her work.

QUESTIONS FOR REFLECTION

Reflecting on Montessori's desire for social change and world peace, what are, in your opinion, the values and beliefs that underpin education for peace?

With regard to creating a peaceable learning environment, how would you go about cultivating 'peace-building' skills in young children?

For an interesting study, examining the training of teachers in facilitating greater peace-building and conflict-resolution strategies, read the journal article by Vestal and Jones (2004) listed below.

Further reading

Anning, A., Cullen, J., & Fleer, M. (2009). *Early childhood education, society and culture* (2nd ed.). London: Sage.

Fielding, M., Moss, P. (2010). *Radical education and the common school: A democratic alternative.* London: Routledge.

Montessori, M. (1995). *Education and peace.* Oxford, UK: CLIO Press.

Rogoff, B. (1990). *Apprenticeship in thinking: Cognitive development in social context.* New York: Oxford University Press.

Vestal, A., & Jones, N. A. (2004). Peace building and conflict resolution in preschoolchildren. *Journal of Research in Childhood Education,* 19 (2): 131–142.

Notes

1 Although geographically united, the socially and economically deprived south and the wealthier industrialising north thwarted any sense of national unity at the time. The lack of stability created by ever-changing coalition governments unable to deal with corruption among government officials eventually led in 1922 to a fascist dictatorship led by Mussolini.

2 The first woman graduate in Italy was Ernestina Paper, who, in 1877, achieved a degree in medicine and surgery from the Superior Institute of Studies of Florence. She opened a medical surgery, treating women and children, in 1877 (Trabalzini, 2003).

3 For political reasons the conference in Naples never actually took place, but its proceedings were published nevertheless (Foschi, 2008).

4 The term was first coined by the Dutch geneticist, Hugo De Vries, and is compared with the notion of 'budding points' used by botanists (source: DeBaldo, 2005).

5 The commission's final report was called *Istruzioni, programmi e orari per gli asili infantili e i giardini d'infanzia* (Instructions, programmes, and schedules for preschools and playgrounds). Commission members included: Camillo Corradini, Luigi Friso, Pietro Cavazzuti, Maria Cleofe Pellegrini, Maria Pia D'Ormea, Pietro Pasquali and Giacomo Merendi (Source: Moretti, 2011).

6 Montessori delivered lectures in 1932 to the International Office of Education in Geneva; in 1936 at the European Peace Congress in Brussels; in 1937 at a congress in Copenhagen entitled Educate for Peace; in 1937, three lectures to the International School of Philosophy in Utrecht; and in 1939, to the World Fellowship of Faiths. These are recorded in her book: *Education and Peace* (1972).

7 The New Education Fellowship, founded in 1921 by Beatrice Ensor with her friends and colleagues, provided a learning community in which educators sought to define their role in the 'new era' within the wider context of an international community of practice (White, 2001).

8 Information retrieved 2 September 2010 from: http://nobelprize.org/nobel_prizes/peace/nomination/nomination.php?action=showandshowid=2806

4

SUSAN ISAACS

Introduction

> We only have to watch his play with a discerning eye, and to listen to his comments and questions in order to realize how his mind is beset with *problems* of one sort and another.
>
> *(Isaacs, 1954: 9)*

Susan Isaacs (1885–1948) shared Montessori's philosophy that everything educators need to know about children is learnt from the children themselves, particularly through the use of careful observations. There was also a strong connection to Montessori's idea of the child having the freedom to choose, but, like Margaret McMillan, Isaacs felt that this freedom was somewhat inhibited by the perceived extreme didacticism brought about by the implementation of the Montessori materials (Graham, 2009; Smith, 1985). Furthermore, although Isaacs would concur with Montessori on the idea of liberating the child towards his or her goal for self-fulfilment, particularly in their shared vision of re-creating a new society, she would disagree with Montessori's marginalisation of children's fantasy and imaginative play. Instead, Isaacs felt that children's play was to be respected and that children should be left free to evolve on their own terms, because, as she explained, 'play has the greatest value for the young child when it is really free and his own' (Isaacs, 1929: 133). Herein lies the tension associated with the understanding of what *freedom* actually means in terms of the child's learning and development and what constitute effective pedagogical approaches.

Susan Isaacs' early life

Susan Isaacs, the ninth – but seventh surviving – child of middle-class parents, was born Susan Fairhurst in Bromley Cross, near Bolton, a Lancashire cotton town.

Her father, a journalist and a Methodist lay preacher, was a person of intellect and scholarship, a disciplinarian who was also capable of inspiring affection (D. E. M. Gardner 1969; Smith, 1985). During the first four years of her life, despite the emotional upset of losing her brother Harry, who was 18 months older than she, to pneumonia, Susan experienced a certain amount of stability during which time her father achieved moderate prosperity, ably supported by his wife who, with strict economy, maintained high standards in the home and care of her large family (Smith, 1985). However, following the birth of her younger sister Alice and the subsequent ill health of her mother, the carefully organised household fell into disorder for a while. This resulted in her older brother William leaving home at the age of 18 to join the Merchant Navy, an event that caused Susan to believe it was she who had driven him away, when the reason was most probably the difficulties William had with his father. Shortly after her mother's death in 1890, her other brother, Archie, left to join the army, aged only 16. Susan, aged five, began attending the local school, which was overcrowded and unsanitary and had low standards of teaching (Graham, 2009). Although at first she welcomed the ordered routine of school life and was eager to show the class teacher what she could do, soon Susan began to find her school life difficult. Her experiences remained with her, as she was often perplexed when the teacher would point out her mistakes without further explanation. For example, Susan recollected a teacher, whom she was eager to please, looking down at her sewing and telling her to make the stitches smaller, and her own bewilderment as to how to achieve this as the stitches were already there and no further advice was given (D. E. M. Gardner, 1969: 19). Later in life Susan developed a deep conviction that children needed to be taught in ways they understood. This can be seen in the following statement regarding, in this instance, the support of young children's behaviour at the Malting House School: 'We never finally enforced any command about which the children had not been quite clear before they undertook the responsibility' (Isaacs, 1930: 31).

Eighteen months after the death of his wife, Susan's father married the housekeeper, and, in keeping with the popular myth of the stepmother, both Susan and her younger sister Alice disliked her. They were often in trouble with their stepmother, who gave them bread and water instead of meals as punishment for their misdemeanours; but when no one was looking Alice, under Susan's direction, would raid the pantry (D. E. M. Gardner, 1969). According to Graham (2009: 25), Susan 'must have found rewarding the responsibility she took upon herself for looking after her younger sister'. Graham further pointed out that all 'four sisters seem to have functioned like a close knit group of intimate friends'. A longitudinal study conducted in England by Gass, Jenkins, and Dunn (2007) revealed that siblings who share an affectionate relationship experience fewer internalising behaviours, such as anxiety and depressive symptoms, after experiencing stressful life events such as separation, loss and divorce. A further factor in developing the sisters' resilience was their love of the surrounding countryside and the freedom of the moors and open spaces they enjoyed together. Susan would later write (Isaacs, 1930, 1933) that children need to have people around them who understand how real their feelings are and how they need realistic experiences in which they are actively engaged (Graham, 2009).

Early career and academic studies

Despite her constantly inquiring mind, Susan remained frustrated by school life, and she left school at the age of 14, which was, at that time, not unusual for girls who were needed to help out in the home (Graham, 2009). Information about what Susan did from the time she left school in 1900 to when she enrolled on a teacher training course in Manchester in 1908 is somewhat hazy. According to Graham (2009), Susan did spend a year tutoring a boy with delicate health who was not well enough to go to school; she then went to Morocco as governess to an English family who were living in Casablanca, and on her return she found work as an assistant teacher. However, recognising the importance of acquiring appropriate training to be able to teach effectively, in October 1908, with her father's financial help, Susan finally embarked on an academic course at Manchester University. When he died in May 1909, Susan's modest share of the estate helped her to continue her studies at Manchester.

From leaving school until the time she started her studies, Susan widened her knowledge by extensive reading. A keen reader, Susan was fortunate to have a home full of books, newspapers and periodicals (Graham, 2009), Furthermore, as an early socialist and member of the Fabian Society, she would most certainly have assimilated ideas similar to those that influenced the McMillan sisters' thinking about welfare reform and social justice. However, it is worth noting at this point that, for Susan, social justice would come to mean an intrinsic and inextricable part of effective teaching, which includes the importance of attending, respectfully and systematically, to everything that children do (Drummond, 2000).

Opportunities for the exchange of ideas were available at the local Birtenshaw Mutual Improvement Society held in the Methodist Sunday School, where speakers from Bolton and Manchester were invited to talk on a range of subjects, which were then thrown open to debate (Graham, 2009; Radcliffe, 1997). In Britain, there was an explosion in mutual improvement societies, which were cooperative ventures in education.

> Typically, at each meeting one member would deliver a paper on any imaginable subject – politics, literature, religion, ethics, 'useful knowledge' – and then the topic would be thrown open to general discussion. The aim was to develop the verbal and intellectual skills of people who had never been encouraged to speak or think. There was complete freedom of expression, the teacher–pupil hierarchy was abolished, and costs were minimal.
>
> *(Rose, 2001: 58)*

This freedom of expression would have appealed to Susan, who had felt stifled by the oppressive education system she had encountered in school. Paolo Freire

(1921–1997), a Brazilian educator best remembered for his seminal text, *Pedagogy of the Oppressed* (Freire, 1968/2002), was critical of what he referred to as 'banking education', wherein pupils or students are asked to silently absorb the deposits that are imparted from the oppressor [teacher] (as cited in Srinivasan, 2006: 355). Links can be made here to Locke's view that children's minds are just empty vessels to be filled. Freire (1968/2002) believed that the great trait all human beings are born with is vocation, the ability to verbalise and articulate their own beliefs and reflections. The Mutual Improvement Society provided the space within Susan's community for this to take place. Susan's participation in the debates not only prepared her for the student debating societies at University, in which she excelled, but also introduced her to the importance of listening and contributing to what people actually had to say. Freire's theory of a liberating education recognises that knowledge is a social construct, not achieved through the transfer of information but co-created through the process of dialogue between teachers and students. This synergy between theory and praxis resonates well with the ideas Susan Isaacs would come to express when discussing the experimental Malting House School in Cambridge, which she had the opportunity to open and manage.

Susan soon became fully immersed in her university studies and joined numerous student societies. By her second year she had established a position as the most outstanding woman student that year, not only due to her intellectual prowess, but also because of her exceptional debating skills (Graham, 2009) Reflecting the McMillan sisters' and Montessori's views about working mothers, Susan, during one of her many successful debates, rebutted the proposal that when a girl accepted marriage, it was her duty to give up her career and devote her time to making her family home comfortable, stating that this was the 'old cry again'. Susan argued that it was wrong for women to give up a career unless the child needed her, and she stated that 'women are struggling for individuality and any curtailment of their liberty is fatal' (Graham, 2009: 37–38). Continuing with this theme as chairman of the Student Societies at Manchester University, Susan arranged for Margaret McMillan to be one of her speakers for the Sociological Society. Listening to Margaret speak about the need of a change of environment, better housing and a healthy diet for the children living in Deptford would most certainly have further fuelled Susan's interest in the importance of nursery education in enhancing children's and their mothers' lives, echoing Montessori's sentiments (Graham, 2009).

In June 1912 Susan gained a first-class honours degree in philosophy, which was an incredible achievement given her lack of schooling prior to starting her university course and, during her studies, her substantial involvement with student societies (Graham, 2009). Susan was one of only two students to gain a first in philosophy, and the quality of her undergraduate dissertation assured her a place at Cambridge as a research student at doctorate level, to study psychology, in which she had become increasingly interested. Susan's mind had been turning from philosophy to biology and then to psychology, and at Cambridge she found many opportunities to study the latter (Smith, 1985). By the time she actually arrived at

Cambridge, Susan knew she wanted to be an educational psychologist, having found that she was increasingly interested in children and child development.

The study of children began with Darwin himself, whose method at arriving at his theory of evolution was as influential as his theory itself. To further establish the study of childhood, Darwin made his own contribution by means of a published article in the journal *Mind,* entitled 'Biographical Sketch of an Infant' (Darwin, 1877). The article was a retrospective account of detailed day-by-day observations of his own child from birth to around three years of age, which he had carried out thirty-seven years earlier. The results provided new insights to changes in behaviour using a biological point of view. It was Darwin's collection of data systematically observed in natural settings that came to be the preferred scientific method of psychologists and researchers studying the growth and development of children (Lorch & Hellard, 2010; Smith, 1985).

Susan's life at Newnham College, Cambridge, was very different from that at Manchester University, as she found the almost exclusively male society oppressive. According to Graham

> Cambridge then, as now, is largely a University for undergraduates. Susan as a twenty-seven-year-old post-graduate was indeed an outsider not merely because she was a woman but because she was older and more senior than the undergraduates, yet hardly able to mix easily with the clannish dons, male or female.
>
> *(Graham, 2009: 54)*

Reading this observation through the lens of the French sociologist and philosopher Bourdieu (1930–2002), it is clear that Susan's transition to a new and very different university environment can be explored usefully through the concept of 'habitus'. The concept of 'habitus' is at the heart of Bourdieu's work and is useful in formulating opinions on how the social, cultural and economic context in which people are raised shapes their attitudes and means of interpreting the world (Bourdieu & Passeron, 1977). In an article she wrote for the *Manchester University Magazine,* which in itself would indicate a desire to remain attached to the familiarity of her own 'habitus', Susan expressed her feelings about Cambridge University and wrote: 'women are essentially intruders. . . nor is it good for the women students to be constantly reminded that they are not merely students but also female ones' (Isaacs as cited in Graham, 2009: 54). Susan appears to articulate a sense of women standing on the edge, as outsiders, observing from afar, or as *fishes out of water*. Bourdieu used the phrase 'fish in water' to describe a sense of belonging:

> when habitus encounters a social world of which it is the product it is like a fish in water, it does not feel the weight of the water, and it takes the world about itself for granted.
>
> *(Bourdieu & Wacquant, 1992: 127).*

When at Manchester Susan still felt attached to the *real world*, as she saw it, with its 'urging sense of the grim hard pressure of life', which for her was far more conducive to meaningful study relevant to the problems that the world faced in 1913 (Graham, 2009: 54). Nevertheless, Susan was able to transcend these views and participate fully in her studies, and although she only spent a year at Cambridge she learned much about general psychology and the fundamentals of research methodology. These experiences would further assist Susan's contribution to the newly emerging international field of education, as she later travelled to countries such as Australia and New Zealand as an active member of the New Education Fellowship (Brehony, 2004).

Before she left Cambridge, Susan was appointed a lecturer at Darlington Teacher Training College, where she was to be remembered for her constant search for the true methods of teaching based on her growing understanding of children's real needs and interests (Smith, 1985). Sharing Plutarch's (c. 46–120 AD) belief that 'the mind is not a vessel to be filled, but a fire to be kindled' (as cited in Willan, 2009: 157) and also influenced by Pestalozzi, Robert Owen and Dewey, Susan promoted the idea of teaching as building on the child's own ideas rather than merely transferring knowledge.

While in her first year of study at Manchester University, Susan was taught by a revisionist Froebelian, Grace Owen (1873–1965), who had introduced her to the work of Froebel and Dewey (Brehony, 1997). As a revisionist, Grace Owen represented a new generation of Froebelian leaders who had an institutional base in teacher training colleges. Far removed from the traditional Froebelians, revisionists looked outward, recognising new opportunities arising from concerns such as those shown by the McMillan sisters about the health and physical conditions of disadvantaged inner-city children and their families (Brehony, 1997).

A leading exponent of Dewey's ideas, John Joseph Findlay, Professor of Education at Manchester University, 'played a pivotal part in introducing Dewey to English audiences when he edited two collections of Dewey's writings in 1906 and 1910' (Brehony, 1997: 431). With such endorsements from those who guided her learning at Manchester University, it was inevitable that Susan would also find inspiration in the works of Dewey. Dewey's conviction about the natural capacity of children to wonder and experiment emerged not only from the ideas of the earlier philosophers, such as Pestalozzi and Froebel, but mainly through the implementation of his psychological theories, which he put into observable concrete practice in his Laboratory School (Smith, 1985). The school, essentially an experiment in understanding and guiding child development towards desired social and intellectual ends, was also instrumental in reinforcing Dewey's views that the task of education was to provide the right conditions to foster growth. Dewey's subsequent publication, *How We Think* (Dewey, 1910), not only provided educators with the results of the process but was also an example of critical reflective inquiry. Dewey was, as Susan described, 'my active inspiration' (Isaacs, 1933: 19).

It was during her time at Darlington that Susan decided to marry William Brierley, whom she had met in her undergraduate days and with whom she had a great deal in common at the time. He, like Susan, qualified to train as a teacher at

Manchester University and then transferred to an honours degree to study Botany as opposed to Philosophy as in Susan's case. They married in July 1914, and on 5 August Britain entered the First World War. As most socialists did at the time, it is likely that Susan and William would initially have opposed the war, but eventually William enlisted in the Artists' Rifles, part of the London Infantry Regiment. He was invalided out in 1916 and returned to his wife, who had by now established herself in London (Graham, 2009). Susan found work by giving a series of guest lectures in psychology for London University tutorial classes and also at the Workers' Educational Association (Smith, 1985). In 1921 she also published her first book, *An Introduction to Psychology,* with strong biological underpinnings, while also becoming increasingly interested in the ideas of Freudian psychoanalysis (D. E. M. Gardner, 1969).

The practice of psychoanalysis was and still is by its very nature complex and difficult to disentangle, as it focuses on those areas of mental functioning that are not directly observable or measurable. Nevertheless Freud's work was a turning point with regard to the constructs of childhood, just as Darwinism had been earlier. The earlier constructs of childhood through welfare and the emphasis on health and physical growth was, in the period between the two world wars, re-defined as the psychological child in terms of emotions, fantasies, dreams, instincts and habits (Hendrick, 1994). At that time psychoanalysis was seen by many psychologists as part of a 'New Psychology', and for pioneering educationists a useful set of ideas from which to develop new teaching methods (Graham, 2009: 70). Recent approaches based on psychoanalytical theory include the work of Hopkins (1988) and Elfer (2007), who both introduced and developed ideas about the importance of considering the emotional interactions and responses that take place within the nursery environment between young children and their primary carers.

For Susan the significance of the newly emerging psychoanalytical theory and its focus on the development of the mind was critical in providing valuable insights into the behaviour of children. This is shown in the interpretations of the many detailed observations she carried out at the Malting House School (discussed in more detail further on in the chapter). Wanting to gain an even deeper insight into what the new discipline of psychoanalysis had to offer her, Susan started upon her first long analysis, which began with J. C. Flugel, who was a founder member of the London Psycho-analytical Society and a psychologist on the staff at University College, London, where Susan also taught as an assistant lecturer (Graham, 2009). In 1920 Susan travelled to Vienna, Austria, hoping to undergo further analysis with Freud himself; Freud was unavailable, so she saw Otto Rank, one of Freud's closest associates. Following these two experiences of analysis and regular attendance at their meetings, in 1921 Susan was elected Associate Member of the British Psycho-analytical Society (Graham, 2009). As Susan's areas of interest spread she began to realise that her marriage was not satisfactory either to herself or her husband, and it was subsequently dissolved. Although this was an unusual occurrence at that time, Susan was driven by her convictions that William Brierley would be happier without her (D. E. M. Gardner, 1969). In 1922 she married Nathan Isaacs, whose intellectual acumen she had admired ever since they first met two years earlier at one of her psychology lectures delivered at the Workers Educational Association (Smith, 1985). That year she also qualified as a psychoanalyst and became a full member of the British Psycho-analytical Society. By 1923 Susan had added a new layer to her 'habitus', as she had finally found in psychoanalysis an ideology she was at home with and was married to a man who met her need for intellectual discussion. Up to this point in time Susan had made serious attempts to understand human growth and development and the best way to provide for children's further development. She would soon be able to put this knowledge and understanding into practice.

QUESTIONS FOR REFLECTION

Reflecting on your own schooling, was there a teacher who made a lasting impression on you? If so in what way?

Considering the factors that influenced Isaacs' early life, can you provide any examples in which Isaacs' experiences in one context influenced her actions and behaviour in another?

Now repeat this process by reflecting on your own life experiences and how they may have impacted on your own learning and development. To help you to do this use Urie Bronfenbrenner's ecological model (1979).

To understand Bronfenbrenner's ecological model, read Swick and Willams' (2006) journal article, available online at http://people.usd.edu/~mremund/bronffamily.pdf.

After reading the article, consider the implications for practitioners working with children and their families experiencing strain or stress. In what ways can practitioners be supportive and caring? If possible, draw on your personal experience of working with children and their families and share your ideas with fellow students or colleagues.

Theoretical aspects of the Malting House School experiment

Susan Isaacs' work, up to this time, had been mainly concerned with understanding children through the use of psychological and educational explanations to those adults who were or would become responsible for them. Her contribution to the study of children stemmed from her wide-ranging reading, the influences of the earlier pioneers and robust debates and lectures, initially attended and latterly prepared as part of her role as a lecturer. By 1924 Susan had arrived at that time in her career when the opportunity arose to become very much part of the broad-scale attempt to improve the learning environment of children. Susan brought with her a new voice in early childhood education, with different things to say and a different understanding.

On 25 March 1924, a full-page advertisement that appeared in the *New Statesman* caught the attention of Susan and Nathan Isaacs (see Figure 4.1).

WANTED—an Educated Young Woman with honours degree—preferably first class—or the equivalent, to conduct education of a small group of children aged 2–1/2–7[1] as a piece of scientific work and research.

Previous educational experience is not considered a bar, but the advertisers hope to get in touch with a University graduate—or someone of equivalent intellectual standing- who has hitherto considered themselves too good for teaching and who has probably already engaged in another occupation.

A LIBERAL SALARY—liberal as compared with research work or teaching—will be paid to a suitable applicant who will live out, have fixed hours and opportunities for a pleasant independent existence. An assistant will be provided if the work increases.

They wish to obtain the services of someone with certain personal qualifications for the work and a scientific attitude of mind towards it. Hence a training in any of the natural sciences is a distinct advantage.

Preference will be given to those who do not hold any form of religious belief but this is not by itself considered to be a substitute for other qualifications.

The applicant chose will be required to undergo a course of preliminary training, 6–8 months in London, in part any rate the expenses of this being paid by the advertisers.

Communications are invited to Box NO 1

[1] As in original advert; however, for clarification this reads: 2½–7.

FIGURE 4.1   The full-page advertisement that appeared in the *New Statesman* (as cited in Gardner, 1969)

The 'young educated woman' . . . 'to conduct the education of a small group of children' aged between two and seven years of age corresponded well to Susan's qualifications, background and experiences. The person who had placed the adver- tisement was Geoffrey Pyke, a wealthy speculator in the commodities market. Dissatisfied with the current education system in England, Pyke wanted to create a school environment that was based on the best psychological and educational thinking then available, in which his son David, aged three at the time, could thrive (Graham, 2009; Smith, 1985). In response to the advertisement, intense three-way discussions took place between the Isaacs and Geoffrey Pyke regarding the educa- tional principles that should guide the running of the school. They agreed that the principles would draw on psychoanalytical theory and the child-centred approaches of progressive education, reflecting Susan's areas of expertise (Graham, 2009). Susan Isaacs would become principal of the school, and Margaret Pyke, Geoffrey's wife, would handle the household and business matters (Smith, 1985). Nathan Isaacs' role was to contribute 'years of philosophical and psychological thought directed particularly to the meaning of knowledge, the process of growth, and the relationship between thought... and language' (D. E. M. Gardner, 1969: 57).

The school opened in October 1924 in a large rented house called Malting House, close to present-day Darwin College, Cambridge, and became another of several progressive or experimental schools popular in the United Kingdom among liberal thinkers in the 1920s and 1930s. As discussed in Part I, progressive education or progressivism stems from the ideas of Rousseau and is a philosophy of teaching and learning that stresses individualism, egalitarianism and learning by discovery. But progressive education is fluid and open to interpretation, as can be seen in the differing emphases within the approaches of, for example, Froebel, Montessori and Dewey. During the early twentieth century, progressive education in the United Kingdom was at its zenith and was promoted by such educational theorists and practitioners as Bertrand Russell (1872–1970) and A. S. Neill (1872–1970), both of whom established their own schools – Beacon Hill School and Summerhill School, respectively – with the latter still open to this day. Russell (1926) advocated the project method and commented on the use of practical lessons in a variety of vocations for the instruction of children, reflecting Pestalozzi's approach.

For Neill (1966), the basic principle in Summerhill was freedom for children to pursue their own academic interests – or not – as they chose. Although certain aspects were similar, such as being informed by psychoanalytical insights (Neill, 1966), the Malting House School was different in that it was planned with both scientific and pedagogical aims and was a living laboratory, in this respect akin to the way Montessori referred to her Children's House in Rome. Although unique in the United Kingdom, there was another school that drew on psychoanalytical theory. This was the Children's Home, founded in May 1921 by the Moscow Institute of Psychoneurology and attended by Stalin's son. Vera Schmidt, a Russian educationist and one of the leading figures in the psychoanalytic movement in Russia, was in charge, with advice from psychologists Alexander Luria, who worked alongside Lev Vygotsky and Sabina Spielrein (Piaget's analyst) (Forrester, 2004). There are many parallels to be drawn between Susan Isaacs and Vera Schmidt, as they were both influenced by Froebel's philosophy and Freud's psychoanalytical theory. Women clearly played a prominent part in the advancement of the psychoanalytical movement, just as they were responsible for spreading Froebel's ideas through the Kindergarten Movement. The close links between networking, organising and institution-building clearly showed how educated women, including those who are the foci of this book, made a substantial contribution to psychology, education, philosophy, policy and practice. Moreover, psychoanalysis offered a new profession that, like the women's movement after 1918, aimed to enhance the individual's capacity for both work and love in exploring sexuality and, increasingly, the relationship between mother and child (Alexander, 1998). The arrival of Melanie

Klein, the Hungarian psychoanalyst, in London in July 1925 was a decisive event in the history of British psychoanalysis (Alexander, 1998), and Klein's lectures on child analysis would have a lasting influence on Susan Isaacs' work with children, particularly with regard to phantasy.[1]

Klein contributed to the debate by enlarging on the concept of unconscious phantasy, focusing more on the imaginative aspect than Freud's emphasis on dreams. Developing the view that phantasy is a mental activity present in rudimentary form from birth onwards and essential for mental growth, in simple terms Klein noted that young children accompany their activities with a constant stream of phantasy (Bott Spillius, 2001). One of Klein's many examples is a young child, Fritz, aged five years:

> For in his phantasies the lines in his exercise book were roads, the book itself was the whole world and the letters rode into it on motor bicycles, i.e. on the pen. Again, the pen was a boat and the exercise book a lake.
>
> *(Klein, 1923/1975: 100)*

Although influenced by Klein, Susan Isaacs was clear in her objectives for her teaching staff at the Malting House School that they should not act as analysts, stressing that:

> Ideally, *no* interpretations should appear in the records. Vague evaluatory comments or summarising phrases, such as 'the children were very interested – polite – quarrelsome,' are best avoided. Only full verbatim records of what was said and full objective records of what was done should be given.
>
> *(Isaacs, 1930: 1)*

However, remaining objective is nigh impossible because, essentially, what the observer sees and records depends on his or her values and the rationale or purpose of the observations. Susan did acknowledge this dilemma and recognised that adults, in selecting what to observe, will always be influenced by their own histories and experiences indicating that any research that has observations as part of the methodology is affected by the values and judgements of the observer. But because of Susan's influence on the field of education and her emphasis on the value of observation-led records for understanding young children, observations have remained the preferred method by early childhood practitioners and researchers (Robson, 2006). But, as Montessori also stressed, the greater the experience and expertise in understanding how children learn and develop, the more valuable the written records are.

With regard to her Malting House School study, it was the application of psychoanalytical theory to child development that was of paramount interest to Susan. So pervasive was Freud's thinking that, according to the *New Statesman* at the time, it would be 'as difficult for an educated person to neglect the theories of Freud and his rivals as it would have been for his father to ignore the equally disconcerting discoveries of Darwin' (as cited in van der Horst, 2011: 25).

Over the next three years, the Malting House School would provide an ideal naturalistic environment in which to observe a small group of children aged between two and seven years of age. These children, described as bright with often challenging behaviour, were mostly the sons and a few daughters of Cambridge dons, albeit the more progressively minded ones, such as G. E. Moore, Professor of Philosophy, while others such as Ernest Rutherford, who helped pioneer nuclear physics, and Percy Nunn, later knighted for services to education, sat on the school's Board (van der Horst, 2011).

Another dominant theoretical position at the time, and one that drew Susan's attention, was behaviourism. The behaviourist perspective considers that everything a person does, such as acting, thinking and feeling, can be regarded as behaviours that are conditioned by their experiences (Doherty & Hughes, 2009). Susan commented that the behaviourist school led by John Watson (1878–1958) was 'making very useful experimental studies of the behaviour of young infants in the nursery by methods exactly comparable to those familiar in the study of the young of other animals' (Isaacs, 1921: 153). However, Susan also believed that 'the refusal of the behaviourists to consider facts of consciousness remains a severe limitation on their final contribution' (Isaacs, 1921: 153). Although both theoretical positions are linked to human growth and development, they are diametrically opposed in their application. The 'facts of consciousness' to which Susan refers are the unconscious feelings and thoughts that are brought to consciousness through a range of complex reactions and, in the case of young children, are often expressed through their free play. For Susan, the technique of psychoanalysis shed a profound illumination upon the outward behaviour of young children (Isaacs, 1933).

The Malting House School (1924–1927)

From Susan's point of view, the major purpose of carrying out detailed observations at the Malting House School, and the two publications that emerged from the study, was to further the understanding of children's behaviour in a way that no other investigation had done at the time, thereby making a significant scientific contribution to the field of child development and psychology (Smith, 1985). As a natural scientist, a philosopher, an educationist and a psychoanalyst, she was extremely well qualified to make new connections about the holistic growth of young children in an essentially child-centred learning environment. Employing ethnographic methods, Susan and her colleagues at the school set about mapping the natural development of children's understanding, and to facilitate this process, the children were encouraged to play freely for their own amusement in the company of attentive adults who were trained to make extensive observational notes of their natural behaviour (Willan, 2009, 2011). Informed by these observations and by what she had learnt from the early philosophers, Susan Isaacs would later write:

> The great educators taught us long ago the child reveals himself in his play. In recent years we have come to understand more fully than ever before the

deeper meaning of the little child's play. if we watch him when he is free to play as he will, the child shows us all that he is wishing and fearing, all that he is pondering over and aiming to do. . . It is through his play that the child tells us most about his needs of growth.

(Isaacs, 1954: 6)

The Malting House School's provision was specifically designed for play and active inquiry, and the children were free to explore their environment both indoors and outdoors. For Susan, play – particularly imaginative or role play – 'was an expression of the child's unique inner psychodrama, requiring time and space for its unrolling, acting out and resolution' (Willan, 2011: 207).

Susan avoided the layout of a formal classroom, as she believed it impeded the children's freedom to make choices. Instead, the children were left to choose their own activities from the equipment and books that were available and from the rich experiences to be found in the various workshops and the large garden (Graham, 2009).

Susan made much of the strong affinity children have with the outdoors, as the McMillan sisters had in their Nursery Garden Schools, and she ensured that the children had much to stimulate their active inquiry through the provision of a range of resources that fired the children's imagination. In Susan's own description of the Malting House School, in her publication *Intellectual Growth in Young Children*, she refers to the children and staff, the school, equipment, educational aims and the actual technique as the conditions of observation (Isaacs, 1930). Although it would seem, on the surface, that the whole undertaking was essentially a piece of educational research, for Susan there was also a deeply held conviction that the school had two essential functions: first, it was to provide for the child's own bodily and social skills and means of expression, and, second, to 'open the facts of the external world (the real external world, that is, not the school "subjects") to him in such a way that he can seize and understand them' (Isaacs, 1930: 20). The first goal is not only reflective of progressive education but is a familiar concept to anyone seriously involved in early childhood education today in the United Kingdom. The second goal, in Susan's view, 'is a little more novel' (Isaacs, 1930: 20) as, at the time, young children actively generating knowledge from daily experiences in this way would not have been taken seriously enough (Smith, 1985). Susan's educational innovations, seen as revolutionary to those teachers who adhered to rote learning as the primary vehicle to academic achievement, were built on the earlier works of Rousseau, Froebel and Dewey in particular and can now be seen in the educational programmes of high-quality early years provision today.

The learning environment

Susan describes at some length the way the large rambling building was adapted for use as a school (Isaacs, 1930: 14). The children and staff met in the large hall, which had access to the garden by means of 'easy steps' for the children's young legs to negotiate. The large hall was used for general purposes, including dramatic play and dressing up, in the same way as perhaps a church or community centre hall would be used nowadays for a pre-school session. At one end of the room was a gallery for visitors who wished to observe the children, and at the other end was a low platform on which the piano stood and was often played by Susan, with the children dancing and interpreting the music through their movements. Susan also noted that the children showed great interest in watching the hammers strike the wires when the keys of the piano were depressed (Isaac, 1930: 121). Other rooms leading off from the hall were used: one as a rest room and another as a reading and writing room for the older children in the group. One large room was fitted up as a combined carpentry room and science laboratory, compete with Bunsen burners. Another room was for handicrafts, painting, modelling and drawing. There was also a smaller rest room for the younger children, with moveable tables and chairs and large floor cushions. The equipment of the school was carefully planned and extensive and included the first 'jungle gym' in Britain (Smith, 1985). In short the children had a wealth of resources with which to build, thread, join, cut, measure, classify, manipulate, examine and explore, both indoors and outdoors. There were low shelves and cupboards that stored a wide range of Montessori equipment, and although initially used as intended, according to Susan they seemed to have stimulated much more easily the desire for their active use in constructive or symbolic play. Susan provides the example of the Montessori rods being used as 'walking sticks' or 'guns' and being used far less readily for their 'proper' value, and she noted that the children needed 'much more stimulus from the teachers to perceive their formal relations' (Isaacs, 1930: 277). This serves to reinforce Montessori's belief that the mere presence of the materials would not be enough and that only under proper guidance would they be educationally effective.

QUESTIONS FOR REFLECTION

Do you agree with Isaacs that through observing children at play we can learn more about their growth and development?

Which aspects of Isaacs' approach can be seen in the EYFS framework?

Reflecting on the range of resources provided in the Malting House School, what is your stance with regard to young children using real equipment such as carpentry tools that include hammers, saws and nails? Share your views with fellow students and colleagues.

What sort of equipment or resources would you provide to fire young children's imagination? Exchange ideas with fellow students or colleagues.

Care of animals

Susan was keen that the children pursued their own interests in the natural world, which was inevitable, given the extensive gardens and close proximity to the pond at the Backs in Cambridge (Willan, 2009). In the garden were kept animals that were cared for by the children, and every child had their own plot for planting vegetables and flowers. On the surface this presents a familiar picture of many early childhood settings today. However, because of the concerns of the Royal Society for the Prevention of Cruelty to Animals (RSPCA) regarding the keeping of vertebrate and invertebrate animals in schools, underpinned by the Animal Welfare Act 2006, the legal responsibility has placed too high a barrier for most schools to overcome with regard to keeping animals on the premises. To some extent this is a pity, as from my recollections the primary justification – although not the only one – is that caring for animals teaches young children responsibility. With no such restrictions to consider, Susan and her staff carried out with absolute impartiality observations of the children's relationships with nature:

> the records themselves are direct and dispassionate observations, recorded as fully as possible under the conditions; and as free as possible from evaluations and interpretations.
>
> *(Isaacs, 1930: 1)*

An altogether more controversial aspect of the children's nature study at the Malting House School was the dissection of dead animals. As a University lecturer in Early Childhood Studies, I have found that this aspect of Susan Isaacs' work raises much heated discussion and debate among the undergraduate students as to the suitability of such an activity, particularly with children aged seven and under. Certainly the RSPCA are opposed to the dissection of any animals in schools as, in their view, it can lead to desensitisation and a lessening of respect for life among the pupils. They suggest the use of alternatives such as models and computer simulations (www. rspca.org.uk, accessed on 5 August 2010).

In 1931 Susan Isaacs, as Chair of the British Psychological Society's Education Section, spoke about her research concerning childhood socialisation and attitudes to animals at 'the Conference of Educational Associations, whose members came together annually to discuss educational theory and practice in Great Britain' (Unti & DeRosa, 2003: 31). Susan's special focus was on children's exposure to the death of animals and on dissection. In defence of dissection, Susan recounted that the children she observed showed greater sympathy with living animals and more consistent care after they 'looked inside' the 'dead ones' and experienced fewer lapses into experimental cruelty such as squashing worms (as cited in Unti and DeRosa, 2003: 32). As Susan further clarifies:

> the impulse to master and destroy was taken up into the aim of understanding. The living animal became much less of an object of power and possession, and much more an independent creature to be learnt about, watched and known for its own sake.
>
> *(Isaacs, 1930: 166)*

Furthermore, through carrying out her observations, Susan discovered that 'the children's minds turned more freely and steadily towards the non-interfering, observational attitude of many modern naturalists towards living animals in their own setting (bird-watchers, big-game observers and photographers)' (Isaacs, 1930: 165–166). From the reaction of outsiders in Cambridge, Susan was also resigned to the fact that so strong was the widely held attitude that it was difficult to get many people even to consider these views. But she also pointed out 'the extra-ordinarily confused and conflicting ways in which adults behave towards animals in the sight of children'; providing a list of examples ranging from eating the meat of dead animals, killing wasps and slugs, to communicating to children phobias about spiders, snakes and mice, to name just a few (Isaacs, 1930: 160). In endeavouring to find a balanced solution, as not all children will come across these inconsistencies, Susan suggested that educators must arrive at a reasonably consistent set of standards and maintain for themselves and the children 'the demand that no living animals. . . shall be allowed any avoidable pain or suffering' (Isaacs, 1930: 164). Clearly, the findings gathered at the Malting House School could not be considered broadly representative or conclusive, given the small sample. However, placing the contentious subject of dissection to one side, the singularity of Susan Isaacs' approach suggests that fruitful research on children's psychological development and on methods by which an attitude of respect and interest in animals could be inculcated (Unti and DeRosa, 2003) are areas worthy of further research. As a point of interest in her writings on whether to start the study of biology through plants or animals, Susan conceded that general opinion at the time inclined to favour plants, particularly with regard to introducing sex education to children (Isaacs, 1930). She posed various questions for the reader to ponder over, including whether

> we favour the study of plants just *because* it is far more remote from the facts of human sexual relations, and we are afraid to make more than a half concession to our conviction of the child's need for knowledge and understanding?
> *(Isaacs, 1930: 159)*

Drawing on her own conclusions from the observations carried out, Susan asserted that, 'children of the ages covered [4–10 years] are on the whole more actively and spontaneously interested in animals than in plants and the facts of the life cycle in animals are far more easily and directly perceived and understood by the child' (Isaacs, 1930: 159). Although there seems to be a paucity of educational or psychological research regarding the connection between young children's interest in animals as a conduit for sex and relationship education (SRE), there is a body of evidence highlighting the importance of connectedness between children and animals (Kahn & Kellert, 2002; Lindemann-Matthies, 2005). Their respective research findings, which resonate well with Susan Isaac's findings, show that if animals are part of a child's immediate environment and cultural heritage, including pets, farm animals and wildlife, they will learn about them and accumulate a body of biological knowledge through a variety of learning processes based on their own observations and interactions with animals. Furthermore, both studies drew the conclusion that the more remote children are from animals, the fewer opportunities they will have to understand them.

Gardening activities

An aspect of the learning environment that is likely to have caused less disagreement to those critical of the Malting House School activities and one that current educators are able to relate to more easily was the children's interest in plants and flowers. Since this was all very familiar ground, Susan felt that her records did not offer anything particularly new, although by grouping them under three different headings: 'Active interest, Phantasy and Flowers as gifts and decorations' (Isaacs, 1930: 171), the findings do provide early years practitioners today with some things to consider in relation to understanding better how best to capture the children's imagination when it comes to gardening activities. At the Malting House School the garden was integral to school life, and everything that could possibly be done outdoors was. Susan incorporated into the activities many of the practical life activities that became part of the Montessori Method as the children helped in the general care of the garden as well as indoors. Each child has their own plot, and through trial and error the children learnt about the best conditions for growing vegetables and flowers. Some of the children even climbed the trees for fruit as the seasons came and went (Isaacs, 1930).

QUESTIONS FOR REFLECTION

Do you agree with Isaacs' view that young children are more actively interested in animals than plants? Can you provide any examples to support your view?

In your experience, do settings provide opportunities for children to play in natural environments where living things might be found? What do you think are the benefits to young children's learning and development?

Consider how you would organise gardening activities with young children to best capture the children's imagination. Share your thoughts with fellow students or colleagues.

How do you use observation, and what do you feel it is important to observe? Reflecting on the way Isaacs used observation, make a list of the kinds of occurrences in your setting that would enable you to observe objectively.

The children were not confined to the school grounds, because if the need arose, they would take trips out into the local community to purchase items, go for long walks, buy wood or follow up their interests in other ways. The entire educational environment was designed to stimulate the active inquiry of the children (Smith, 1985).

Finding out, feelings and fantasy

In her analysis of the data gathered by means of a wide range of narrative-style observations, Susan articulated principles of children's inquiry into the natural world that are reflected in the early learning goals of the educational programme: 'Understanding of the World' (one of the seven areas of learning in the Early Years Foundation Stage, Department for Education, 2012). In describing the actual technique implemented in the school, Susan derived the principle that children have strong, spontaneous *interests* in and raised *questions* about the things and events of the natural world:

> our technique was to meet the spontaneous inquiries of the children, as they were shown day by day, and to give them the means of following these inquiries out in sustained and progressive action. So the facts of their behaviour with fire and water and ice, with pulleys and see-saw and pendulum, and later with drilling machine and Bunsen burner, can be taken as immediate evidence of the spontaneous direction of their interests. We did not 'teach' our children about these things, nor try to create an interest in them, nor introduce any experiments or apparatus until the need for them had actually arisen. . . It was. . . their eager questions. . . that led me gradually to give them material that would allow of these interests being followed out for their own sake. And these were children (then) all under five years of age.
>
> *(Isaacs, 1930: 80–81)*

Evelyn Lawrence, who became a member of the teaching staff in 1927, recollected that there was an underlying feeling, emanating from the promoters of the school, that an indispensable preliminary to learning and development was to foster a scientific attitude to life, intellectual curiosity and vigour (Ecken & Turner, 1969). Thus it was the actual world around the child that Susan sought to clarify: the world of people and things, and of his or her own inner and outer responses. In this respect the Malting House School, was unique among progressive schools of the time, in that 'finding out about things' and 'feelings and fantasy' were never separated (Smith, 1985: 67). Susan noted that the younger children, although directly concerned with physical objects and changes, spent a great deal of time in 'dramatic representation of their own wishes and phantasies', which, she concluded, was the 'characteristic type of mental activity in these years' (Isaacs, 1930: 98). It is Susan's observations of children left free to occupy themselves as they wished that has provided a greater understanding of the vital role of spontaneous, imaginative play in early childhood education. Susan classified young children's spontaneous activity into three main types: (a) the perfecting of bodily skills of all sorts and joy in movement and the control of movement for its own sake; (b) make-believe play, varying in form according to age, sex, recent real experiences and the material to hand; (c) the 'direct concern with physical things and with animals and plants for their own sake and direct inquiry into their "why's" and "wherefore's"' (Isaacs, 1930: 98). Susan also noted that through play children moved in and out of reality and began to get a balance in their ideas: 'What imaginative play does, in the first place is to create practical situations which may often then be pursued for their own sake, and this leads on to actual discovery or to verbal judgment and reasoning (Isaacs, 1930: 99).

This can be seen in the following extract, just one the numerous records Susan made in dealing with imaginative play:

> The children had made 'trains' with chairs, and Dan [aged five years] told the others, 'I'm going to London to-day – *really'* with much emphasis. Alfred said, 'I've been to London once'. Dan: No, you have *not!'* Alfred: 'Oh, yes, I've been once, *really'*. Then there was general talk about Dan going to London to-day *really,* while they were all *pretending* to go to Hunstanton, America and India, now.
>
> *(Isaacs, 1930: 100)*

In this extract can be seen the way that playing at 'trains' allows children to weave together their emerging knowledge, skills and understanding as they move between the real and imagined 'train journeys'. They are also learning the skills of friendship and ways of playing together in groups. Dewey believed that true education occurs as a social process happening in any social situation where children are using their cognitive abilities to meet the demands of participating in a group. Furthermore, cooperating and communicating in this way enables children to find their own position in life, moving from an egocentric view to a more congenial picture of the world (Dewey, 1916). Susan grasped, as Dewey did, that the work of schools, to be effective in building good intellectual growth, must be based on and proceed from children's natural tendencies, and that helping children to be reasonable and effective in their surroundings would have long-term social and moral benefits (Smith, 1985).

Behaviour guidance approach

As is often the case when uninitiated adults do not see the underlying learning potential of proceeding from young children's natural tendencies exhibited mainly in their play, the Malting House School was seen by some outsiders as having a rather laissez-faire approach to schooling. In addition to this the prevailing view among some of the fault finders was that children of such an early age did not need any kind of *schooling* or special attention.

> Cambridge, to which Pyke had turned as a centre of enlightenment, proved to be as insular, as parochial and as opposed to educational adventures as any other small town. Stories about the activities at the scandalous Malting House grew over the coffee cups, until, inflated with distortions, exaggerations and sheer lies, they blew through the community on a wind of gossip.
>
> *(Eyken & Turner, 1969: 36)*

The criticism the school attracted and the discussions that ensued served to clarify further the aims of the school. As the philosophy of the school ensured that children should use their own initiative, Susan continued to pay great attention to the use of the learning space and how it increased the children's imagination and complexity of play through their communication and cooperation. Rather than suppressing child-initiated play through a predominantly adult-regulated environment, the emphasis on supporting the children's freely chosen activities in such a way as not to dampen their natural curiosity remained. Even so, the belief that children should be constrained as little as possible was heavily tested, and the greatest challenge for the staff came from the behaviour of some of the more aggressive children, despite there being rules about time-keeping and about the avoidance of dangerous situations and limitations placed on physical aggression between children (Graham, 2009).

It was Melanie Klein's visit to the school in July 1925 that led to some modifications in the approach to discipline. Klein was greatly impressed with what she saw, but despite her earlier writings, which had inspired the removal of constraints in the first place, she reinforced the doubts that Susan Isaacs had been feeling about the amount of verbal abuse that was permitted, which was having a detrimental effect on both victims and perpetrators (Graham, 2009). Subsequently, verbal aggression, alongside physical aggression, would no longer be tolerated, and in order to assist in regulating children's own emotions, an element of guiding firmness was introduced. Susan recognised that in terms of guiding children's behaviours, this translated into the acceptance of where children are in terms of their intellectual growth and their need to explore social rules in the same way they explore their physical world. These ideals form part of the core values for early childhood education today, and Susan's guidance approach to supporting young children's behaviour can be seen in quality early years provision and practice today, which is encapsulated in the following sentiment:

> We saw then no obedience for obedience sake. On the other hand, we held on psychological grounds that once a particular demand was definitely made as such, it was important to carry it through. For both these reasons we were careful not to put into the form of a definite demand or prohibition anything that was not in itself important enough to be worth insisting upon...This was our general way of influencing the direction of the children's growth towards such desirable behaviour as gentle manners, positive consideration for others, and active social co-operation.
>
> *(Isaacs, 1930: 28)*

Susan Isaacs and Jean Piaget

By the late 1920s Susan's work at the Malting House School was making a key contribution to thinking on how children learn and develop and attracted the

QUESTIONS FOR REFLECTION

How do you value children's spontaneous activity and imaginative play? Share your views with fellow students or colleagues.

What might be the barriers or challenges that practitioners face in creating opportunities for children's imaginative play?

What would you say to those parents who would prefer to see their child sitting down and doing 'work' rather than 'wasting their time playing'?

What behaviour guidelines would you establish in supporting young children's personal, social and emotional development? How far would you set the boundaries? Discuss your ideas with fellow students or colleagues.

attention of many visitors, reminiscent of the interest shown in Pestalozzi's approach to education. One such visitor was Jean Piaget (1896–1980), a Swiss psychologist who has, of course, had a profound influence on the progress of cognitive development theories in both psychology and educational fields. Susan was keenly interested in Piaget's research and is credited with bringing his work to the attention of the British educational establishment in the first place through written reviews of his published work in the late 1920s (Willan, 2011). Despite not always being in agreement in the way they perceived young children's cognitive development, Piaget's and Susan Isaacs' association was always marked with the greatest of respect, since each knew they were breaking new and important ground in the study of children's thinking (Smith, 1985). Susan saw Piaget's methods first-hand when she visited the *Maison des Petits*[2] of the Jean-Jacques Rousseau Institute in Geneva, which became the principal venue for his research. Piaget, in turn, had the opportunity to visit Susan Isaacs' school when he came to give a lecture at Cambridge in the same year of 1927 (Beatty, 2009). Piaget was interested in the evidence the Malting House School provided that very young children can sometimes reason in a logical and realistic way in situations where they are personally involved and deeply interested (Gardner, 1969). Piaget was able to see this first-hand during his visit to Malting House School as, while he was talking to Susan outdoors, a boy aged five years nine months passed by on his tricycle, backpedalling. When asked why the tricycle was not moving forward, the boy gave an accurate explanation of the mechanical action, pointing to each part of the mechanism in turn.

Piaget acknowledged that the children were indeed making good progress, but in later years, when referring to the incident at the Malting House School, he wrote that even these exceptionally favourable circumstances, because of the various features of children's mental structure, did little more than accelerate development (Graham, 2009). This seems, though, a contradiction, and Susan asserted that 'different levels of functioning co-exist even in young children' (Isaacs, 1930: 88). Susan also held the view that Piaget's conclusions were lessened in value because he did not use the concept of maturation 'expressed as the structure of the mind at different ages' either sparingly or critically enough, a position that was at odds with the ages and stages work coming out of Piaget's observations of young children's learning in Geneva (Isaacs, 1930: 88). Instead, Susan held the view that children's learning and development is a continuous curve, with peaks and troughs of development and ways of functioning (Isaacs, 1930: 58). Piaget's evidence from the Maison des Petits was based mainly on children's answers to psychologists' questions during what Piaget referred to as clinical interviews. However, Susan was critical of his interview method, stating that 'sustained conversations between one child and one adult in one place do not provide the circumstances which would provoke questions demanding causal explanations or inquiries about inanimate objects'. Instead, the circumstances would occur 'in the course of free practical activity in a varied setting, and in play with other children and with adults who share in the practical pursuits' (Isaacs, 1930: 83). With regard to holding sustained conversations, Susan pointed out that there were errors in the kinds of questions Piaget posed to children, and she wrote in her review of his work: 'which one of us would not be thrown into confusion at having to make a shot at explaining "how the sun came" or "how the moon began"?' (Isaacs, 1929: 606).

Another of Susan's criticisms was that Piaget exaggerated young children's egocentrism as he put forward the view that only when children reached seven or eight could they form relationships with other children. In Susan's experience the capacity of children to learn from one another and through friendships is present in children much younger, and there are numerous verbatim examples in her records to support this view (Graham, 2009). One such example, useful in counteracting Piaget's later conclusion that because of their egocentrism children under the age of eight could not decentre refers to a remark that Christopher, aged five years eight months, made after looking at an aerial photograph that the man in the aeroplane would 'see some little specks walking about' (Isaacs, 1930: 115).

Susan Isaacs and Piaget reviewed each other's publications, and their long-running theoretical conversations centred mainly around whether the child's intellectual growth and development were due to heredity or to the environment. Obviously this is an over-simplification of two people's research into how children learn and develop, but an examination of Susan Isaacs' writing in *Intellectual Growth in Young Children* (Isaacs, 1930) reveals an argument that seems to have been composed deliberately to expose the poverty of Piaget's earliest theory and empirical findings as developed in the 1920s (Piaget, 1926; 1928). Susan Isaac's criticism of his work was important and influential (Hall, 2000; Smith, 1985) – so much so that Piaget took it into account when he extended his work in later publications (brought to a British public through the efforts of Nathan Isaacs, after Susan's premature death in 1948). In later years the Piagetian notion of fixed stages, which set clearly defined limits on children's use of reasoning or logic, began to circulate alongside Susan Isaac's view that children can use reason, ask questions, hypothesise and experiment when conditions stimulate their interests (Hall, 2000; Isaacs, 1930). Piaget was not impervious to Susan's criticisms, which made a lasting impression on his later work as he moved towards focusing on the way children acquired new knowledge (Graham, 2009). For Piaget, intellectual development (reflective of Montessori's sensitive periods) is ensured as long as the child has an adequate aliment or diet of active experiences. He believed that if you equip a child with the conceptual means of making a leap to a higher level, then he would be able to reason and transfer his knowledge to new problems entirely on his own.

This notion gave rise to the phrase commonly used and attributed to Piaget: *The Child as a Lone Scientist* (Lindon, 2001). This linear understanding of learning, where development moves along at a slow and steady pace, was not in keeping with Susan's thinking, and had she not died prematurely, she would probably have found more in common with the works of the Russian psychologist Lev Vygostsky (1896–1934), which were only translated into English in 1962. Vygotsky was preoccupied during his short working life with how others provide the cultural patterning that makes the process of development possible (Bruner, 2006). He incorporated his thinking into a theory, called Zone of Proximal Development, which is the gap between what a person can do on his/her own, unassisted, and what one can do with hints and aids from a knowledgeable other. Vygotsky also believed that it was through play that children operated at a higher intellectual ability, echoing Isaacs' sentiments. Susan Isaacs would concur with the view that young children are born into a social world that shapes their development in countless ways, and this is one of the fundamental differences between Piaget's thinking and that of Isaacs and Vygotsky (Robson, 2006).

After the publication of *Intellectual Growth in Young Children* (1930), Susan Isaacs' interest in Piagetian psychology lessened, although she remained conversant with it and praised later studies that Piaget carried out on moral reasoning (Graham, 2009). It would be through her appointment at the newly created Department of Child Development at the Institute of Education, London, discussed further on in this chapter, that Susan would find a further challenge as she sought to help student teachers value the observation of children's play as the key to understanding a child's whole experience. Rather than what she felt was the Piagetian approach of identifying what children cannot do, it was through her Kleinian perspective that she explained that play is a powerful way to show what children can do (Smith, 1985). As this capacity did not change at five years of age, Susan Isaacs saw no justification for compelling children to give up their play in order to sit quietly at their desks and devote their time to formal learning.

QUESTIONS FOR REFLECTION:

Reflecting on the criticism that Susan Isaacs made of Piaget's formal technique in assessing children's cognitive development, consider the pedagogical and observational skills needed to be able to assess children informally, for example through self chosen open-ended play.

In your view do developmental tick sheets based on ages and stages of development reinforce a 'deficit' model of assessment? When could they be usefully employed? Discuss this with fellow students or colleagues

Considering Isaacs' view that a child's social world shapes their development, how might children's exposure to popular culture, media and new technologies impact on their social, emotional and cognitive development? To help answer this question access Marsh *et al's* report (2005) available online at: http://www.digitalbeginnings.shef.ac.uk/DigitalBeginningsReport.pdf

For a further insight into young children's social world and applying Bourdieu's concept of 'habitus', explore what it means to be a 'digital native' as opposed to a 'digital immigrant'. Locate and read Zevenbergen's (2007) journal article (listed in further reading) and discuss with fellow students or colleagues the implications for practitioners in relation to practice and provision.

Life after The Malting House School

Susan and Nathan Isaacs decided to move back to London when the conditions at The Malting House School were no longer tenable, mainly due to Geoffrey Pyke's rapidly deteriorating financial situation. During the six years from 1927 until 1933, when she joined the Institute of Education, Susan concentrated on writing up the data she had accumulated over the four years of observing the children at the school. In 1930 *Intellectual Growth of Young Children* appeared and in 1933 the second of her Malting House contributions, *Social Development of the Child*. In the intervening years Susan, following in the footsteps of the early philosophers, published a book specifically for parents, entitled *The Nursery Years* (1929). In the book she provides advice on child-rearing practices and discusses ways of managing children's behaviour and the value of play. The ideas presented, although only revised in 1932, are remarkably similar to those appearing in the child-care books of the present time. When reading through the book, one can almost hear Susan's voice as she provides gentle advice on such issues as value of movement, curiosity and interests in events, let's find out, making things, and jealousy and rivalry, to name just some of the sections. Susan also reminds her readers of the importance of learning by doing as she writes:

> Children *learn* by their fingers – without active touch their vision as yet tells them little; and without their actual sensory experience of things, what other people tell them means hardly anything at all. There could not be a more cruel or a more stupid thing said to little children than, 'don't touch'. It simply means 'don't learn, don't grow, don't be intelligent'.
>
> *(Isaacs, 1929: 73)*

During this period Susan also began writing – under the pseudonym Ursula Wise – a regular advice column for *The Nursery World*, a weekly magazine aimed initially at the trained children's nurse or nanny but eventually at all early years practitioners. With her considerable practical experience, Susan was well placed to respond to parents who were concerned about their children's behaviour or about their own perceived lack of parenting skills.

In 1932, Sir Percy Nunn, then Head of the Institute of Education, who had sat on the Malting House School Board, discussed with Susan the possibility of founding a Department of Child Development within the Institute. There were important centres of research elsewhere in the world – for example, under Gesell in the United States and Piaget in Geneva, but surprisingly there was no university-based centre for training and research in the United Kingdom at the time (Smith, 1985). At first, because of considerable commitments, she declined the offer, but following the success of Nunn in persuading the university to establish such a department, Susan agreed to work on a part-time basis. One of the aims of the Institute of Education, as opposed to the London Day Training College, which it replaced in 1932, was to establish a centre for research into human development in general and sound teaching methods. Susan would be the key person to supply this need, and her teaching methods at the Institute were just as innovative as her work with children, encouraging discussions, seminars and active observation and inquiry as part of the task (May, 1997). Susan's lectures and publications would soon ensure that child development would become an integral part of teacher training courses across the country (Aldrich, 2009).

It had been hoped that a laboratory school could be attached to the department with opportunity for direct observation; financial constraints made that impossible at first but, later, space was found for a small group of children to come each morning (Smith, 1985). Fortuitously, Susan had also made special links with the Chelsea Open Air Nursery School, privately funded by Natalie Davis, an American benefactor. Susan took over the educational supervision of the school and became a trustee. As a result her students at the Institute of Education were able to visit the Chelsea Open Air School to carry out observations of the children (Graham, 2009).

Susan, who was by now having an enormous influence on the development of nursery education, supplied evidence to the 1933 Hadow Report on *Infant and Nursery Schools* (Hadow, 1933) and, together with Cyril Burt, a distinguished psychologist whom she had first met at Cambridge University, drafted the chapter on the psychological development of children up to seven years of age (Aldrich, 2009). In this chapter Susan ensures that the view is reinforced that young children of around three years of age benefit from playing with other children, particularly in relation to their emotional development:

> At this stage of emotional development the child begins to turn from his parents and even from adults generally, and to find his chief source of interest in other children or in the objects of the outside world. A feeling of comradeship with his playfellows begins to develop, which gives him a greater sense of confidence and independence.
>
> *(Hadow, 1933: 85)*

From 1935 until her death Susan fought a long battle against cancer, but her commitment to children and to research never wavered. Despite being treated with radiotherapy, which was a much more invasive treatment then than it is today, Susan was otherwise able to function well, with limited time away from work (Graham, 2009).

Susan Isaacs and the New Education Foundation

In 1937, shortly after a period of convalescence, Susan Isaacs was invited to be one of a team of lecturers for a conference, organised by the Educational Research Councils of Australia and New Zealand and sponsored by the New Education Foundation (NEF), to be held in Australia and New Zealand during July, August and September. At the time, key figures at the Institute of Education made important contributions to the work of the NEF and its national section, the English New Education Fellowship (ENEF), established in 1927.

For example, both Sir Percy Nunn and Fred Clarke, a distinguished historian who was to succeed Nunn as Head of the Institute, served as presidents of the ENEF, while Susan took on the role of chairman. Her particular contribution was that extensive empirical research enabled her to interpret situations from the child's point of view (Aldrich, 2009). While at the Malting House School, Susan promoted the importance of actively listening to the children, and later she wrote that 'by patient listening to the talk of even little children, and watching what they do... we can wish their wishes, see their pictures and think their thoughts' (Isaacs, 1929: 15). In recent years, particularly following the ratification of the UNCRC by the United Kingdom government when the committee responsible for this process added the following general comment to Article 12, there has been much written about the importance of listening to children, not only to further understand their learning and development but also from a children's rights perspective.

> Respect for the views and feelings of the young child. The Committee wishes to emphasize that article 12 applies to both younger and to older children. As holders of rights, even the youngest children are entitled to express their views.
>
> *(Office of the High Commissioner for Human Rights, 2005: 7)*

The 1937 NEF Conference tour

Susan travelled to the NEF Conference by boat via the United States, going first to New York, where the Child Study Associations had arranged visits for her, and then to the Institute of Human Development at the University of Berkeley in California, where she was able to see the work of Jean Walker Macfarlane (1894–1989) whose classical studies of child development she greatly admired and which are well known among child development experts today (Gardner, 1969; Graham, 2009). From there Susan travelled with other members of the group to New Zealand, giving lectures in Auckland, Wellington and Christchurch. Such was the anticipation of the lectures that schools were closed to enable teachers to go to them, and nearly 6,000 of them attended, along with parents, officials and members of the general public (Campbell, 1938). According to May (2003), Susan Isaacs was particularly popular, and many of the lectures were broadcast on the radio. Beatrice Beatty, one of the educationists promoting progressive ideas in New Zealand during these early years, recollects 'that Susan Isaacs' presentations at the conference had a considerable impact on audiences and later on early childhood education initiatives in New Zealand' (as cited in Middleton & May, 1997: 89).

The following is a statement from one of Susan's talks on the lecture tour: it encapsulates her values and beliefs and clearly shows the influences earlier philosophers and educators such as Froebel, Dewey and Montessori had upon her thinking at the time.

> The principle of activity expresses the empirically discovered truth that the child grows by his own efforts and his own real experiences. Whether it be in skill or knowledge, in social feeling or spiritual awareness, it is not what we do to the child or for the child that educates him, but what we enable him to do for himself.
>
> *(Isaacs, 1938: 504)*

The conference also provided an opportunity to re-appraise the educational system in both Australia and New Zealand. A reform agenda, partly based on the recommendations of Susan Isaacs and others in the international group, was created, proposing that for the first time education recognised children under the compulsory school age as part of its vision (Alcorn, 1999; Graham, 2009).

The remaining years and lasting legacies

At the end of the conference tour Susan returned to London to a full schedule of activities, including following up requests from the numerous people she had met on her tour. She also added to her teaching commitments by leading a course in child psychology at the London School of Economics for those training to be psychiatric social workers (Gardner, 1969).

In the time she was head of the department, Susan had built up its international reputation, but the threat of war brought about changes to the fortunes of the department. During the Second World War the Institute of Education was evacuated from London to Nottingham, but Susan returned to Cambridge. In October 1939 Susan brought together a team of psychologists and social workers to assess the effects of wartime evacuation on children. The migration from town to country disrupted family life and relationships on a large scale, and Susan realised that a qualitative study of reactions to the evacuations would provide invaluable data as to how children coped with separation (Graham, 2009). The results of the survey were published in 1941, and the main recommendations were: that much greater attention should be paid to the emotional well-being of the children; brother and sisters should be placed together; and parents should be encouraged to visit their children even if it was a stressful process. Through this unique study Susan provided insightful information that furthered the understanding of how best to ensure that children are fully supported in times of emotional upheaval. Susan concluded her study with strong words for the authorities, and they are just as pertinent today as they were then, given the rioting and looting by disaffected youths in England's major cities in August 2011, particularly in London, when the last time it saw such destruction was during the wartime Blitz:

> We feel justified. . . in stressing our conclusion that a true understanding of the feelings and aims of ordinary human beings is an essential condition of success whether we are concerned with the replanning and re building of our great cities. . . the humanising of our town schools, the training and teaching of youth, the education of adult citizens, the revision of the economic structure. Every one of these purposes not only requires a cooperative effort from the departments and sectional authorities now so often working isolatedly; it demands also the full knowledge and understanding of human nature as a whole.
>
> *(Isaacs, 1941: 11)*

Susan Isaacs was an unusual combination of many professions: a teacher, a childhood researcher, a psychoanalyst and a university lecturer, and because of this she was at the forefront of innovative educational ideas. Clearly influenced by Froebel, she reinvigorated thinking about the value of play – in particular, imaginative play. In fact, Susan raised the status of play, giving teachers today the confidence to regard play as an absolute essential and redeeming it from any suggestion of triviality. However, for Susan, play was not about harnessing children's learning and development along a path of pre-determined outcomes or expectations. In contrast, for Susan play should be truly open-ended, unpredictable and controlled and directed by the players – that is, the children. Susan's view was that the free flow of play enabled children to produce higher level thinking skills, and although unknown to Susan at the time, Lev Vygotsky (1962) also shared this view and developed this concept.

Susan Isaacs, like Montessori, demonstrated the importance of carrying out observations and keeping careful records. But she also made it clear that it would be easy as adults to focus our observations on what interests us or on the aesthetically pleasing rather than on those things that are of deep concern to young children. Susan had a great ability in synthesising an enormous amount of information from a wide range of sources. She was keen that adults accompany rather than direct the children on their learning journey. In this way a picture of the child's learning can be built up. From these observations the significance of individual differences between children has led to an appreciation of the value of individual records in early childhood settings and schools today. Many early childhood settings today are now producing learning stories or journeys based on the learning narratives as devised by Carr (2001). Susan taught us the lesson of '*looking*' and to see children as she saw them: whole, vividly and dramatically, with all their strengths and weaknesses intact (Drummond, 2000).

Susan lost her long battle with cancer; she died, aged 63, on 12 October 1948, with her husband Nathan by her side (Gardner, 1969).

Although Susan Isaacs lived her professional life in the somewhat rarefied atmosphere of Cambridge, followed by life in academia, her most substantial educational and theoretical contributions came from the realities of children's lived experiences, both at the Malting House School and the Cambridge Evacuation Study (Isaacs, Clement, & Thouless, 1941). Susan's emphasis on the importance of play in children's learning and healthy emotional development has left a lasting legacy on the pedagogy of play.

QUESTIONS FOR REFLECTION

Having reflected on the ideas presented in this chapter, how would you define a pedagogy of play?

Reflecting on how Isaacs stressed the importance of 'active' listening, consider what being a good listener to young children involves and what the implications are for practitioners in terms of opportunities and challenges in improving practice and provision.

Consider how you would support young children's emotional well-being. Investigate the role of the key person, and consider the strategies used in your setting to ensure that young children feel secure and form positive attachments.

Further reading

Clark, A., & Moss, P. (2011). *Listening to young children: The mosaic approach* (2nd ed.). London, UK: NCB.

Dowling, M. (2010) *Young children's personal, social and emotional development* (3rd ed.). London, UK: Sage.

Elfer, P., Goldshmied, E., & Selleck, D. (2011). *Key persons in the early years.* Abingdon, UK: Routledge.

Rogers, S. (2011) *Rethinking play and pedagogy in early childhood education.* Abingdon, UK: Routledge.

Zevenbergen, R. (2007). Digital natives come to preschool: Implications for early childhood practice. *Contemporary Issues in Early Childhood*, 18, 19–21.

5

THE PIONEERS' LEGACIES TO UK AND INTERNATIONAL POLICY ON EARLY CHILDHOOD EDUCATION

This concluding chapter provides a useful summary of each of the women's most significant contributions to early childhood education in the United Kingdom as discussed in earlier chapters of this book and moves on to discuss the pioneers' impact on policy and provision in other countries and also considers their contribution to early childhood education from the perspective provided by Foucault's 'regimes of truth'.

Summaries of the work of Rachel and Margaret McMillan, Maria Montessori and Susan Isaacs and the significance of their work for UK policy on early childhood education

Rachel and Margaret McMillan

The McMillan sisters' contribution to early childhood education was built on the understanding that good health and well-being were essential for all young children to learn and develop effectively. Both Rachel and Margaret McMillan believed in the potential of nursery education to transform the lives of children and families from disadvantaged backgrounds, living in overcrowded, poor housing conditions, with little opportunity to access green spaces. They set about establishing *camp schools* and *open-air nurseries* with an emphasis on outdoor learning where children could flourish both physically and cognitively, while ensuring that the parents were integral to the day-to-day activities. In this way the parents themselves were benefiting from opportunities provided to develop their parenting skills while learning how to be self-sufficient.

Both sisters' aspirations can be seen to have influenced current policy and provision in the United Kingdom. For example, in July 2011, as part of a wider vision for families with children under five, the Government published details

(Department for Education, DfE, 2011) of its planned reforms to existing Sure Start Children's Centres. The reforms include the overall aim to identify, reach and help children and families in greatest need through focusing on promoting good physical and mental health for both children and their families; supporting parents to improve the skills that enable them to access education, training and employment; addressing risk factors; supporting parents' aspirations to be free from poverty; and improving both their immediate well-being and their future life chances (DfE, 2011). As discussed in earlier chapters, combating the effects of poverty still remains and is one of education's biggest challenges. The McMillans' interventionist approach to early childhood education is as relevant today as it was with the opening of the first open-air nursery school in Deptford in 1914.[1]

The fact that early childhood education has never been compulsory and early education specialist knowledge in the training of students in teacher training institutions is often lacking has resulted in a certain lack of confidence in its implementation among practitioners (Bilton, 2010). This has often resulted in provision more aligned to infant classes with timetabled outdoor play that staff have not planned for with regard to the children's use of the space and their learning (Bilton, 2010). There are also implications here for the understanding of the value of outdoor play that is such an integral part of the EYFS (Department for Education, 2012b). The title of a 'nursery garden', introduced by Froebel and the McMillan sisters, has more or less disappeared in England, having been replaced with terminology such as the 'outdoor area' or 'outdoor classroom' (Bilton, 2010).[2]

The two terms do not imply the same as a 'garden' with its living growing space in which children become the 'gardeners' as well as the 'players'; the idea of a garden conjures up a place of beauty – however, whatever the terminology used, it is the outdoor design and layout that need careful consideration. In the United Kingdom in the twenty-first century the current concerns with obesity, behaviour problems and poor social skills have set in motion new responses to the provision of outdoor play in many early childhood settings, Forest Schools[3] being one of them (Knight, 2009).

Developing the early thinkers' and educators' conviction that nursery education was a different form of education that required specialist training, Margaret McMillan set up the Rachel McMillan Training College. Margaret McMillan recognised that the unique characteristics of a play-based nursery education required teachers whose approaches were far removed from the monotonous, repetitive teaching methods associated with elementary school at the time (Alexander, 2010; Straw, 1990). The training that the student teachers undertook in the Rachel McMillan Training College was a combination of childcare and education training. Margaret placed considerable emphasis on teaching students how to observe and understand the holistic nature of child development.

The need for properly trained early years teachers was one of the key findings from the EPPE study (Sylva et al., 2004). However, since the inception of the National Childcare Strategy in 1998 (after thirty years of neglect at policy level) and the expansion of childcare provision, particularly across the private and voluntary sectors, there has been increasing concern about the variability of quality early years provision (Baldock, Fitzgerald, & Kay, 2009). In 2008, although early years practitioners were becoming better qualified, only 65 per cent of childcare staff and 79 per cent of early years staff in maintained schools had at least a Level 3 qualification (Pugh, 2009).

The recently introduced graduate-level Early Years Professional (EYP) has been welcomed in the childcare sector, but there still remain concerns that funding is only available to work in the private and voluntary sectors (Alexander, 2010). Furthermore, there is a lack of clarity over how the EYP status relates to qualified teachers. Margaret wanted the Rachel McMillan Teacher Training College to be a centre that drew together people wanting to work in different child-related professions from all walks of life (Bradburn, 1976), but she also acknowledged that this approach had added to the confusion about the fundamental aims of nursery education. Nevertheless within present-day Children's Centres there is an emphasis on collaborative and cooperative working in order to provide an integrated range of services to meet the health, social and educational requirements of children and their families. This emphasis resonates well with the McMillan sisters' vision for Nursery Centres, as indeed with Robert Owen's before them.

In order to clarify the existing situation within the *Children's Workforce,* an independent review of early years qualifications, headed by Professor Cathy Nutbrown, was carried out to consider how to strengthen current qualifications and to examine career progression of people working in the foundation years (Children's Workforce Development Council, CWDC, 2011). This move by the government emphasises yet again the importance of training and qualification for those working with young children. However, at the time of writing this book, the government have yet to produce a response to proposals put forward in the Nutbrown Report (Department for Education, 2012a) to raise the quality of childcare across the board.

Maria Montessori

Maria Montessori's contribution to early childhood education stemmed from the great respect she had for the potential of each and every child. Montessori's approach to early childhood education is summed up in two words: *freedom* and *structure*. Seeing education as a process in setting children free, Montessori's principle of a revolutionary new pedagogy was built on the understanding that children could be free to teach themselves, first through the senses and then through the intellect, within an environment that was carefully prepared. Many of Montessori's approaches can be seen in the principles that underpin the EYFS (Department for Education, 2012b). For example: 'The Unique Child' and 'Enabling Environments' are two of the four guiding themes of the EYFS that provide the context for the children's learning and development. These include 'principles' that recognise children as competent learners who 'develop in the context of relationships and the environment around them' (Early Education, 2012: 4). The remaining two themes of the EYFS are 'Learning and Development' and 'Positive Relationships', which echo Montessori's beliefs regarding the role of the adult in supporting children's active learning in all areas of learning and development. For example, fostering the child's own efforts and independence through child-initiated activities and knowing when to stand back or intervene are a vital part of the role of the adult as envisaged by Montessori.

Having lived through turbulent times, Montessori's hope of peace lay in the education of young children. She believed that when the value of the child's personality has been recognised and he or she has been given room to expand spiritually as well as intellectually, then 'we have had the revelation of an entirely new child whose astonishing characteristics are the opposite of those that had hitherto been observed' (Montessori, 1972/1948: 3).

Montessori's objectives of education for peace were expressed in the following statement:

> Peace is a goal that can only be attained through common accord, and the means to achieve this unity for peace are twofold: first, an immediate effort to resolve conflicts without recourse to violence – in other words, to prevent war – and second, a long-term effort to establish a lasting peace among men. Preventing conflicts is the work of politics; establishing peace is the work of education.
>
> *(Montessori, 1972/1948: 27)*

Montessori was aware that in order for peace to flourish, basic human dignity needed to be sustained. Consequently, her work included consideration of children's rights. This aligns with those of several United Nations organisations, including UNESCO (Montessori, 1965/1917), and Montessori had a clear vision of what those rights should be (Duckworth, 2006). The United Nations adoption of the Convention on the Rights of the Child (United Nations, 1989) was the watershed for children's participatory rights (Chawla & Johnson, 2004). When translated into practice with young children, Montessori's emphasis on empowering children by focusing on developing their independence prepares children to be autonomous learners and acknowledges their right to be seen as powerful individuals now rather than adults in waiting (Montessori, 1965/1917).

Montessori's approach could be seen in the way the previous EYFS framework supported children's participatory rights, with its endorsement of the importance of 'making time to listen to children's views and to act on them even when they do not match adult views' (DCSF, 2008, Principles into Practice cards 2.3). However, the fact that the statement was placed under the heading *Challenges and Dilemmas* rather than under the heading *Effective Practice* implied a certain degree of wariness towards the idea that children may wish to express a contrasting view from that of an adult. Interestingly, this statement no longer appears in the reformed framework, and although the current EYFS briefly mentions the rights of the child, it does so from a protective rather participatory stance, as can be seen in the statement: 'help children to understand their rights to be kept safe by others, and encourage them to talk about ways to avoid harming or hurting others' (Early Education, 2012: 13). The current EYFS framework should draw a clearer distinction between the needs-based approach and the participatory-based approach to children's rights if young children's views are to be taken seriously. According to Garrick et al. (2010), the EYFS should also make stronger links to those experiences and activities that follow individual and/or group interests, particularly those that are sustained over time and/or across context. Every attempt to find out the best interests of the child must be confirmed by paying attention to the child so as to capture the views and feelings the child expresses in verbal and non-verbal ways. The sense of *freedom* that Montessori created in her *Casa dei bambini* is evident in those settings where children are able to express their opinions and follow their own interests or preoccupations without fear or favour.

Susan Isaacs

As a teacher, a childhood researcher and a psychoanalyst, Susan Isaacs was able to contribute ideas to early childhood education from a variety of perspectives. However, her greatest contribution to early childhood education stemmed from her belief in the potential of play in children's learning. There is currently a well-established consensus among early childhood educators and key authors in the field that play provides benefits in the holistic development of young children (Broadhead, 2004; Moyles, 1989, 2010). It was Susan, clearly influenced by Froebel, who renewed thinking about the value of play, raising its status and giving educators, then and now, the confidence to regard play as an absolute essential, thus redeeming it from any suggestion of triviality. She was clear in her thinking that play should not be about harnessing children's learning along the path of pre-determined outcomes, but should be truly open-ended and directed by the children themselves.

In current times, in the face of often perceived pressure to concentrate on the teaching of the 3Rs in the earliest stages of the children's early learning experiences, the haste to formalise is sometimes attributed to a lack of understanding of how young children learn and develop (David, 1999). But, as Susan clearly demonstrated, it is only through a play-based curriculum that children demonstrate higher level thinking skills, and free-flow play can also develop young children's social skill and problem-solving skills. Spontaneous self-directed free-flow play often led to confrontation and conflict between children at the Malting House School, but if they were left to work things out for themselves, Susan demonstrated that more often than not they found a solution. This is when the expertise of early years practitioners is vital in developing children's confidence in becoming 'master player and learners. . . who value and extend children's ways of knowing, thinking, reasoning and understanding' (Wood & Attfield, 2005: 231). As a psychoanalytically trained teacher, Susan used her considerable skill in carrying out naturalistic observations of the children. Her understanding of psychoanalytical theories, such as those of Sigmund Freud (1907) and Melanie Klein (1923), would have had a direct impact on what she felt about a child's emotional well-being and in the way she noted the child's interactions and relationships as well as their learning.

Understanding the importance of 'tuning in to' children's social and emotional well-being owes much to psychoanalytical theories (Underdown, 2007: 35) and is reflected in the Key Person approach, which is now required practice in UK government-funded early childhood provision (Department for Education, 2012b) One of the roles of a Key Person is to carefully record the children's development and progress, to be shared with other professionals and parents alike. Susan certainly contributed to the importance of recording in detail everything that children do and say in order to build up an accurate picture of the children's learning. The terminology of *Look, Listen and Note* in the 2008 EYFS framework would not look out of place in Isaacs' writings. This can be seen in the numerous detailed observations that she carried out at the Malting House School, which form a major part of her writing in relation to children's intellectual growth and social development (Isaacs, 1930, 1933).

As Susan was keen that adults accompany rather than direct the children on their learning journey, she would most likely have approved of *documentation* as defined in both the Swedish curriculum (*Lpo98*: Skolverket, 2006) and the Reggio Emilia approach (Edwards et al., 1998). Dahlberg refers to *documentation* as the reflexive problematising approach that makes it possible for adults to enter into dialogue with the child and his or her parents, so that it becomes an arena for discussing critical questions and reflection (Dahlberg, Moss, & Pence, 1999: 145). Documentation provides a record of the learning and reveals connections between events in much the same way as Susan did in her detailed observations. She clearly adopted a reflexive problematising approach when working on the two books based on the observations she recorded. The observations made then are just as relevant to practice and provision today, as they capture vividly all the nuances of children's progress in learning and development. Susan also acknowledged the vital role of parents in supporting their children's learning and development, particularly in relation to the often difficult task of supporting young children's behaviour.

In her role as university lecturer when she was head of the Child Development Department at the Institute of Education, London, Susan was able to provide considerable insights into young children's learning, thus influencing and informing students' pedagogical understanding. No doubt she would have expressed her belief that attending a nursery school should be a natural part of a child's early life: 'Experience has shown that it can be looked upon as a normal institution in the social life of any civilised community' (Isaacs, 1952: 31). These words resonate well with current thinking among educationalists and fit with those of policymakers who recognise the value of early childhood education.

Table 5.1 identifies the ways in which the key ideas of Rachel and Margaret McMillan, Maria Montessori and Susan Isaacs relate to play, the role of the adult and the learning environment and the links to UK policy and the EYFS.

The pioneers' influences on policy and provision in other countries

In different ways, each of these pioneers has had considerable influence on the development of policies for early childhood education, particularly in Western societies and English-speaking countries. The discussions that follow are by no

TABLE 5.1 The key ideas of the McMillan sisters, Montessori, and Isaacs

Early childhood education dimensions	Rachel and Margaret McMillan	Maria Montessori	Susan Isaacs
Play	• promoted children's health and well-being through outdoor play • understood the value of outdoor play in enabling the children to make scientific and environmental discoveries while developing their language skills	• acknowledged play as a means by which children could express their inner needs • placed emphasis on *Practical Life Exercises* and didactic materials as tools for the child's self-construction	• believed strongly in the potential of play in children's learning and development • advocated free play that should be truly open-ended, unpredictable and controlled and directed by the children
The role of the adult	• considered children's changes over time in terms of discrete stages of growth and development • understood that children learn better when well nourished and appropriately clothed • introduced the idea of providing breakfast before school • ensured the nursery became part of the local community • encouraged parents to participate with the activities and develop skills alongside their children • introduced concept of multi–professional working by placing emphasis on having the right combination of staff in supporting both education and care	• introduced the concept of 'teacher as director': to demonstrate procedures and show the correct use of the self-correcting didactic materials • respected the unique individuality of each child recognising the potential that they possessed within themselves • stressed importance of intervening only when necessary or asked to by the child • placed emphasis on observing and keeping records of the children's activities, recognising children's growth at crucial developmental moments • consideration of children's rights • emphasis on empowering children by focusing on developing their independence in preparing children to be autonomous learners	• supported children's freely chosen activities in such a way as not to dampen their natural curiosity • placed importance on need for children to have adults around them who understand how real their feelings are and are able to provide meaningful experiences for the children to engage with within their learning • promoted the importance of actively listening to the children • recognised importance of guiding children's behaviours, according to where children are in terms of their intellectual growth and their need to explore social rules in the same way they explore their physical world

	• fostered a love of taking care of living things	• viewed provision as freedom for children and parents	• stressed importance of observing everything that children do and say in order to build up an accurate picture of the children's learning
The learning environment	• developed the provision of nurseries with gardens • gave prominence to sensory training within a natural environment • placed importance on ample space for children to move around freely • placed importance on providing a provocative outdoor environment • organised garden into different sections in order for children to follow own interests • saw importance of creating positive risk-taking opportunities within a safe environment • importance of nursery schools being integral to the local community	• demonstrated that within a carefully structured environment children could be free to teach themselves, first through the senses and then through the intellect • the environment should be meticulously prepared before the children arrive • careful use of space and separate work areas created a classroom which was a child-friendly environment and included small tables and chairs, light enough for a child to carry, low washstands, and low cupboards for the children to access materials	• provision specifically designed for free play and active inquiry • the garden was integral to school life and everything that could possibly be done outdoors was • children free to explore their environment both indoors and outdoors ensured that children had much to stimulate their active inquiry through the provision of a range of resources that fired the children's imagination • attention paid to use of the learning space to ensure it increases children's imagination and complexity of play through communication and cooperation

Continued

TABLE 5.1 (Cont'd)

Early childhood education dimensions	Rachel and Margaret McMillan	Maria Montessori	Susan Isaacs
Present policy links	ECM: • Stay safe • Be healthy • Achieve economic well being • Sure Start Children's Centres	ECM: • Enjoy and achieve • Make a positive contribution • Organisation • UNCRC: The Rights of the Child	ECM: • Enjoy and achieve • Be healthy [mentally] • Make a positive contribution • Social and Emotional Aspects of Learning (SEAL)[a]
English EYFS links	Enabling Environment: • The outdoor environment • Children's needs • The community A Unique Child: • Child development • Growing and developing • Physical well-being • Making choices	Enabling environment: • The indoor environment • Observation starting with the child • The wider context A unique child: • Child development • A competent learner • Children's entitlements	Enabling environment: • The indoor and outdoor environment • The emotional environment • Observation • Working together A unique child: • Child development • Discovering boundaries • Emotional well-being

Learning and development:

- Play and exploration
- Mental and physical involvement

Positive relationships:

- Shared care
- Learning together
- Professional relationships

Learning and development:

- Decision making
- Transforming understanding

Positive relationships:

- Effective teaching
- Respecting diversity
- Positive interactions
- Listening to children

Learning and development:

- Play and exploration
- Learning through experience
- Adult involvement
- Making connections

Positive relationships:

- Understanding feelings
- Learning together
- Listening to children

[a] SEAL is a comprehensive whole-school approach to promoting the social and emotional skills that are thought to underpin effective learning, positive behaviour, regular attendance, and emotional well-being (Department for Education and Skills, 2005).

means a complete and comprehensive account of the impact the four women pioneers have had on early childhood policy and provision abroad. For the sake of brevity the intention therefore is to focus on certain examples of the ways in which the ideas of the four women have played a major part in developing effective early childhood practice and provision within differing cultural contexts.

Margaret McMillan's ideas became widespread through her many public lectures and numerous publications, including *The Nursery School,* with its broad readership, particularly in English-speaking nations, including Australia, New Zealand and the United States. In her foreword to the first edition, Professor Patty Smith Hill (1868–1946) of Columbia University, New York, and a founding member of the Progressive Education Movement in America described McMillan's publication as: 'an epoch-making book which all who have to do with the welfare of children cannot afford to overlook' (Smith Hill as cited in McMillan, 1921: xi). Reflecting further on McMillan's attention not only to education but also to the health and welfare of all children, Smith Hill recommended that 'civilisation demand a new environment for our youngest children, a new type of nurture and education – a high standard of teaching, and teacher nurses. . . who understand the right of the youngest in our democratic society to 'life, liberty and the pursuit of happiness' (ibid.). At that time some of the class, ethnic and racial biases were haunting democracy in the United States, and there was a great need to address these issues. McMillan's strongly held view that teachers should have a wider training and a greater understanding of how to work not only with the children but also their families drew much attention, and a flow of students travelled from the United States to Deptford to learn more. Abigail Adams Eliot, a significant figure in the American nursery-school movement, was one of the earliest students who benefited from studying and working at the Deptford Open Air Nursery School in 1921. On her return to Boston in 1922 she applied her newly acquired pedagogical expertise at the Ruggles Street Nursery School in Roxbury, Massachusetts, and would eventually become part of the leadership that formed the National Association for Nursery Education (NANE), which now exists as the National Association for the Education of Young Children (NAEYC). The pedagogical values and principles that underpinned practice and training at the Deptford Open Air Nursery School shaped the NANE/NAEYC standards for early childhood professional preparation (Staples-New & Cochran, 2008). NAEYC expresses its mission in terms of three broad goals: (a) improving professional practice and working conditions in early childhood education; (b) supporting early childhood programs by working to achieve a high-quality system of early childhood education; and (c) building a high-performance, inclusive organisation of groups and individuals who are committed to promoting excellence in early childhood education for all young children (National Association for the Education of Young Children, 2009). Although expressed in twenty-first-century terminology, these goals are reflective of Margaret McMillan's underlying principles and key objectives for the professionalisation of early childhood teachers and practitioners.

Not only the nursery-school movement, but also child socioeconomic and welfare policies in the United States and around the world owe much to the innovative work of the McMillan sisters. To this day poverty, social inequalities and inequity in health continue to remain high on the political agenda and, in the face of the persistent education gap, most industrialised countries in the twenty-first century provide compensatory early childhood education programmes targeted at low-income and ethnic or sociolinguistic minority groups (Organization for Economic Cooperation and Development, 2001). These programmes with their roots in the McMillans' approach to education involve child-focused and child-centred-based education, together with strong parent involvement, parent education, programmed educational home activities and measures of family support. One such example is the Head Start Project, which began in 1965 and is still providing, in addition to its educational services, social, health and nutritional services to children and their low-income parents. In 1994, when Early Head Start was established, the programme expanded to serve children from birth to three and their families (Barnett & Hustedt, 2005). These projects and those elsewhere in the world – for example, the Early Child Care Development Education (ECCDE) policy in Nigeria (David, 2001) and Sure Start in the United Kingdom – are clearly an extension to the services that were provided by Rachel and Margaret McMillan in Deptford almost a century ago.

Maria Montessori's philosophies and the internationalisation of the Montessori Method has had a huge world-wide influence on early childhood education. In 1909, Montessori published the first edition of *The Montessori Method*, and it was soon translated into all of the major world languages. The spread of her ideas was further aided by a series of stimulating lectures held in all parts of the world. In 1929 Montessori established the Association Montessori Internationale (AMI) to give structure to her work and to ensure that her standards for teacher training would be continued long after her death, in accordance with her pedagogical and scientific principles. The AMI headquarters are in Amsterdam, Holland, and, in affiliation with the United Nations Educational, Scientific and Cultural Organization (UNESCO), overview the activities of the teacher-training courses in the Montessori Method in all corners of the world. Nevertheless, there is diversity in Montessori educational communities around the world, with their differing interpretations and practices responding to the local needs of children and their families. However, the essential elements of Montessori's philosophy with regard to the role of the adult and the learning environment can be found in all early childhood education approaches where the practitioners are skilled in 'following' the child, fostering independence through a carefully prepared environment, and responding to the changing interests, needs and democratic rights of the child. For example, ideas about the democratic rights of the child and the importance of a prepared environment are fundamental to what the protagonists of the internationally renowned Reggio Emilia Approach feel are at the centre of their educational vision. Loris Malaguzzi (1920–1994), founder of the Reggio Emilia Approach in Northern Italy, said that they meditated on the work of Montessori, describing her reverentially as: 'Montessori – she is our mother, but as all children, we have had to make ourselves independent of our mothers' (as cited in Rinaldi, 2006: 7). Rinaldi refers to how Malaguzzi 'loved to recall the genesis of the Reggio experience: the pre-school in Villa Cella and the declaration which is still inscribed on the school as the place where peace building is achieved by educating the new generations (Rinaldi, 2006: 146). Manifest in this inscription is the prominence Montessori gave to education for peace.

Susan Isaacs' international influence was also wide-reaching through her lecture tours and publications, the overseas students who were attracted to her courses and through her correspondence with the many colleagues she met across the English-speaking world (Willan, 2011). Isaacs' attendance at the 1937 New Education Fellowship (NEF) conferences in New Zealand, and later that summer in Australia, gave a great stimulus to early childhood education initiatives taking place at the time. These initiatives stemmed from the worldwide revulsion, following the First World War, at the notion of violence as a way of settling disputes at any level and the strong tide in favour of education as a means to international understanding. Education for young children would play a significant part in achieving that end (Gregg, 1993). Isaacs' lectures were very popular, as she used jargon-free language and chose case studies from her own practice to illustrate points made, which resonated well with both educators' and parents' concerns' alike. In fact, such was Isaacs' influence on primary schoolteachers that when she died in 1948, a memorial fund was established in her honour (Alcorn, 1999). The impact of the conferences was immense in instigating a period of questioning and anticipated reform, resulting in the recognition that children under five years of age were part of the new educational vision for New Zealand and Australia. The value Issacs placed on play and the use of observations to assess children's learning and development was to leave a lasting legacy on the new wave of educational policy and provision. Her emphasis on real and active experiences in supporting children's development as the basis for an appropriate curriculum became the core of Australian early childhood education (McLean, Bailey, & Wolery, 1992). Isaacs' ideals also became central to early childhood education provision in New Zealand, not least through the Playcentre movement, which was based on her philosophies. The New Zealand Playcentres reflect Isaacs' ideals in their focus on developing the whole child – intellectually, emotionally and socially – and by involving parents and the community in the process of learning (Alvestad & Duncan, 2006). The ensuing development of the Playcentre movement, with its recognition of the value of play, combined with the importance of observing children's existing skills and understanding, supported the early childhood education programmes' move towards a less formal structure with greater opportunities for children to explore their own ideas and interests (Sewell & Bethall, 2009).

A significant milestone in response to initiatives from the early childhood sector was the creation of the Te Whariki progressive curriculum document in which Isaac's ideals are clearly visible. Playcentres follow the play-based *Te Whāriki* (Māori for woven mat), which contains 'curriculum specifically for Māori immersion services in early childhood education and establishes, throughout the document as a whole, the bicultural nature of curriculum for all early childhood services' (Ministry of Education, 1996: 7). Nuttall and Edwards (2007: 20) describe *Te Whāriki* as prescribing 'a series of four *inviolate* principles (empowerment, holism, family and community, relationships) and five strands (well-being, belonging, contribution, communication, exploration)'. However, *Te Whāriki* differs from other curricula in that it does not prescribe content or methods but leaves it to the teachers to weave their own *Whāriki* (mat). In this way, each early childhood service can maintain its own 'ways of working' with children and families, which are in keeping with their setting (Alvestad, Duncan, & Berge, 2009: 5). This freedom in providing relevant learning experiences for the children and families using the service mirrors the way in which Isaacs worked with the children and their families in the Malting House School.

Having shown how contemporary early childhood education has been influenced by the work of the pioneers, the chapter now moves on to discuss the notion that their legacies produced a particular 'regime of truth' (Foucault, 1980) to current understandings of what constitutes effective practice and provision.

Legacies as a 'regime of truth'

This section discusses the four key women's legacies to early childhood education from the perspective provided by Foucault's regimes of truth. 'Regimes of truth' is how Foucault describes a set of rules that produce an authoritative directive on what needs to be done and how it should be done and are based on a collection of dominant discourses that govern ideas, thoughts and actions in a specific direction (Gore, 1993). Foucault argued that they constitute boundaries, within a given field, through processes of inclusion and exclusion, for what, during a specific time and in a specific place, is seen as a truth and the right thing to do (Foucault, 1980).

Foucault's notion of 'regimes of truth' is a helpful tool in reconceptualising the legacies of the four key women pioneers in relation to current contexts of early childhood education, policy and provision in the United Kingdom and elsewhere. In Foucault's terms, the four key women produced a particular 'regime of truth' by means of their historically and socially specific contribution to current understandings of early childhood education and in relation to their values and beliefs concerning young children's learning and development. The intensive industrialisation of the late nineteenth and early twentieth centuries brought about new socioeconomic conditions in inner cities areas across the United Kingdom and Europe that resulted in the emergence of new societal attitudes, which eventually led to social reforms and a new role for education. With emerging scientific discourses and new understandings of the importance of health and physical and emotional well-being in early childhood, in formulating their ideas the four women shared a consensus understanding about 'the nature of the child' and what early childhood education should look like and what it should achieve. Their pedagogical aim was to maximise young children's learning through the creation of an enabling environment where optimum growth and development would take place, unhindered by unnecessary intervention. Influenced by the ideas of Froebel and the early key thinkers, as explored in this book, the four women established common pedagogical approaches that, although regarded as radical and often controversial at the time, link directly to current policy on early childhood education in the United Kingdom. The key women pioneers' 'reforming' philosophical approach to early childhood education is clearly reflected within the broad principles and flexible approaches of not only the EYFS but other early childhood education approaches as their ideas link directly with the model of a child as an active learner (MacNaughton, 2003: 160).

When particular understandings – such as, for example, the valorisation of play as a vehicle for young children's learning; the use of child observations to inform teaching and learning decisions; and young children learning best through active exploration – are legitimately sanctioned as true by sociocultural normative knowledge, it becomes an expert dominant discourse with a power to inform and direct (Foucault, 1972). Foucault is useful in that he provided many insights into the relationships between power, knowledge and discourse. Not that Foucault believed that power is necessarily oppressive, as it is possible to have relations of power that are open and reciprocal. Foucault suggested that 'any attempt to analyse power should not be directed towards the position of power, nor to those upon whom it is exercised, but to its effects' (Foucault, 1980: 97).

In the field of early childhood education, 'regimes of truth' assist policymakers and educators to define what constitutes good-quality practice and provision – for example, whether to allow free play, both indoors and outdoors, with little adult interference, as advocated by the McMillan sisters, or to allow the child to choose from a variety of didactic materials and resources, as seen in Montessori settings, or to accompany the child or children in co-constructing knowledge together while carefully observing learning, as advocated by Susan Isaacs. However, this also places enormous responsibility on the shoulders of policymakers and educators, as very often they are participating in acts of power in the decision-making processes. In helping to make these decisions, officially sanctioned truths are woven together into a regime or system of regulation – for example, the EYFS framework that governs what is held to be a desirable way to act and feel in early childhood settings (MacNaughton, 2005). Nonetheless, L. R. Williams (1994: 156) points out that '... when a professional organisation [in this case the Department for Education] takes a stand regarding excellence in education, the resulting document will embody the values of its writers or, in a larger sense, the values of the culture(s) that influence those writers'. Given this viewpoint, policymakers and educators need to question whether they can hold diverse views within a shared vision. From a Foucauldian perspective the EYFS framework should take into account 'multiple processes which constitute' working with very young children in early years settings (Foucault, 1981: 6). For example, standards and frameworks need to include the current social contexts within which children develop in relation to gender, class, race and ethnicity (Cohen, 2008).

In arriving at decisions about children and their education, more and more researchers and educationalists are seeing early childhood settings as a space where knowledge, power and desire are woven into complex relationships between children and their peers and children and adults (MacNaughton, 2005). Becoming post-structurally active in this way means being able to contest 'regimes of truth' and to theorise new possibilities in working with young children. Nevertheless, in the language of evaluation linked to effective early childhood education, it is essential that policymakers and educators privilege those 'truths' that produce both the intellectual and practical tools for articulating what it is that early childhood education should be and what early childhood educators should be doing (Ailwood, 2003). In this respect the legacies of the four key women pioneers provide a comprehensive source of theoretical, philosophical and pedagogical knowledge on which to build for the future.

Final reflections

The contribution of the contents of this book to a current understanding of early childhood education lies in the way it has synthesised the lives and work of the four women and shown how much of what constitutes effective early childhood provision has been shaped through the course of history. As clearly shown in Table 5.1, current United Kingdom early childhood provision and practice owes much to the key ideas and work of the four women pioneers.

During the last two decades, UK government policies have impacted on early childhood practice and provision with an inspection regime of all settings offering educational experiences for under-fives, run and managed by Ofsted (Anning, Cullen, & Fleer, 2004). When first introduced, inspections emphasised the importance of the quality of learning experiences in literacy and numeracy (Office for Standards in Education, 1998/9), and many early years practitioners focused their attention on teaching only those parts of the early years curriculum for which they would be held publicly accountable (Anning & Edwards, 1999). The understanding that early childhood education was different from the demands of formal schooling was in danger of being overlooked until the introduction of the play-based EYFS, which now offers practitioners the opportunity to re-engage with a broader curriculum framework – based on key aspects of children's learning and development.

The pioneers were fortunate enough to live through a time when they were able to set their own high standards and able to take risks through opportunities to experiment with ideas and take risks within a generally less risk-averse society. In their time, these women raised the status of early childhood education, and those of us involved in the field of early childhood education owe a great deal to them. Now, in the twenty-first century, as nations and cultures become ever more intertwined, it is imperative that policy decisions regarding practice and provision in early childhood education look to the future by examining how things were done in the past in order to understand the effectiveness of current approaches.

Future research questions that have arisen as a result of the background doctoral study informing the contents of this book and that practitioners or post-graduate students might find useful, are the following:

- In what way does planning for play-based approaches allow children the opportunity to engage in free play that is firmly rooted in their sociocultural experiences and stems from their own interests?

- How do educators work with others to build a socially just learning community, with particular emphasis on recognising each person's unique social and cultural histories?
- What opportunities are available within early childhood settings to promote children's health and well-being through meaningful and respectful engagement with animals and plants?
- In what ways can educators ensure that both the indoor and the outdoor environment promote children's understanding of the importance of a sustainable society through child-initiated approaches?

What the pioneers have shown us is that working with our youngest children is an enjoyable, rewarding and yet intensely challenging commitment, which requires knowledgeable educators who know how best to create an inspiring environment in which young children are free to learn and develop.

Notes

1 Nowadays most British analysts use the *ph* spelling for all phantasies. The reason given is that it is sometimes difficult to be sure whether phantasies are conscious or unconscious (Source: Bott Spillius, 2001, p. 364).
2 Maison des Petits was a French rendition of Montessori's *Casa dei bambini* or Children's House, and two Montessori teachers had given classes at the Institute (Beatty, 2009: 443).
3 The Forest School movement in the United Kingdom, which came into being before the EYFS, is loosely based on the Danish way of facilitating learning outdoors with young children.

REFERENCES

Abbott, L., & Langston, A. (2004). *Birth to three matters: Supporting the framework of effective practice*. Maidenhead, UK: Open University Press.

Adamson, J. W. (1922). *The educational writings of John Locke*. Cambridge, UK: Cambridge University Press.

Adelman, C. (2000). Over two years, what did Froebel say to Pestalozzi. *History of Education, 29*, 103–114. doi:10.1080/004676000284391

Ailwood, J. (2003). Governing early childhood education through play. *Contemporary Issues in Early Childhood, 4*, 286–299. doi:10.2304/ciec.2003.4.3.5

Albisetti, J. C. (2009). Froebel crosses the Alps: Introducing the kindergarten in Italy. *History of Education Quarterly, 49*, 159–169. doi:10.1111/j.1748-5959.2009.00193.x

Alcorn, N. (1999). *'To the fullest extent of his powers': C. E. Beeby's life in education*. Wellington, New Zealand: VUP.

Aldrich, R. (2009). The new education and the Institute of Education, University of London, 1919–1945. *Paedagogica Historica, 45*, 485–502. doi:10.1080/00309230903100882

Alexander, R.. (Ed.). (2010). *Children, their world their education, final report and recommendations of the Cambridge Primary Review*. London, UK: Routledge.

Alexander, S. (1998). Psychoanalysis in Britain in the early twentieth century: An introductory note. *History Workshop Journal, 45*, 135–143. Retrieved from http://www.jstor.org/stable/4289553

Alvestad, M., Duncan, J. and Berge, A. (2009). New Zealand ECE teachers talk about Te Whāriki. *New Zealand Journal of Teachers' Work, 6* (1), 13–19.

Alvestad, M., & Duncan, J. (2006). New Zealand preschool teachers' understandings of early childhood curriculum in New Zealand – A comparative perspective. *International Journal of Early Childhood, 38*, 31–45.

Anning, A. (2004). The co construction of an early childhood. In A. Anning, J. Cullen, & M. Fleer (Eds.), *Early childhood education: Society and culture*. London: Sage Publications.

Anning, A., Cullen, J., Fleer, M. (Eds.) (2004). *Early childhood education: Society and culture*. London: Sage Publications.

Anning, A., & Edwards, A. (1999). *Promoting children's learning from birth to five: Developing the new early years professional*. Maidenhead, UK: Open University Press.

140 References

Aristotle (2009). *The Nicomachean ethics.* (D. Ross., Trans.). Oxford, UK: Oxford University Press. (Original work published c. 334 BC.)

Armitage, M. (2005). The influence of school architecture and design on the outdoor play experience within the primary school. *Paedagogica Historica,* 41, 535–553.

Armytage, W. H. G. (1952). Friedrich Froebel: A centennial appreciation. *History of Education Journal,* 3 (4), 107–113. Retrieved from http://www.jstor.org/stable/3659205

Ayres, L. P. (1910). *Open air schools.* Retrieved 31 May 2011, from http://www.archive.org/stream/openairschools00ayreuoft/openairschools00ayreuoft_djvu.txt

Babini, V. (2000). Science, feminism and education: The early work of Maria Montessori. *History Workshop Journal,* 49, 44–67. Retrieved from http://www.jstor.org/stable/4289658

Bacon, F. (1627). *The New Atlantis.* Retrieved 30 March 2013 from: http://www.gutenberg.org/catalog/world/readfile?fk_files=3274948

Baldock, P., Fitzgerald, D., & Kay, J. (2009). *Understanding early years policy.* London: Sage Publications.

Bales, K. (1999). Popular reactions to sociological research: The case of Charles Booth. *Sociology,* 33, 153–168. doi:10.1177/S0038038599000085

Ball, S. J., & Vincent, C. (2005). The 'childcare champion'? New Labour, social justice and the childcare market. *British Educational Research Journal,* 31, 557–570. doi:10.1080/0141192 0500240700

Barlow, T. A. (1977). *Pestalozzi and American education.* Boulder, CO: University of Colorado Libraries Press.

Barnett, S., & Hustedt, J. (2005). Head Start's lasting benefits. *Infants & Young Children,* 18, 16–24. Retrieved August 2012, from http://depts.washington.edu/isei/iyc/barnett_hustedt18_1.pdf

Barres, V. (2007). *Widening the commitment to the child in today's global world: Montessori principles contribute to an international movement of social reform.* Retrieved 6 June 2007, from http://montessoricentenary.org

Beatty, B. (2009). Transitory connections: The reception and rejection of Jean Piaget's psychology in the nursery school movement in the 1920s and 1930s. *History of Education Quarterly,* 49, 442–446. doi:10.1111/j.1748-5959.2009.00225

Bennett, C. (1909). An ancient schoolmaster's message to present-day teachers. *The Classic Journal,* 4, 149–164. Retrieved 31 March 2010, from http://www.jstor.org/stable/496881

Bertram, T., & Pascal, C. (2002). *Early years education: An international perspective.* Retrieved 30 June 2011, from http://www.inca.org.uk/pdf/early_years.pdf

Bilton, H. (2010). *Outdoor learning in the early years.* Abingdon, UK; Routledge.

Bird, W. (2007). *Natural thinking: Investigating the links between the natural environment, biodiversity and mental health.* Retrieved 31 May 2011, from http://www.rspb.org.uk/Images/naturalthinking_tcm9-161856.pdf

Blackstone, T. (1974). Some issues concerning the development of nursery education in Britain. *Paedagogica Europaea,* 9 (1), 172–183. Oxford, UK: Blackwell Publishing. Retrieved from http://www.jstor.org/stable/1502397

Blakemore, S. J., & Frith, U. (2005). *The learning brain: Lessons for education.* Oxford, UK: Blackwell Publishing.

Board of Education. (1905). *Report on children under five years of age in public elementary schools.* London, UK: Her Majesty's Stationery Office (HMSO).

Booth, C. (1889) *Life and labour of the people in London.* Retrieved 30 March 2013 from http://booth.lse.ac.uk/static/a/3.html

Booth, C. (1989). *Life and labour of the people in London.* London, UK: Macmillan and Company.

Bott Spillius, E. (2001). Freud and Klein on the concept of phantasy. *International Journal of Psychoanalysis*, 82, 361–373. doi:10.1516/5PWR-57TK-VT2U-3XU8/

Bourdieu, P., & Passeron, J. C. (1977). *Reproduction in education, society and culture.* London, UK: Sage Publications.

Bourdieu, P., & Wacquant, L. (1992). *Invitation to reflexive sociology.* Bristol, UK: Policy Press.

Bowers, F. B. & Gehring, T. (2004). Johann Heinrich Pestalozzi: 18th century Swiss educator and correctional reformer. *The Journal of Correctional Education*, 55 (4), 306–320.

Bowlby, J. (1969). *Attachment and loss. Vol. 1: Attachment.* New York, NY: Basic Books.

Bradburn, E. (1976). *Margaret McMillan: Framework and expansion of nursery education.* Redhill, UK: Denholm House Press.

Bradburn, E. (1989). *Margaret McMillan: Portrait of a pioneer.* London, UK: Routledge.

Brehony, K. J. (1994). The school masters parliament: The origins and formation of the Consultative Committee of the Board of Education 1868–1916. *History of Education*, 23 (2), 171–193. doi:10.1080/0046760940230203

Brehony, K. J. (1997). An 'undeniable' and 'disastrous' influence? John Dewey and English Education (1895–1939). *Oxford Review of Education*, 23 (4), 427–445. Retrieved from http://www.jstor.org/stable/1050860

Brehony, K. J. (2003). A 'socially civilising influence'? Play and the urban 'degenerate'. *Paedagogica Historica*, 39, 87–106. doi:10.1080/00309230307453

Brehony, K. J. (2004). A new education for a new era: creating international fellowship through conferences 1921–1938. *Paedagogica Historica*, 40, 733–755. doi:10.1080/003092 3042000293742

Brehony, K. J. (2009). Lady Astor's campaign for Nursery Schools in Britain, 1930–1939: Attempting to valorize cultural capital in a male-dominated political field. *History of Education Quarterly*, 49, 196–210. doi:10.1111/j.1748-5959.2009.00196.x

Broadhead, P. (2004). *Early years play and learning: Developing social skills and cooperation.* London: RoutledgeFalmer.

Broughton, H. (1914). *The open air school.* Retrieved 31 May 2011, from http://core.roehampton.ac.uk/digital/froarc/bropenair/

Brown, G. (2004). The Chancellor's Spending Review Statement. Retrieved 30 March 2013 from http://news.bbc.co.uk/1/hi/uk_politics/3887877.stm

Bruce, T. (2010). *Early childhood: A guide for students.* London, UK: Sage.

Brühlmeier, A. (2010). *Head, heart and hand: Education in the spirit of Pestalozzi.* Retrieved 30 May 2011, from http://www.pestalozziworld.com/images/HeadI IeartandI Iand.pdf

Bruner, J. (2006). *In search of pedagogy* (Vol. II). Abingdon, UK: Routledge.

Bryder, L. (1992). 'Wonderlands of buttercup, clover and daisies': Tuberculosis and the Open-Air School Movement in Britain, 1907–39. In R. Cooter (Ed.), *In the name of the child: Health and welfare, 1880–1940* (pp. 72–95). London, UK: Routledge.

Burnett, A. (1962). Montessori education: Today and yesterday. *The Elementary School Journal*, 63 (2), 71–77. Retrieved from http://www.jstor.org/stable/1000044

Campbell, A. (Ed.). (1938). *Modern trends in education: The proceedings of the New Education Fellowship Conference held in New Zealand in July 1937.* Wellington, New Zealand: Whitcombe and Tombs.

Capkova, D. (1970). The recommendations of Comenius regarding the education of young children. In C. H. Dobinson (Ed.), *Comenius and contemporary education.* Retrieved 18 August 2010, from http://eric.ed.gov/PDFS/ED079212.pdf

Carpenter, B. (2005). Early childhood intervention: Possibilities and prospects for professionals, families and children. *British Journal of Special Education*, 32, 176–185. doi:10.1111/j.1467- 8578.2005.00394

Carr, M. (2001). *Assessment in early childhood settings: Learning stories.* London, UK: Paul Chapman Publishing.

Catarsi, E. (1985). *Il dibattito sul metodo: Rosa Agazzi e Maria Montessori* [The debate on the method: Rosa Agazzi and Maria Montessori]. In E. Catarsi & G. Genovesi (Eds.), *L'infanzia a scuola, l'educazione infantile in Italia dalle sale di custodia alla materna statale* [Infants at school, Infant education in Italy from custodial rooms towards a state maternal (Nursery)] (pp. 92–120). Bergamo, Italy: Juvenlia.

Catarsi, E. (1995). *La giovane Montessori [The young Montessori].* Ferrara, Italy: Corso Editore.

Central Advisory Council for Education (CACE). (1967). *Children and their primary schools (Plowden Report).* London, UK: HMSO.

Champkin, J. (2007). Henry Mayhew: The statistical Dickens. *Significance,* 4, 136–138. doi:10.1111/j.1740-9713.2007.00250.x

Chancellor's Spending Review Statement (2004). Retrieved 30 March 2013 from http://news.bbc.co.uk/1/hi/uk_politics/3887877.stm

Charlton, K (1968). *Education in Rennaisance England.* London, UK: Routledge and Kegan Paul.

Chartier, A., & Geneix, N. (2006). *Pedagogical approaches to early childhood education.* Retrieved 25 August 2011, from http://unesdoc.unesco.org/images/0014/001474/147448e.pdf

Chawla, L., & Johnson, V. (2004). Not for children only: Lessons learnt from young people's participation. In N. Kenton (Ed.), *Participatory learning and action: Critical reflections, future directions.* London, UK: International Institute for Environment and Development.

Chernin, M. (1986). A practical application of an eighteenth-century aesthetic: The development of Pestalozzian education. *College Music Symposium,* 76, 53–65. Retrieved from http://www.jstor.org/stable/40373822

Children's Workforce Development Council (CWDC). (2011). Graduate leaders 'drive up standards' in nursery provision. Retrieved 7 September 2011, from http://www.cwdcouncil.org.uk/news/6027_graduate-leaders-drive-up-standards-in-nursery-provision

Chisnall, N. (2008). Montessori through the eyes of newly qualified teachers in Aotearoa New Zealand. In P. L. Jeffery (Ed.), *Changing climates: Education for sustainable futures. Proceedings of the AARE 2008 International Education Research Conference 2008, Queensland University of Technology* (pp. 1–12). Brisbane, Australia: Queensland University of Technology.

Chistolini, S. (2009). *Maria Montessori and Giuseppina Pizzigoni pioneers of the century in scholastic modernisation, Università Roma Tre.* Retrieved from https://ccie-media.s3.amazonaws.com/wf09_agenda/chistolini.pdf

Clements, R. D. (1981). Modern architecture's debt to creativity education: A case study. *Gifted Child Quarterly,* 25, 119–121. doi:10.1177/001698628102500307

Cohen, L. E. (2008). *Foucault and the early childhood classroom.* Retrieved 19 December 2011, from http://issuu.com/gfbertini/docs/foucault_and_the_early_childhood_classroom

Comenius, J. A. (1907). *Comenius's school of infancy: An essay on the education of youth.* Retrieved 20 June 2010, from http://onlinebooks.library.upenn.edu/webbin/book/lookupid?key=olbp34683 (Original work published 1633.)

Comenius, J. A. (1910). *Orbis sensualium pictus* [The visible world in pictures]. Mannheim, Germany: Harenberg Kalender Verlag. (Original work published c. 1657.)

Comenius, J. A. (1628/1967). *The great didactic of J. A. Comenius* (M. W. Keatinge, Trans., 2nd ed.). New York, NY: Russell and Russell. (Original work published c. 1628.)

Compayre, G. (1907). *Johann Heinrich Pestalozzi.* Retrieved 21 July 2010, from http://ia331318.us.archive.org/3/items/pestalozziandele00compuoft/pestalozziandele00-compuoft.pdf

Compayre, G., & Payne, W. H. (2003). *History of pedagogy 1889.* Whitefish, MT: Kessinger Publishing Co.

Connolly, C. (2004). Pale, poor and 'pretubercular' children: A history of paediatric antituberculosis efforts in France, Germany, and the United States, 1899–1929. *Nursing Inquiry*, 11, 138–147. doi:10.1111%2Fj.1440-1800.2004.00225.x

Cremin, L. A. (1961). *The transformation of the school: Progressivism in American education, 1876–1957*. New York: Random House.

Cuberley, E. P. (2005). *The Project Gutenberg ebook of the history of education*. Retrieved 20 June 2010, from http://www.gutenberg.org/dirs/etext05/8hsed10.txt

Cunningham, P. (2006). Early years teachers and the influence of Piaget: Evidence from oral history. *Early Years*, 26, 5–16. doi:10.1080/09575140500507769

Dahlberg, G., Moss, P., & Pence, A. (1999). *Beyond quality in early childhood education and care*. Abingdon, UK: Routledge.

Darwin, C. (1877). Biographical sketch of an infant. *Mind*, 2 (7), 285–294. doi:10.1093/mind/os-2.7.285

David, T. (1993). Educating children under 5 in the UK. In T. David (Ed.), *Educational provision for our youngest children: European perspectives*. London, UK: Paul Chapman Publications.

David, T. (Ed.). (1999). *Young children learning*. London, UK: Sage Publications.

David, T. (Ed.). (2001). *Promoting evidence-based practice in early childhood education*. Oxford, UK: Elsevier Science.

Davis, R. A., & O'Hagan, F. (2010). *Robert Owen*. London, UK: Continuum.

Deacon, R. (2006). From confinement to attachment: Michel Foucault on the rise of the school. *The European Legacy: Toward New Paradigms*, 11 (2), 121–138. doi:10.1080/10848770600587896

DeBaldo, A. C. (2005). *Genetics and gene science (classical)*. *Van Nostrand's Encyclopedia of Chemistry*. Wiley Online Library. doi:10.1002/0471740039.vec1148

Dent, N. J. H. (2005). *Rousseau*. London, UK: Routledge.

Department for Children, Education, Lifelong Learning and Skills. (2008). *The Foundation Phase: Framework for Children's Learning for 3 to 7-year-olds in Wales*. Retrieved 1 April 2013 from http://wales.gov.uk/dcells/publications/policy_strategy_and_planning/early-wales/whatisfoundation/foundationphase/2274085/frameworkforchildrene.pdf?lang=en

Department for Children, Schools and Families. (2008). *Early Years Foundation Stage*. Annesley, UK: DCSF Publications.

Department for Education. (2010). *Sure Start children's centre statutory guidance:* Retrieved 28 August 2011, from https://www.education.gov.uk/publications/eOrderingDownload/SSCC%20statutory%20guidance-2010.pdf

Department for Education. (2011). The core purpose of Sure Start children's centres. Retrieved 7 September 2011, from http://www.education.gov.uk/childrenandyoungpeople/earlylearningandchildcare/a00191780/core-purpose-of-sure-start-childrens-centres

Department for Education. (2012a). *Nutbrown Review: Foundations for Quality. Final Report*. London: Department of Education.

Department for Education. (2012b) *The Statutory Framework for the Early Years Foundation Stage*. London: Department for Education.

Department for Education and Skills. (2003). *Every child matters*. London, UK: The Stationery Office.

Department for Education and Skills. (2004). *Every child matters: Change for children* London, UK: The Stationery Office.

Department for Health and Social Security. (January 1976). *Low cost day provision for under fives*. Papers presented at a conference held at the Civil Service College, Sunningdale Park, UK.

Department for Works and Pensions. (2010). *State of the Nation Report: Poverty, worklessness and welfare dependency in the UK*. Retrieved 31 August 2010, from http://www.marmotreview.

org/AssetLibrary/resources/new%20external%20reports/cabinet%20office%20-%20state%20of%20the%20nation.pdf

Descartes, R. (1998). *Meditations and other metaphysical writings* (D. M. Clark, Trans.). London, UK: Penguin Group. (Original work published 1627.)

Dewey, J. (1910). *How we think*. Retrieved 10 September 2010, from http://www.archive.org/details/howwethink000838mbp

Dewey, J. (1916). *Democracy and education: An introduction to the philosophy of education*. New York, NY: Macmillan.

Dobrin, A. (2001). Finding universal values in a time of relativism. *The Educational Forum*, 65, 273–276. Retrieved 9 January 2011, from http://arthurdobrin.files.wordpress.com/2008/08/finding-universal-values-in-a-time-of-relativism2.pdf

Doherty, J., & Hughes, M. (2009). *Child development: Theory and practice 0–11*. Harlow, UK: Pearson Education.

Donnachie, I. (2000). *Robert Owen: Owen of New Lanark and New Harmony*. East Linton, UK: Tuckwell Press.

Drummond, M. J. (2000). *Comparisons in early years education: History, fact, and fiction*. Retrieved 4 September 2010, from http://ecrp.uiuc.edu/v2n1/drummond.html

Duckworth, C. (2006). Teaching peace: A dialogue on the Montessori method. *Journal of Peace Education*, 3, 39–53. doi:10.1080/17400200500532128

Early Education (2012). *Development matters in the Early Years Foundation Stage (EYFS)*. London: Department for Education.

Ecken, W., van der, & Turner, B. (1969). *Adventures in education*. London, UK: Penguin Press.

Edwards, C., Gandini, L., & Forman, G. (1998). *The Reggio Emilia approach – Advanced reflections*. London, UK: JAI Press.

Eichhoff, J. (1988). 'Kindergarten' and its progeny in American English. *Monatshefte*, 80 (1), 82–95. Retrieved from University of Wisconsin Press website: http://www.jstor.org/stable/30153053

Elfer, P. (2007). Babies and young children in nurseries: Using psychoanalytic ideas to explore tasks and interactions. *Children & Society*, 21, 111–122. doi:10.1111/j.1099- 0860.2006.00034.x

Erichsen, V. (1993). *The health of the school child? An historical comparison of inspection schemes in Britain and Norway*. Retrieved 4 March 2011, from http://www.raco.cat/index.php/Dynamis/article/viewFile/105933/149937

Eyken, W., & Turner, B. (1969). *Adventures in education*. London: Allen Lane.

Field, F. (2010). *The foundation years: Preventing poor children from becoming poor adults*. Retrieved 28 August 2010 from http://www.nfm.org.uk/component/jdownloads/finish/74/333

Fjørtoft, I., & Sageie, J. (2001). The natural environment as a playground for children: The impact of outdoor play activities in pre-primary school children. *Early Childhood Education Journal*, 29 (2), 111–117. doi:1082-301/01/1200-0111.x

Forrester, J. (2004). Freud in Cambridge. *Critical Quarterly*, 46, 1–26. doi:10.1111/j.0011-1562.2004.t01-1-00560.x

Foschi, R. (2008). Science and culture around Montessori's first 'children's houses' in Rome (1907–1915). *Journal of the History of the Behavioral Sciences*, 44, 238–257. doi:10.1002/jhbs.20313

Foucault, M. (1972). Preface. In G. Deleuze & F. Guattari (Eds.), *Anti-Oedipus: Capitalism & schizophrenia* (pp. xi–xiv). London, UK: The Anthole Press.

Foucault, M. (1975). *Discipline and punish: The birth of the prison*. New York, NY: Random House.

Foucault, M. (1976). *The birth of the clinic: An archaeology of medical perception*. London, UK: Taylor and Francis.

Foucault, M. (1980). *Power/knowledge: Selected interviews and other writings, 1972–1977* (C. Gordon, L. Marshall, J. Mepham, & K. Soper, Trans.). London, UK: Wheatsheaf.

Foucault, M. (1981). The order of discourse. In R. Young (Ed.), *Untying the text: A post-structural anthology* (pp. 48–78). Boston, MA: Routledge & Kegan Paul

Foucault, M. (1985). *History of sexuality: Vol. 2. The use of pleasure.* New York, NY: Pantheon.

Franzé, G. (2000). *Fancuilli oggi uomini domani: Agazzi, Pizzigoni, Montessori – Itinerati didatici* [Children today, men tomorrow: Agazzi, Pizzigoni, Montessori – *Didactic* itineraries]. Rome, Italy: Edizione Magi.

Freire, P. (2002). *Pedagogy of the oppressed* (M. Bergman Ramos, Trans.). New York, NY: Continuum. (Original work published 1968.)

Freud, S. (1907). The sexual enlightenment of children (An open letter to Dr. M. Furst). *Standard Edition, 7,* 1901–5.

Froebel, F. (1826/1906). *The education of man* (W. N. Hailman, Trans.). London, UK: Appleton. (Original work published 1826.)

Froebel, F. (1920). *Mother's songs, games and stories.* Retrieved 30 August 2010, from http://core.roehampton.ac.uk/digital/froarc/fromoth/ (Original work published 1846.)

Frost, J. (2010). *A history of children's play and play environments.* Abingdon, UK: Routledge.

Gardner, D. E. M. (1969). *Susan Isaacs.* London, UK: Methuen Educational.

Garrick, R., Bath, C., Dunn, K., Maconochie, H., Willis, J., & Wolstenholme, C. (2010). *Children's experiences of the Early Years Foundation Stage.* Retrieved 12 September 2011, from https://www.education.gov.uk/publications/eOrderingDownload/DFE-RB071.pdf

Gass, K., Jenkins, J., & Dunn, J. (2007). Are sibling relationships protective? A longitudinal study. *Journal of Child Psychology and Psychiatry, 48,* 167–175. doi:10.1111/j.1469-7610.2006.01699.x

Gay, P. (1998). Locke on the education of paupers. In A. Oksenberg Rorty (Ed.), *Philosophers on education: Historical perspectives.* New York, NY: Routledge.

Gelbier, S., & Randall, S. (1982). Charles Edwards Wallis and the rise of London's School Dental Service. *Medical History, 26,* 395–404. Retrieved from http//:ncbi.nlm.nih.gov/pmc/articles/PMC1139219/pdf/medhist00085-0033.pdf

Giardiello, P. (2006). *An exploration of 'circle time' as a pedagogical tool in developing young children's emotional literacy* (Unpublished master's dissertation). University of Lancaster, Lancaster, UK.

Gilbert, A. (2007). Inequality and why it matters. *Geography Compass, 1,* 422–447. doi:10.1111/j.1749-8198.2007.00021.x

Glennester, H., Hills, J., Piachaud, D., & Webb, J. (2004). *One hundred years of poverty and policy.* York, UK: Joseph Rowntree Foundation.

Goodman, J., & Harrop, S. (2000). *Women, educational policy making, and administration in England.* London, UK: Routledge.

Gorb, P. (1951). Robert Owen as a business man. *Bulletin of the Business Historical Society, 25,* 127–148. Retrieved 8 August 2010, from http://www.jstor.org/stable/3111280

Gordon, P. (1994). *Robert Owen (1771–1858) prospects: The quarterly review of education.* Retrieved 20 October 2010, from http://www.ibe.unesco.org/fileadmin/user_upload/archive/publications/ThinkesPdf/owenf.PDF

Gore, J. (1993). *The struggle for pedagogies: Critical and feminist discourses as regimes of truth.* London, UK: Routledge.

Graham, P. (2009). *Susan Isaacs: A life freeing the minds of children.* London, UK: Karnac Books.

Gregg, A. (1993). The hope of the future: The Kindergarten Union and the campaign for children's libraries in Western Australia. *Issues in Educational Research, 3,* 17–33.

Gregor, J. A. (2005). *Mussolini's intellectuals: Fascist. Social and Political Thought.* Princeton, NJ: Princeton University Press.

Gundem, B. B. (1992). 'Vivat Comenius': A commemorative essay on Johan Amos Comenius 1592–1670. *Journal of Curriculum and Supervision,* 8, 43–55.

Gutek, G. L. (2000). *Historical and philosophical foundation of education: A biographical introduction.* Upper Saddle River, NJ: Merrill Prentice Hall.

Gutek, G. L. (2003). *Philosophical and ideological voices in education.* London, UK: Allyn and Bacon.

Hadow, H. (1933). *Infant and nursery schools: Report of the Consultative Committee.* London, UK: HMSO.

Hall, J. S. (2000). Psychology and schooling: The impact of Susan Isaacs and Jean Piaget on 1960s science education reform. *History of Education,* 29, 153–170. doi:10.1080/004676 000284436

Hamilton, D. (1989). *Towards a theory of schooling.* London, UK: Falmer Press

Hampson-Patterson, M. (2007). *Domesticating the Reformation: Protestant best sellers, private devotion, and the revolution of English piety.* Cranbury, NJ: Rosemont Publishing and Printing Corporation.

Harris, J., Treanor, M., & Sharma, N. (2009). *Below the breadline: A year in the life of families in poverty.* Retrieved 31 March 2011, from http://www.barnardos.org.uk/11325_breadline_report_final.pdf

Harris, R. (2009). Freedom of speech and philosophy of education. *British Journal of Educational Studies,* 57, 111–126. doi:10.1111/j.1467-8527.2009.00431.x

Hatfield, G. (2003). *Philosophy guidebook to Descartes and the meditations.* London, UK: Taylor and Francis.

Hendrick, H. (1994). *Child Welfare: England 1872–1989.* London: Routledge.

Hendrick, H. (1997). Construction and reconstruction of British childhood: An interpretive survey, 1800 to present. In A. James & A. Prout (Eds.), *Constructing and reconstructing childhood: Contemporary issues in the sociological study of childhood* (2nd ed.). London, UK: Falmer Press.

Hewes, D. W. (1990). Historical foundations of early childhood teacher training. The evolution of kindergarten teacher preparation. In B. Spodek & O. N. Saracho (Eds.), *Early childhood teacher preparation* (pp. 1–22). New York, NY: Teachers College Press.

Hewes, D. W. (1992). *Pestalozzi: Foster father of early childhood.* Retrieved 21 October 2012, from http://www.eric.ed.gov/PDFS/ED353067.pdf

Hewes, D. W. (2005). Maintaining the median in early childhood educational methodology. *Journal of Early Childhood Teacher Education,* 26, 157–169. doi:10.1080/10901020590955789

Higgins, P. (2010). Why indoors? The value of outdoor learning. In M. Fleurot (Ed.), *Education in the outdoors: Proceedings of the Countryside Recreation Network, 2010 Centre in the Park, Sheffield* (pp. 7–15). Retrieved from http://www.countrysiderecreation.org.uk/events/Education%20in%20the%20Outdoors%202010%20Proceedings.pdf#page=7

Hilton, M. (2001). Revisioning Romanticism: Towards a women's history of progressive thought 1780–1850. *History of Education,* 30, 471–487. doi:10.1080/00467600110064744

Hinchliffe, G. (2006). *Re-thinking lifelong learning.* Studies in Philosophy and Education, 25, 93–109. doi:10.1007/s11217-006-0004-1

Hopkins, J. (1988). Facilitating the development of intimacy between nurses and infants in day nurseries. *Early Child Development and Care,* 33, 99–111.

House of Commons, Children, Schools and Families Committee. (2009). *National Curriculum: fifth report of session 2009–2010.* London, UK: HMSO.

Hummel, C. (1993). Aristotle 384–322 BC. *Prospects: The Quarterly Review Of Comparative Education,* 23, 39–51. Retrieved 3 March 2010, from http//:www.ibe.unesco.org/fileadmin/user_upload/archive/publications/ThinkesPdf/aristote.pdf

Ingall, C. K. (1994). Reform and redemption: The Maharal of Prague and John Amos Comenius. *Religious Education,* 89, 358–375. doi:10.1080/0034408940890304

Iovan, M. (2010). Characteristics of the ideal Christian education. *European Journal of Science and Theology*, 6 (4), 5–20.

Isaacs, S. (1921). *An introduction to psychology*: London, UK: Methuen Press.

Isaacs, S. (1929). *The nursery years: The mind of the child from birth to six years*. London, UK: Routledge.

Isaacs, S. (1930). *Intellectual growth in young children*. London, UK: Routledge & Kegan Paul.

Isaacs, S (1932) *The nursery years: The mind of the child from birth to six years* (Revised Edition). London: Routledge & Kegan Paul.

Isaacs, S. (1933). *Social development in young children: A study of beginnings*. London, UK: Routledge & Kegan Paul.

Isaacs, S. (1938). The principle of activity in modern education. In A. E. Campbell (Ed.), *Modern trends in education: Proceedings of the New Zealand N.E.F Conference* (p. 504). Wellington, New Zealand: Whitcombe and Tombs.

Isaacs, S. (Ed.). (1941). *The Cambridge Evacuation Survey*. London, UK: Methuen.

Isaacs, S. (1952). *The educational value of the nursery school*. London: Headly Brothers.

Isaacs, S. (1954). *The educational value of the nursery school*. London, UK: BAECE Publication.

Isaacs, S., Clement, S., & Thouless, H. (1941). *The Cambridge evacuation survey, a wartime study in social welfare and education*. London, Methuen.

Kahn, P. H., & Kellert, S. R. (2002). *Children and nature: Psychological, sociocultural and evolutionary investigations*. Cambridge, MA: MIT Press.

Kamm, J. (1971). *Indicative past: A hundred years of the Girls' Public Day School Trust*. London, UK: George Allen and Unwin,

Kasper, B. (2005). Educational Reform 1983–1994: New ideas or the rebirth of Quintilian's ideologies. *American Educational History Journal*, 32, 175–182. Retrieved 31 March 2010, from http://proquest.umi.com.eresources.shef.ac.uk/pqdweb?did=1039251381&sid=1&Fmt=3&clientId=29199&RQT=309&VName=PQD

Kean, H., & Oram, A. (1990). Men must be educated and women must do it: The National Federation (later Union) of Women Teachers and contemporary feminism 1910–1930. *Gender and Education, 2,* 147–167. doi:10.1080/0954025900020202

King, P., & Howard, J. (2010). Understanding children's free play at home, in school and at the After School Club: A preliminary investigation into play types, social grouping and perceived control. *The Psychology of Education Review*, 34 (1), 33–41.

Klein, M. (1923). The role of the school in the libidinal development of the child. In *The Writings of Melanie Klein, Volume 1, Love Guilt and Reparation and Other Works, 1921–1945*. London: Hogarth Press, 1975.

Klein, M. (1975). Early analysis. In M. Klein (Ed.), *The writings of Melanie Klein: Vol. 1. Love, guilt and reparation* (pp. 77–105). London, UK: Hogarth Press. (Original work published 1923.)

Knapper, C. K., & Cropley, A. J. (2000). *Lifelong learning in higher education*. London, UK: Kogan Page.

Knight, S. (2009). *Forest schools and outdoor learning in the early years*. London, UK: Sage Publications.

Kontio, K. (2003). The idea of autarchy in Rousseau's natural education: Recovering the natural harmony? *Scandinavian Journal of Educational Research, 47,* 3–19.

Koven, S. (2004). *Slumming: Sexual and social politics in Victorian London*. Princeton, NJ: Princeton University Press.

Koven, S., & Michel, S. (1990). Womanly duties: Maternalist politics and the origins of welfare states in France, Germany, Great Britain, and the United States, 1880–1920. *The American Historical Review*, 95 (4), 1076–1108. Retrieved from http://www.jstor.org/stable/2163479

Kramer, R. (1976). *Maria Montessori*. London, UK: Montessori International Publishing.

Krentz, A. (1998). *Play and education in Plato's Republic*. Retrieved 21 March 2010, from http//:www.bu.edu/wcp/Papers/Educ/EducKren.htm

Lathom, J. (2002). Pestalozzi and James Pierrepont Greaves: A shared educational philosophy. *History of Education, 31*, 59–70. doi:10.1080/00467600110102327

LeBlanc, M. (2000). *Johann Heinrich Pestalozzi*. Retrieved 20 October 2010, from http://www.communityplaythings.co.uk/resources/articles/pestalozzi.html

Lee, J. S., & Bowen, N. K. (2006). Parent involvement, cultural capital, and the achievement gap among elementary school children. *American Educational Research Journal, 43* (2), 193–218. doi:10.3102/00028312043002193

Lee, S. W., Evans, R., & Jackson, P. (1994). Froebel and Christianity. *Early Child Development and Care, 100*, 1–42. doi:10.1080/0300443941000101

Levine, R. F. (1987). *Recapturing Marxism: An appraisal of trends in sociological theory*. New York, NY: Greenwood Press.

Liebschener, J. (1991). Foundations of progressive education: The history of the National Froebel Society. *Cambridge, UK: Lutterworth Press.*

Lindemann-Matthies, P. (2005). 'Loveable' mammals and 'lifeless' plants: How children's interest in common local organisms can be enhanced through observation of nature. *International Journal of Science Education, 27*, 655–677. doi:10.1080/09500690500038116

Lindon, J. (2001). *Understanding children's play*. Cheltenham, UK: Nelson Thorne.

Lloyd, E., & Hallet, E. (2010). Professionalising the early childhood workforce in England: Work in progress or missed opportunity? *Contemporary Issues in the Early Years, 11* (1), 75–88.

Locke, J. (1910). *Some thoughts concerning education*. Retrieved 21 July 2010, from http://www.fordham.edu/halsall/mod/1692locke-education.html (Original work published 1692.)

Locke, J. (1959). *An essay concerning human understanding* (A. Campbell, Ed.). New York, NY: Dover Publications. (Original work published 1690.)

Lombardo-Radice, G. (1934). *Nursery schools in Italy: The problem of infant education*. London, UK: George Allen and Unwin.

Lorch, M., & Hellard, P. (2010). Darwin's 'Natural Science of Babies'. *Journal of the History of the Neurosciences, 19*: 140–157. doi:10.1080/09647040903504823

Løvlie, L., & Standish, P. (2002). Bildung and the idea of liberal education. *Journal of Philosophy of Education, 36* (3), 317–340.

Lowndes, G. A. N. (1960). *Margaret McMillan 'The Children Champion'*. London, UK: Museum Press.

Luke, C. (1989). *Pedagogy, printing and protestantism*. Albany, NY: State University of New York Press.

Luther, M. (1889). *Luther on education: A translation of the reformer's two most important education treatises* (F. V. N. Painter, Trans.). Retrieved 30 September 2010, from http://www.archive.org/stream/lutheroneducati00luthgoog#page/n6/mode/thumb (Original work published 1532.)

MacNaugton, G. (2003). *Shaping early childhood*. Maidenhead, UK: Open University Press.

MacNaughton, G. (2005). *Doing Foucault in early childhood studies*. Abingdon, UK: Routledge.

Malaguzzi, L. (1996). The right to environment. In T. Filippini & V. Vecchi (Eds.), *The hundred languages of children: The exhibit*. Reggio Emilia, Italy: Reggio Children Publications.

Mansbridge, A. (1932). *Margaret McMillan*. Letchworth, UK: The Temple Press.

Manning, J. P. (2005). Rediscovering Froebel: A call to re-examine his life & gifts. *Early Childhood Education Journal, 32* (6), 371–376. doi:10.1007/s 10643-005-0004-8

Martensson, F., Boldemann, C., Soderstrom, M., Blennow, M., Englund, J., & Grahn, P. (2009). Outdoor environmental assessment of attention promoting settings for preschool children.

Health and Place, 15 (4), 1149–1157. Retrieved from http//:www.elsevier.com/locate/healthplace

May, H. (1997). *The discovery of early childhood: The development of services for the care and education of very young children, mid eighteenth century Europe to mid twentieth century.* Auckland, New Zealand: Bridget Williams Books.

May, H. (2003). *Concerning women considering children. Battles of The Childcare Association 1963–2003.* Wellington, NZ: Te Tari Puna Ora o Aotearoa, New Zealand Childcare Association.

Mayhew, H. (1861/1967). *London labour and the London poor: A cyclopaedia of the condition and earnings of those that will work, those that cannot work, and those that will not work.* New York, USA: A.M. Kelley.

Mazzoleni, D. (1993). The city and the imaginary (J. Koumantarakis, Trans.). In E. Carter, J. Donald, & J. Squires (Eds.), *Space and place: Theories of identity and location.* London, UK: Lawrence & Wishart.

McCann, P. (1966). Samuel Wilderspin and the early infant schools. *British Journal of Educational Studies,* 14 (2), 188–204. Retrieved from http://www.jstor.org/stable/3118652

McCann, P., & Young, F. A. (1982). *Samuel Wilderspin and the infant school movement.* London, UK: Taylor & Francis.

McGrath, A. E. (2001). *Christian theology: An introduction* (3rd ed.) Oxford, UK: Blackwell Publishers.

McLaren, D. J. (1996). Robert Owen, William Maclure and New Harmony. *History of Education, 25,* 223–233. doi:10.1080/00467609602503

McLean, M., Bailey, D.B., & Wolery, M. (1992). *Assessing infants and pre-schoolers with special needs.* Columbus, OH: Merrill/Prentice Hall.

McMillan, M. (1904). *Education through the imagination.* London, UK: J. M. Dent and Sons.

McMillan, M. (27 January 1911). Faith and fear, Labour leader. *Guardian.* Retrieved from http://archive.guardian.co.uk/Default/Skins/DigitalArchive/Client.asp?Skin=DigitalArchive&enter=true&AW=1314895065648&AppName=2

McMillan, M. (1919). *The nursery school.* London, UK: J. M. Dent and Sons.

McMillan, M. (1921). *The nursery school.* New York: Dutton.

McMillan, M. (1927). *The life of Rachel McMillan.* London, UK: J. M. Dent and Sons.

McMillan, M. (1930) *The Nursery School* (Revised Edition). Retrieved 30 March 2013 from http://core.roehampton.ac.uk/digital/froarc/mcmnur/

Mearn, A. (1883). *The Bitter Cry of Outcast London: An Inquiry into the conditions of the abject poor.* London, UK: James Clarke.

Middleton, S., & May, H. (1997). *Teachers talk teaching 1915–1995: Early childhood, school and teachers' colleges.* Palmerston North, New Zealand: Dunmore Press.

Miliband, R. (1954). The politics of Robert Owen. *Journal of the History of Ideas,* 15 (2), 233–245. Retrieved from http://www.jstor.org/stable/2707769

Ministry of Education (1996). *Te Wh riki: Early childhood curriculum. He Wh riki Matauranga mo nga Mokopuna o Aotearoa.* Wellington, NZ: Learning Media.

Montessori, M. (1913). *Pedagogical anthropology* (trans. F.T. Cooper). University of Michigan: Stokes Publications.

Montessori, M. (1948). *The discovery of the child* (M. A. Johnstone, Trans.). Madras, India: Kalakshetra Publications.

Montessori, M. (1964). *The Montessori method* (A. E. George, Trans.). New York, NY: Schocken Books. (Original work published 1912.)

Montessori, M. (1965). *Dr. Montessori's own handbook* (F. Simmonds, Trans.). London, UK: Schocken Books. (Original work published 1917.)

Montessori, M. (1967). *The absorbent mind* (C. A. Claremont, Trans.). New York, NY: Dell Publishing Co.

Montessori, M. (1972). *Education and peace* (trans. H. R. Lane). Chicago, IL: Henry Regnery. (Original work published 1948.)

Moretti, E. (2011). *Recasting Il Metodo: Maria Montessori and early childhood education in Italy (1909–1926).* Retrieved 2 September 2011, from http://www.cromohs.unifi. it/16_2011/moretti_montessori.html

Morris, I. (1989). *Burial and ancient society: The rise of the Greek city-state.* Cambridge, UK: Cambridge University Press.

Mosley, J., & Murray, P. (1998). *Quality circle time in the Primary classroom: Your essential guide to enhancing self-esteem, self-discipline and positive relationships.* London, UK: LDA Publication.

Moss, P. (2006). Farewell to childcare? *Journal of the National Institute of Economic and Social Research, 195,* 70–83. doi:10.1177/0027950106064040

Moyles, J. (1989). *Just playing? The role and stus of play in early childhood education.* Buckingham, UK: Open University Press.

Moyles, J. (2010). *The excellence of play* (3rd ed). Maidenhead, UK: Open University Press.

Moyles, J., Adams. S., & Musgrove, A. (2001). *Study of pedagogical effectiveness in early learning.* Retrieved 20 August 2010, from https://www.education.gov.uk/publications/ eOrderingDownload/RR363.pdf

Mussolini, B (1933). The schools of Italy. *The High School Journal,* 16 (7), 261–265. Retrieved from: http://www.jstor.org/stable/40360948?origin=JSTOR-pdf

National Association for the Education of Young Children (2009). *Developmentally appropriate practice in early childhood programs serving children from birth through age 8: A position statement.* Retrieved 1 April 2013 from http://www.naeyc.org/files/naeyc/file/positions/PSDAP.pdf

Nawrotski, K. D. (2007). 'Like sending coals to Newcastle': Impressions from and of the Anglo-American kindergarten movements. *Paedagogica Historica,* 43, 223–233. doi:10.1080/00309230701248321

Neill, A. S. (1966). *Summerhill: A radical approach to education.* London, UK: Gollancz.

Nutbrown, C., Clough, P., & Selbie, P. (2008). *Early childhood education.* London, UK: Sage Publications.

Nuttall, J., & Edwards, S. (2007). Theory, policy and practice: Three contexts for the development of Australasia's early childhood curriculum documents. In L. Keesing-Style & H. Hedges (Eds.), *Theorising early childhood practice: Emerging dialogues* (pp. 3–22). Castle Hill, Australia: Pademelon Press.

Organization for Economic Cooperation and Development (2001). *Starting strong: Early childhood education and care.* Paris: OECD.

Oelkers, J. (2002). Rousseau and the image of modern education. *Journal of Curriculum Studies,* 34, 679–698. doi:10.1080/00220270210141936

Office of the High Commissioner for Human Rights (OHCHR). (2005). *General Comment No. 7: Implementing child rights in early childhood.* Retrieved 4 September 2011, from www. ohchr.org/english/bodies/crc/comments

Office for Standards in Education (1998/9). *Annual Report of Her Majesty's Chief Inspector of Schools.* London, UK: HMSO.

O'Hagan, F. (2007). Robert Owen and the development of good citizenship in 19th century New Lanark. Retrieved 10 August 2010 from Glasgow University Eprint Service http://eprints.gla.ac.uk/3801/

Ornstein, A.C. & Levine, D.U. (2008). *Foundations of education* (9th ed.). Boston, MA: Houghton Mifflin Company.

Owen, R. (1813). *A new view of society: Essays on the principle of the formation of human character.* London, UK: Cadell & Davies.

Owen, R. (1842). *Book of the new moral world, Part 3.* Glasgow: H. Robinson.

Owen, R. D. (1874). *Threading my way: Twenty-seven years of autobiography.* London, UK: Trubner. Retrieved 11 November 2010, from http://www.archive.org/stream/threadingmywayt01owengoog#page/n117/mode/2up

Pacey, M. (2011). *Early education welcomes Dame Clare Tickell's overwhelming endorsement of the Early Years Foundation Stage* [Press release]. Retrieved 30 May 2011 from http://www.early-education.org.uk/press_release_30-03-11.htm

Parekh, A., MacInnes, T., & Kenway, P. (2010). *Monitoring poverty and social exclusion 2010.* Retrieved 31 January 2011, from http://www.jrf.org.uk/sites/files/jrf/poverty-social-exclusion-2010-full.pdf

Pascal, N. (1984). The legacy of Roman education. *The Classic Journal.* Retrieved 31 March 2010, from http://www.jstor.org/pss/3297030

Peltzman, B. R. (1998). *Pioneers of early childhood education: A bio-bibliographical guide.* Westport, CT: Green Press.

Penn, H. (2002). Round and round the mulberry bush. In R. Aldrich (Ed.), *Public and private in the history of education.* London, UK: Woburn Press.

Penn, H. (2007). Childcare market management: How the United Kingdom Government has reshaped its role in developing early childhood education and care. *Contemporary Issues in Early Childhood,* 8 (3). doi:10.2304/ciec.2007.8.3.192

Pestalozzi, J. H. (1819/1827). *Letters on education: Addressed to J. P. Greaves, Esq.* Retrieved 30 July 2010, from http://www.archive.org/stream/lettersonearlyed00pestiala#page/4/mode/2up

Pestalozzi, J. H. (1894). *How Gertrude teaches her children* (L. E. Holland & F. C Turner, Trans.). Retrieved 18 August 2011, from http://www.archive.org/details/howgertrudeteach-00pestuoft (Original work published 1801.)

Petrie, P. (2004). *Pedagogy: A holistic, personal approach to work with children and young people across services: European models for practice, training, education and qualification.* Unpublished manuscript, Thomas Coram Research Unit, IoE University of London, London, UK.

Petrina, S. (2006). The medicalization of education: A historiographic synthesis. *History of Education Quarterly,* 46 (4), 503–531. Retrieved from http://proquest.umi.com.eresources.shef.ac.uk/pqdweb?index=32&did=1206582181&SrchMode=1&sid=1&Fmt=6&VInst=PROD&VType=PQD&RQT=309&VName=PQD&TS=1314804455&clientId=29199

Piaget, J. (1926). *Language and thought of the child.* London, UK: Routledge and Kegan Paul.

Piaget, J. (1954). *The construction of reality in the child.* New York: Basic Books.

Pike, E. R. (1963). *Pioneers of social change.* London, UK: Pemberton Publishing.

Plato. (2008). *The Republic* (B. Jowell, Trans.). New York, NY: Cosimo Classics. (Original work published c. 360 BC.)

Pollard, A. (1989). British primary education: A response to Karl Heinz Gruber. *Comparative Education,* 3, 365–368. Retrieved from http://www.jstor.org/pss/3099212

Popper, K. R. (1952). *The Open Society and its enemies* (2nd ed.). London: Routledge and Kegan Paul.

Poskoff, P. (1952). Quintilian in the late Middle Ages. *Speculum,* 27 (1), 71–78. Retrieved from http://www.jstor.org/pss/2855295

Pramling-Samuelsson, I., & Kaga, Y. (2008). *The contribution of early childhood education to a sustainable society.* Retrieved 12 September 2010, from http://unesdoc.unesco.org/images/0015/001593/159355e.pdf

Pugh, G. (2009). The policy agenda for early childhood services. In G. Pugh & B. Duffy (Eds.), *Contemporary issues in Early Years* (pp. 5–20). London, UK: Sage Publications.

Radcliffe, C. (1997). Mutual improvement societies and the forging of working-class political consciousness in nineteenth-century England. *International Journal of Lifelong Education,* 16, 141–155. doi:10.1080/0260137970160206

Read, J. (2003). Froebelian women: Networking to promote professional status and educational change in the nineteenth century. *History of Education, 32,* 17–33. doi:10.1080/004676 0022000032396

Read, J. (2006). Free play with Froebel: Use and abuse of progressive pedagogy in London's infant schools, 1870–c.1904. *Paedagogica Historica, 42,* 299–323. doi:10.1080/0030923 0600622717

Read, J. (2010). Gutter to garden: Historical discourses of risk in interventions in working class children's street play. *Children and Society, 1,* 1–14. doi:10.1111/j.1099-0860. 2010.00293.x

Riley, P. (1991). Rousseau's general will: Freedom of a particular kind. *Political Studies, 39* (1), 55–74.

Rinaldi, C. (2006). *In dialogue with Reggio Emilia: Listening, researching and learning.* Abingdon, UK: Routledge.

Robb, F. (1943). Aristotle and education. *Peabody Journal of Education, 20,* 201–213. Retrieved 3 March 2011, from http://www.jstor.org/pss/1489937

Roberts, A. (1976). The development of professionalism in the early stages of education. *British Journal of Educational Studies, 24* (3), 254–264. Retrieved from http://www.jstor. org/stable/3119909

Robson, S. (2006). *Developing thinking and understanding in young children.* Abingdon, UK: Routledge.

Röhrs, H. (1994). *Maria Montessori (1870–1952).* PROSPECTS, 24 (1/2, 89–90) 169–183. Paris, France: UNESCO: International Bureau of Education. Retrieved 2 September 2011, from http://www.ibe.unesco.org/fileadmin/user_upload/archive/publications/ ThinkersPdf/montesse.pdf

Rose, J. (2001). *The intellectual life of British working classes.* New Haven, CT: Yale University Press.

Rousseau, J. (1979). *Emile or on education.* (A. Bloom, Trans.). New York, NY: Basic Books. (Original work published 1762.)

Royal Society for the Prevention of Cruelty to Animals (RSPCA) *Animal friendly schools.* Retrieved 30 March 2013 from: http://www.rspca.org.uk/ImageLocator/LocateAsset?a sset=document&assetId=1232721467391&mode=prd

Russell, B. (1926). *On education: Especially in early childhood.* London, UK: George Allen and Unwin.

Sandsmark, S. (2002). A Lutheran perspective on education. *Journal of Education and Christian Belief, 6,* 97–105. Retrieved 28 August 2010, from http://ezproxy.hope.ac.uk:2071/ ehost/pdfviewer/pdfviewer?vid=3&hid=21&sid=284c09ae-66ca-493e-8cb7- b7a309b63e32%40sessionmgr11

Saracho, O., & Spodek, B. (1995). Children's play and early childhood education: Insights from history and theory. *Journal of Education, 177,* 129–148. Retrieved from http:// ebschost/detail?sid=0de08436-b44d-460a-9541-bbcf3b064190%40sessionmgr13&vid= 4&hid=11&bdata=JnNpdGU9ZWhvc3QtbGl2ZQ%3d%3d#db=ehh &AN=9705281799

Saracho, O., & Spodek, B. (2009). Educating the young mathematician: A historical perspective through the nineteenth century. *Early Childhood Education Journal, 36,* 297–303. doi:10. 1007/s10643-008-0292-x

Sayle, A. (1929). The nursery school: A factor in the health of the nation, by Miss A. Sayle, M.B.E., M.A., Chairman, Women Sanitary Inspectors and Health. *The Journal of the Royal Society for the Promotion of Health, 50,* 588–592. doi:10.1177/146642402905000903

Sewell, A., & Bethall, K. (2009). Building interests: A 1940s story of curriculum innovation and contemporary connections. *New Zealand Journal of Teachers' Work, 6* (2), 93–110.

Sharpe, K., & Van Gelder, L. (2004). Children and Paleolithic 'art': Indications from Rouffignac Cave, France. *International Newsletter on Rock Art*, 38, 9–17. Retrieved 15 October 2010, from http://www.ksharpe.com/Word/ArchBib.htm

Shepherd, J. (2004). A life on the Left: George Lansbury (1859–1940): A case study in recent labour biography. *Labour History*, 87, 146–165. Retrieved from http://www.jstor.org/stable/27516003

Singer, E. (1992). *Child-care and the psychology of development*. London, UK: Taylor & Francis.

Siraj-Blatchford, I., Sylva, K., Muttock, S., Gildewn, R., & Bell, D. (2002). *Researching effective pedagogy in the Early Years*. London, UK: HMSO.

Skolverket. (2006). *Lpo 98 curriculum for the preschool*. Retrieved 3 March 2010, from http://www.skolverket.se/

Smith, L. (1996). The shoe-black to the crossing sweeper: Victorian street Arabs and photography. *Textual Practice*, 10, 29–55. doi:10.1080/09502369608582238

Smith, L. A. H. (1985). *To understand and to help: The life and work of Susan Isaacs (1885–1948)*. London, UK: Fairleigh Dickinson University Press.

Smith, L. G., Smith, J. K., & Pergo, F. M. (1994). *Lives in education: A narrative of people and ideas*. New York, NY: St Martin Press.

Smith, M., & Whyte, B. (2007). Social education and social pedagogy: Reclaiming a Scottish tradition in social work. *European Journal of Social Work*, 11, 15–28. doi:10.1080/13691450701357174

Smith, R. (2010). Half a language: Listening in the city of words. *Educational Research*, 4, 149–160. doi:10.1007/978-90-481-3249-2_11

Sobe, N. (2010). Concentration and civilisation: Producing the attentive child in the age of enlightenment. *Paedagogica Historica*, 46, 149–160. doi:10.1080/00309230903528520

Soëtard. M. (1994). Johann Heinrich Pestalozzi (1746–1827). *Prospects: The Quarterly Review of Comparative Education*. Retrieved 31 October 2010, from http://www.ibe.unesco.org/fileadmin/user_upload/archive/publications/ThinkersPdf/pestaloe.PDF

Spodek, B., & Saracho, O. (2003). On the shoulder of giants: Exploring the traditions of early childhood education. *Early Childhood Education Journal*, 31 (1), 3–10. Retrieved from http://search.proquest.com.eresources.shef.ac.uk/docview/751591345?accountid=13828

Srinivasan, R. (2006). Where information society and community voice intersect. *The Information Society*, 2, 355–365. doi:10.1080/0197224060090432

Staples-New, R., & Cochran, M. (2008). *Early childhood education*. Westport, CT: Praeger Publishers.

Steedman, C. (1990). *Childhood, culture and class in Britain: Margaret McMillan 1890–1931*. London, UK: Virago Press.

Stephenson, A. (2003). Physical risk-taking: Dangerous or endangered? *Early Years*, 23, 35–43. doi:10.1080/03004270701602632

Stewart-Steinberg, S. (2007). *The Pinocchio effect: On making Italians (1860–1920)*. Chicago, IL: University of Chicago Press.

Straw, H. (1990). The nursery garden. *Early Child Development and Care*, 57, 109–119.

Suchodolski, B. (1970). *Comenius and teaching method*. Retrieved 12 November 2010, from http://unesdoc.unesco.org/images/0013/001319/131996eo.pdf

Sylva, K., Melhuish, E., Sammons, P., Siraj-Blatchford, I., & Taggart, B. (2004). *Effective pre-school provision*. London, UK: Institute of Education.

Sylva, K., Melhuish, E., Sammons, P., Siraj-Blatchford, I., Taggart, B., & Elliot, K. (2003). *The Effective Provision of Pre-School Education (EPPE) project: Findings from the pre-school period*. London, UK: DfES Publications.

Taylor Allen, A. (1988). 'Let us live with our children': Kindergarten movements in Germany and the United States, 1840–1914. *History of Education Quarterly*, 28 (1), 23–48. Retrieved from http://www.jstor.org/stable/368282

Thomson, J., & Smith, A. (1877). *Street life in London.* Retrieved 25 January 2011, from http://www.victorianlondon.org/publications/thomson.htm

Thorndike, L. (1940). Elementary and secondary education in the Middle Ages. *Speculum*, 15, 400–408. Retrieved 18 August 2011, from http://www.jstor.org.eresources.shef.ac.uk/stable/pdfplus/2853459.pdf?accept

Tickell, C. (2011). *The Early Years: Foundations for life, health and learning. An independent report on the Early Years Foundation Stage to Her Majesty's Government.* Retrieved 29 August 2011, from http://outdoormatters.co.uk/wp-content/uploads/2011/04/The-Early-Years-Foundations-for-life-health-and-learning.pdf

Toynbee, P. (28 January 2011). Our children will inherit a far worse legacy than mere debt. *Guardian*, p. 33.

Trabalzini, P. (2003). *Maria Montessori: da Il Metodo a La scoperta del bambino* [Maria Montessori: from The Method to The discovery of the child]. Rome, Italy: Aracne.

Turner, D. A. (1970). *The State and the infant school system,* 18 (2), 151–165. Retrieved 27 August 2011, from http://www.jstor.org/stable/3120306

Underdown, A. (2007). *Young children's health and well-being.* Maidenhead, UK: Open University Press.

United Nations. (1989). *Conventions on the rights of the child.* Retrieved 11 October 2010, from http://www.unicef.org.uk/Documents/Publication-pdfs/crcsummary.pdf?epslanguage=en

Unti, B., & DeRosa, B. (2003). Humane education: Past, present, and future. In D. J. Salem & A. N. Rowam (Eds.), *The State of the Animals II.* Washington, DC: Humane Society Press.

Vag, O. (1975). The influence of the English infant school in Hungary. *International Journal of Early Childhood,* 7 (1), 132–136. Retrieved from http://www.springerlink.com/content/9248527032015273/

Valkanova, Y., & Brehony, K. J. (2006). The gifts and 'contributions': Friedrich Froebel and Russian education (1850–1929). *History of Education*, 35, 189–207. doi:10.1080/00467600500528065

van der Horst, F. C. P. (2011). John Bowlby – From psychoanalysis to ethology: Unraveling the roots of attachment theory. *History of Psychology*, 13, 25–45. doi:10.1037/a0017660

Vaughan, G., & Estola, E. (2007). The gift paradigm and theory. *Educational Philosophy & Theory*, 39, 246–263. doi:10.1111/j.1469-5812.2007.00326.x

Vecchi, V. (2005). *The right to beauty.* Reggio Emilia, Italy: Grafitalia.

Vernon, J. (2005). The ethics of hunger and the assembly of society: The techno-politics of the school meal in modern Britain. *The American Historical Review,* 110 (3), 693–725. Retrieved from http://www.jstor.org/stable/10.1086/ahr.110.3.693

Vygotsky, L. (1962). *Thought and language.* Cambridge, MA: MIT Press.

Walsh, D. J., Chung, S., & Tufekci, A. (2001). Friedrich Froebel. In J. A. Palmer., D. E. Cooper, & L. Breseler (Eds.), *Fifty major thinkers in education: from Confucius to Dewey.* London, UK: Routledge.

Watts, B. (2008). *What are today's social evils? The results of a web consultation.* York, UK: Joseph Rowntree Foundation.

White, H. (2001). The New Education Fellowship: An international community of practice. *New Era in Education* Vol 82 (3) 74. Retrieved 30 March 2013 from: http://www.neweraineducation.co.uk/PDFs/v82n03%20p71-75%20Margaret.pdf

White, S. H., & Buka, S. L. (1987). Early education: Programs, traditions and policies. In E. Z. Rothkopf (Ed.), *Review of research in education* (Vol. 14). Washington, DC: American Educational Research Association.

Wilderspin, S. (1840). *A system for the education of the young.* Retrieved 27 August 2011, from http://babel.hathitrust.org/cgi/pt?id=mdp.39015022627981;page=root;view=image;size=100;seq=1

Wilderspin, S. (1993). *On the importance of educating the young.* London, UK: Routledge/Thoemmes. (Original work published 1824.)

Willan, J. (2009). Revisiting Susan Isaacs – A modern educator for the twenty-first century. *International Journal of Early Years Education,* 17, 151–165. doi:10.1080/09669760902982356

Willan, J. (2011). Susan Isaacs (1885–1948): Her life, work and legacy. *Gender and Education,* 23, 201–210. doi:10.1080/09540253.2011.553822

Williams, L. R. (1994). Developmentally appropriate practice and cultural values: A case in point. In B. L. Mallory & R. S. New (Eds.), *Diversity and developmentally appropriate practices: Challenges for early childhood education.* New York, NY: Teachers College Press.

Williams, R. (1961). *The Long Revolution.* London, UK: Chatto and Windus.

Wilson, E. O. (1984). *Biophilia: The human bond with other species.* Cambridge, MA: Harvard University Press.

Winterer, C. (1992). 'Hothouse system of education': Nineteenth-century early childhood education from the infant schools to the kindergartens. *History of Education Quarterly,* 32 (3), 289–314. Retrieved from http://www.jstor.org/stable/368547

Wood, E., & Attfield, J. (2005). *Play, learning and the early childhood curriculum.* London, UK: Sage Publications.

Woodham-Smith, P. (1952). History of the Froebel Movement in England. In E. M. Lawrence (Ed.), *Friedrich Froebel and English education* (pp. 34–94). London, UK: University of London Press.

Woodhead, M. (1985). Pre-school education has long-term effects: But can they be generalised? *Oxford Review of Education,* 11, 133–155. doi:10.1080/0305498850110202

Wright, F. L. (1957). *A testament.* New York, NY: Horizon Press.

Wylie, W. (2008). *Montessori and the Theosophical Society.* Quest 96(2): 53–55. Retrieved 30 March 2013 from: http://www.theosophical.org/publications/quest-magazine/1409

Zufiaurre, B. (2007). Education and schooling: From modernity to 99postmodernity. *Pedagogy, Culture & Society,* 15, 139–151. doi:10.1080/14681360701403490

INDEX

Adelman, C. 31, 32, 44
Agazzi, C. 86, 90
Agazzi, R. 86, 90
AMI, *see* Association Montessori
    Internationale (AMI)
Animal Welfare Act (2006) 107
anthropology, pedagogical 80
apperception: learning through 31;
    self-activity through 31; self-driven
    activity through 40
Aristotle 5, 9, 11, 13–16, 89; key ideas 10;
    The Nicomachean Ethics 10, 14
arithmetic 38, 40, 41
Arundale, G. 88
Asquith, H. 58
Association Montessori Internationale
    (AMI) 80, 91, 133
Astor, N. 71, 72
attachment theory 72, 73
audio-visual techniques 22

Bacon, F. 22
Barnett, W.S. 74, 133
Bathurst, K. 60
Beacon Hill School 102
Beatty, B. 113, 119, 138
behaviourism 104
Belle Vue School, Bradford 59
Berkeley, University of, Institute of
    Human Development 118
biophilia 67
Bird, W. 67
Birtenshaw Mutual Improvement Society
    95, 96

Blatchford, R. 37, 55, 75, 77
block play, value of 45, 48
Board of Education, Medical Branch 68
Boer War 61
Booth, C. 57
botany 21, 34
Bott Spillius, E. 103, 138
Bourdieu, P. 69, 97
Bowlby, J. 72, 73
brain-imaging technology, neurological
    research with 65
Brehony, K.J. 46, 56, 59, 60, 62, 68, 72,
    74, 89, 98
Brierley, W. 98, 99
British Association for Early Childhood
    Education 5
British Infant School System 37
British Psycho-Analytical Society 99, 100
British Psychological Society, Education
    Section 107
Brown, G. 55, 74; Spending Review
    Statement (2004) 75
Brühlmeier, A. 32
Brunswick, T. 42
Buchanan, J. 37
'Building Gifts' 45
Burt, C. 117

Cambridge Evacuation Study 119, 121
Cambridge University 97, 117
camp schools 122
Carr, M. 121
Casa dei bambini 81, 126, 138
catechism 19

Champkin, J. 56
Charlemagne 16
Charlton, K. 21
Chelsea Open Air Nursery School 117
chemistry 34
child(ren) (*passim*): actively listening to
    128; cognitive development of 113;
    disadvantaged 58, 61, 69, 70, 85, 90;
    earliest years of, importance of 2, 49;
    environment of, importance of (Locke)
    25; holistic development of 126; learning
    of, importance of play in 121; listening
    to, actively 118, 128; natural stages of
    development of 28; nature of 88, 135;
    observations, *see* observations, child;
    play of, importance of 46, 93, 115; rights
    of 76, 90, 118, 125, 126, 128, 133;
    working-class 34, 37, 60, 61, 63, 64, 76
Child Benefit 77
child-centred learning 59, 104
child development 26, 58, 59, 65, 97, 98,
    103, 104, 117, 118, 123
Child Development Department, Institute
    of Education, London 127
child-focused education 133
child-initiated learning 85
child-initiated play 112
child poverty 57, 74, 76
child prostitution 53
child sexual abuse 53
Child Study Associations, New York 118
Child Tax Credit 77
Children Act (2004) 75
Children's Home, Moscow 102
Children's House(s), Italy 81, 82, 86,
    89, 102
children's learning, *see* learning
children's picture book, first illustrated 21
Christian Socialism 58
Cicero 15
'circle time' 39
Clarke, E. 26, 118
Columbia University, New York 132
Comenius, J.A. 5, 16, 28, 44, 62, 81, 89;
    Didactica Magna 21; father of modern
    pedagogy 22; key ideas of 23; legacy of
    22; maternal school 20; *Orbis Pictus: The
    World in Pictures* 21, 22, 23; phases of
    child's development 19–20; School
    of Infancy 20, 22, 23; Universal
    Education 21; Universal Wisdom 21
Compayre, G. 19, 27
compensatory education 69
compulsory school age 119
Congregational Union 56

constructivism 32
Corradini, E. 86
Council of the National Froebel Society 62
critical didactics 85
curriculum, design of (Owen) 36–7

Dahlberg, G. 127
dancing 36, 106
Darlington Teacher Training College 98
Darwin, C. 59, 97, 103
Darwinian theory 62
Darwinism 71, 99
David, T. 85
Davis, N. 34, 117
Daycare Trust 74
delinquency 62
Department of Child Development,
    Institute of Education, London 115, 117
Depretis, A. 79
Descartes, R. 25
De Vries, H. 92
development, child's: phases of (Comenius)
    19–20; stages of 18, 23, 28, 71
    [psychological notion of 65]
developmental psychology 26, 29, 84
Devi, R. 88
Dewey, J. 22, 27, 85, 89, 98, 102, 105,
    111, 119
didactic materials and resources 136
didacticism 93
Dunn, J. 94

Early Child Care Development Education
    (ECCDE), Nigeria 133
Early Head Start 133
Early Years Foundation Stage 2, 3, 13
Early Years Professional (EYP) 124
East End of London: life in 56;
    working-class housing conditions in,
    in late nineteenth to early twentieth
    centuries 55
ECCDE, *see* Early Child Care
    Development Education, Nigeria
ECM, *see* Every Child Matters: Change for
    Children
education (*passim*): as central to
    regeneration of community (Pestalozzi)
    31; child-centric approach to 27; early
    childhood, play-based 2; for peace and
    social justice 90; progressive 85, 89, 102,
    105; as social justice (Pestalozzi) 31;
    starting early, importance of 20–1;
    three principles of (Rousseau) 28–30;
    for under-fives, state-funded 1;
    women's 19

Education Act (1918) 68
Education Act (1986) 13
Education Act (1992) 18
Education (Administrative Provision)
  Act (1907) 60
education for peace, Montessori 90, 91,
  125, 134
Education (Provision of Meals) Act
  (1906) 60
Education Reform Act (1988) 13
Educational Research Councils of Australia
  and New Zealand 118
Edwards, S. 134
Effective Provision of Pre-School
  Education (EPPE) project 46, 75, 123
Elementary Education Act (1870) 60
Elfer, P. 99
Eliot, A.A. 132
ENEF, see English New Education
  Fellowship
English Early Years Foundation Stage 1
  (EYFS) 2–5, 12, 13, 20, 23, 67, 123–7,
  130, 136–8; 'Enabling Environments'
  124; 'Learning and Development' 124;
  play-based 137; 'Positive Relationships'
  124; 'The Unique Child' 124
English New Education Fellowship
  (ENEF) 118
English Socialism, Owen as father of 34
Enlightenment 24, 25
Ensor, B. 92
EPPE project, see Effective Provision of
  Pre-School Education project
ethnography 56, 104
Every Child Matters: Change for Children
  (ECM) 75, 130
evolution, theory of 97
experiential learning 34, 45, 65
EYFS, see English Early Years Foundation
  Stage 1
EYP, see Early Years Professional

Fabian Society 54, 77, 95
facilitator, teacher as 84–5
Fairhurst, S., see Isaacs, S.
feminism 55, 79, 82
Field, F. 75
Findlay, J.J. 98
Fjørtoft, I. 66
Flugel, J.C. 99
FMM, see Franciscan Missionaries of Mary
Forest School movement 138
Forest Schools 123
Foucault, M. 19; 'regime of truth' 5, 122,
  135, 136

Foundation Stage Early Learning Goals and
  Profile 3
Franciscan Missionaries of Mary (FMM) 82
free play 104, 128, 129, 136
Freire, P. 95, 96
French Revolution 29
Freud, S. 27, 99, 102, 103, 126
Froebel, F. 22, 27–8, 63, 65, 70, 85–9;
  block play, value of 45; 'Building
  Gifts' 45; child observations 45; early
  education, importance of 2; *The
  Education of Man* 43, 44, 47, 48;
  gardening activities 46; gifts and
  occupations 45–6, 83; Montessori
  critical of 83; Helba plan 43–4; idea
  of nursery garden 123; ideas on
  child-centred learning and play 59;
  influence of [on Grace Owen 98; on
  Isaacs 102, 105, 119, 120, 126; on Locke
  25; on McMillan sisters 73; on M.
  McMillan 59; on Montessori 80, 90;
  on women pioneers 4, 5, 9, 135];
  influenced by [Comenius 22; Rousseau
  27, 28]; key ideas 48; kindergarten(s) 47,
  51, 87; kindergarten as call to action 47;
  kindergarten movement 42–3; life and
  contributions 42–8; *Mother's Songs,
  Games and Stories* 46, 48; open-air school
  movement, influence on 62; potential
  of play 44; visit to Pestalozzi's Yverdon
  32, 47
Froebel Certificate 72
Froebel Society, National 47, 62

galleried infant schoolroom, Spitalfields
  (Wilderspin) 39
gardening activities 46, 48, 109
Garrick, R. 126
Gass, K. 94
German Kindergarten 42
Gesell, A. 117
gifts and occupations (Froebel) 45–6, 48
Graham, P. 94, 95, 97, 119
Greaves, J.P. 33, 35
Greek city state, rise of 11
Gruener, A. 43

'habitus', concept of 97, 116
Hadow Report 73, 117
half-time system in schooling 58
Hall, S. 71, 114
Hardie, J.K. 54
Head Start, USA 74, 133
Helba plan (Froebel) 43–4
Hendrick, H. 61, 99

Hewes, D.W. 17, 28, 29, 31, 47
Hinchliffe, G. 14
Hopkins, J. 99
Hungary 42
Huss, J. 49
Hustedt, J.T. 74, 133

ILP, *see* Independent Labour Party
imaginative play 93, 110, 111, 113, 120
Independent Labour Party (ILP) 58
industrial revolution 34, 39, 64
innate ideas, Descartes' theory of 25
Institute of Education, London 91, 115–19,
    127; Department of Child Development
    115, 117, 127
Institute of the Formation of Character,
    The 35
Institute of Human Development 118
integrated learning 73
intellectual curiosity 110
International Council of Women, London
    (1899) 78
International Institute of Education 91
Inverness High School and Academy 53
IRBS, *see* Roman Institute of Real Estate
Isaacs, N. 99, 100, 102, 114, 116, 121
Isaacs, S. 1, 2, 15, 36, 47, 90, 112–36;
    care of animals 106–9; contribution to
    early childhood education and effect
    on UK policy 126–7; early career and
    academic studies 95–100; early life
    93–5; experiment, theoretical aspects
    of 100–104; finding out, feelings and
    fantasy 110–11; gardening activities 109;
    Intellectual Growth in Young Children 105,
    114–16; key ideas [adult, role of 128;
    learning environment 129; play 128];
    lasting legacy of 119–21; learning
    environment of 105–6]; legacy of,
    as 'regime of truth' 135–7; life and
    contributions of 93–111; Malting House
    School 104–5 [behaviour guidance
    approach 111–12; move to London
    116–18; NEF Conference tour 118–19;
    New Education Foundation 118;
    The Nursery Years 116; and Piaget
    112–15; *Social Development of the
    Child* 116
Itard, J. 83

Jean-Jacques Rousseau Institute, Geneva,
    Maison des Petits 113, 114, 138
Jena, University of 43
Jenkins, J. 94
Joseph Rowntree Foundation 15

Jowett, F. 58
joy in movement 110

Kaga, Y. 67
Kerr, J. 59, 60, 61
Key Person approach 127
kindergarten(s) (Froebel) 42, 44, 46–8, 51,
    63, 87; as call to action 47
kindergarten movement 42, 51, 102
Klein, M. 103, 112, 126
knowledge, origins and extent of 25
Kramer, R. 80, 84, 87
Krentz, A. 11, 12

La Sapienza the University of Rome 79
laboratory school 98, 117
Lansbury, G. 54
Lathom, J. 33, 35
Lawrence, E. 110
learning (*passim*): through apperception 31;
    child-centred 59, 104; child-initiated
    85; experiential 34, 45, 65; through
    first-hand experiences 26, 29;
    importance of play in 121; integrated 73;
    through senses 21, 22, 26, 29;
    subject-by-subject-based 73; visual aids
    for 21; whole-group 85
learning environment, purpose-built 36
learning space, use of 112, 129
LeBlanc, M. 34
Lega Nazionale per la Protezione dei
    Deficienti (National League for Care and
    Education of Mentally Deficient
    Children) 80
lifelong learning 10, 20; Aristotle 14
literacy 5, 19, 21, 46, 137
Locke, J. 24–7, 30, 59, 62, 88, 96; child's
    environment, importance of 25, *An Essay
    Concerning Human Understanding* 25; key
    ideas 29; *Reflections* 25; *Sensations* 25;
    Some Thoughts Concerning Education 26,
    29; sound mind in sound body 26, 73
Lombardo-Radice, G. 84, 85, 86, 90
London, violent demonstrations
    (mid-1880s) 57
London Day Training College 117
London Dock Strike (1889) 58
London Psycho-analytical Society 99
Løvlie, L. 28
Lowndes, G.A.N. 55, 78
Luria, A. 102
Luther, M. 16, 17–19, 22–4, 28, 49; *Lesser
    Catechism – Luther's Little Instruction Book*
    19; *Letters to the Mayors and Aldermen* 18;
    key ideas of 23

Macfarlane, J. W. 118
Maison des Petits, Jean-Jacques Rousseau
 Institute, Geneva 113, 114, 138
make-believe play 110
Malaguzzi, L. 32, 133
Malting House School, Cambridge 1, 36,
 94, 96, 99, 102–5, 107–13, 116–18,
 121, 126, 127, 135; behaviour guidance
 approach 111–12; care of animals
 106–9; experiment, theoretical
 aspects of 100–4; finding out, feelings
 and fantasy 110–11; gardening
 activities 109
Manchester University 95–9
Manning, J.P. 42, 43, 45, 46
Mansbridge, A. 71, 76
marching 38
Marenholtz-Bulow, B. von 47
Martensson, F. 66
Marx, K. 54
Marxist theory 81
maternal school (Comenius) 20
mathematics 5, 34
May, H. 117, 119
Mayhew, H. 56
Mayo, C. 33
McMillan, M. 1, 2, 26, 47, 78, 79, 90, 93,
 95–8, 105, 127, 133; Bradford years
 58–60; committed to the socialist
 philosophy 54; contribution to early
 childhood education, and UK policy
 122–4; Deptford years 61–2; early life
 53–6; *Education through the Imagination*
 63; key ideas 128–31 [adult, role of 128;
 learning environment 129; play 128];
 lasting legacy 73–6; legacy of, as 'regime
 of truth' 135–7; life and contributions of
 53–77; London years 60–1; *The Nursery
 School* 55, 68, 76, 132; nursery garden
 school 63–71; nursery school as agent
 of change 67–71; open-air camp 62–3;
 see also McMillan sisters
McMillan, R. 1, 2, 26, 47, 78, 95–8,
 105, 127, 133; Bradford years 58–60;
 committed to the socialist philosophy
 54; contribution to early childhood
 education and UK policy 122–4; early
 life 53–6; key ideas 128–31 [adult, role
 of 128; learning environment 129; play
 128]; lasting legacy 73–6; legacy of,
 as 'regime of truth' 135–7; life and
 contributions of 53–77; London years
 60–1; nursery garden school 63–71;
 open-air camp 62–3; Rachel McMillan

Teacher Training College 71–3, 123; *see
 also* McMillan sisters
McMillan sisters: concern for the children
 of poor and working-class families 55,
 57, 74, 98; importance of garden 64; life
 and work 53–76; London Dock Strike
 of 1889 as turning point 58; open-air
 camp 63; Open Air Nursery Schools
 26; parallels with Montessori 78;
 pioneering work in London 2;
 progressive movement within the field
 of early childhood education 2; as
 social reformers 58, 66; views about
 working mothers 96; vision for
 Nursery Centres 124; work in socialist
 movement 58
McMillans' open-air nursery, Deptford 54
Mearns, A. 56, 57
Melanchthon, P. 49
memorising 73
Meux, H. 54, 55
modern movement 27
Mompiano Nursery, Trieste 86
Montesano, G.F. 80
Montessori, Maria 2, 47, 55, 73, 74, 103,
 115, 119, 120, 122, 127, 138; *The
 Absorbent Mind* 88; child having
 freedom to choose 93; Children's House
 81–2; children's rights 125; Comenius's
 influence on 22; concept of early
 childhood education as distinct phase 1;
 constructive social reform 91;
 contribution to early childhood
 education, and effect on UK policy
 124–6; early years 78–80; education
 for peace 90, 91, 125, 134; feminism,
 politics and social medicine 79; freedom
 and structure 89, 124; influence of early
 key thinkers on 32; influenced by
 [Locke 26; Plato, 12; Quintilian, 15;
 Seguin, 59]; key ideas 128–31 [adult,
 role of 128; learning environment 129;
 play 128]; lasting legacy 89–91; legacy
 of, as 'regime of truth' 135–7; life and
 contributions of 78–92; Marxist theory
 81; and Mussolini 87–8; Pedagogical
 Anthropology 80; and progressive
 education 102; scientific pedagogy 83;
 sensory learning, materials for 83;
 social function of mother 82; teacher as
 facilitator 84–5; views about working
 mothers 96
Montessori, Mario 80, 88
Montessori educational communities 133

Montessori equipment 106
Montessori materials 93, 106
Montessori Method 32, 82, 85–7, 109, 133
Montessori rods 106
Moore, G.E. 104
moral education 13, 44
moral reasoning 115
Moscow Institute of Psychoneurology 102
mother(s) (*passim*): role of in early
    education 47, 48; social function of
    (Montessori) 82; vital role of, in earliest
    stages of education 33
music 12, 36, 46, 48, 106
Mussolini, B. 87, 88, 90, 91

NAEYC, *see* National Association for the
    Education of Young Children
NANE, *see* National Association for
    Nursery Education
Napoleonic Wars 32
National Association for the Education of
    Young Children (NAEYC) 132
National Association for Nursery Education
    (NANE) 132
National Childcare Strategy (1998) 3,
    75, 123
National Curriculum 12, 13
National Nursery Examination Board
    (NNEB) 77
nature, concept of, in education 28
NEF, *see* New Education Fellowship (NEF)
Neill, A.S. 102
neurological research with brain-imaging
    technology 65
New Education Fellowship (NEF) 90,
    92, 98; conferences in New Zealand
    (1937) 118, 134
New Education Foundation 118
New Lanark community school 36
New Lanark cotton mills 34, 35
Newnham College, Cambridge 97
NNEB, *see* National Nursery Examination
    Board
nuclear physics 104
numeracy 137
Nunn, P. 104, 117, 118
nursery education (*passim*): fundamental
    aims of 124; in UK 73; universal 68, 73
nursery garden school(s) 63–71, 105
nursery school, as agent of change 67–71
nursery-school movement 72; in USA 132
Nutbrown, C. 1, 11, 31, 51
Nutbrown Report 124
Nuttall, J. 134

Object Lessons 38, 41
observation(s), child 108, 110, 136; Froebel
    44, 45; Isaacs 93, 97, 99, 115, 117, 120,
    126, 127, 134 [Malting House School
    103–7]; McMillan sisters 70–1;
    Montessori 82–3, 130 [methodical
    scientific 89]; Piaget 114
occupations and gifts (Froebel) 45–6, 48
Oelkers, J. 27
Office for Standards in Education (Ofsted)
    3, 18, 137
Ofsted, *see* Office for Standards in
    Education
open air, importance of 26, 63, 64, 68
open-air camp (M. & R. McMillan)
    62–3
open-air nursery garden 54, 63, 66, 67, 70
open-air nursery school, Deptford 63, 117,
    123, 132
open-air nursery schools/nurseries 26, 63,
    68, 69, 70, 73, 122
outdoor environments, use of, in early
    childhood education, 67
outdoor learning 37, 73, 122
outdoor play 66, 123, 128; value of 123
outdoor play areas, importance of 66
Owen, G. 98
Owen, R. 32, 40–2, 59, 65, 70, 98, 124:
    'The Application of the Principle to
    Practice' 35; design of curriculum 36–7;
    as father of English Socialism 34;
    Institute of the Formation of Character,
    The 35; key ideas 40; life and work
    34–7; 'A New View of Society, or
    Essays on The Principle of the
    Formation of the Human Character' 35,
    37, 41; parenting classes 37; Pestalozzi's
    influence on 35, 38; purpose-built
    learning environment 36

Pacey, M. 3
Paper, E. 92
Parekh, A. 67, 75
parenting, poor, effects of (Quintilian) 15
parenting classes (Owen) 37
Parker, F.W. 85
Pasquali, P. 87
Payne, W.H. 19
pedagogical anthropology 80
pedagogy: as form of play, anticipatory (or
    proactive) socialisation 12; fundamental
    principles of experimental sciences
    applied to 82; modern, Comenius as
    father of 22

Pestalozzi, J.H. 22, 41, 42 62, 102, 113; Comenius's influence on 22; creating self through play 44; education as social justice 31; experiential learning 45; *How Gertrude Teaches Her Children* 32, 40; influence of [on Froebel 43, 44, 47; on Isaacs 98; on McMillan sisters 59, 60, 65; Montessori 80, 90; on Owen 35, 38; on Wilderspin 38; on women pioneers 5]; influenced by, Rousseau 27; key ideas 40; *Leonard and Gertrude* 31, 40; life and work of, 30–4; Model School in Frankfurt 43; reflective practice 71; reforming society position 28

Pestalozzi Institute, Yverdon 31–4, 43, 47

Pestalozzi method 31–2

Pestalozzi Model School, Frankfurt 43

Petrarca, F. 17

phrenology 62

physical drill, regimented 39

physical games 12

physical punishment 26, 29

physics 34

Piaget, J. 27, 84, 102, 112–17

Piagetian psychology 115

Plato 4, 5, 9–15, 21, 27, 49, 59, 88; early childhood education, suggested design for 12; key ideas 10; *Republic* 10, 11 [as greatest treatise on education 12]; state as educator 12–13

play: free-flow, self-directed 126; potential of, Froebel 44; structured guided 42, 48; value/importance of 16, 21, 116, 120, 126, 134 [in children's learning 121]; as vehicle for learning 13

Playcentre movement, New Zealand 134

Plutarch 98

Pollard, A. 13

Popper, K. 12, 88

positivism 81, 83

Poskoff, P. 17

Pramling-Samuelsson, I. 67

Preyer, W. 71

primary-school playground 70

printing press revolution 18–19

progressive education 85, 89, 102, 105

Progressive Education Movement, USA 132

psychoanalysis 99, 100–4

psychoanalytical theory(ies) 101–3, 126

psychology 26, 29, 84, 96–100, 102, 104, 113

Pyke, G. 101, 111, 116

Pyke, M. 102

Quintilian 5, 9–11, 14–15, 17, 89; *De Institutio Oratori* 10, 15; key ideas 10

Rachel McMillan Teacher Training College 71–3, 123

Rank, O. 99

reading 14, 38, 40, 41

Reale Scuola Technica Michelangelo Buonarroti 79

reflective learning 40; Pestalozzi 32

reflective practice 71

Reggio Emilia Approach to early childhood education 32, 36, 90, 127, 133

'regime of truth' (Foucault) 5, 122, 135, 136

religious education 38

research methodology 98

Rinaldi, C. 36, 90, 133, 134

risk-averse society 34, 67, 137

Risorgimento 81, 87

Robb, F. 13

Rogoff, B. 88

Roman Institute of Real Estate (IRBS) 81

rote learning 26, 29, 37, 44, 73, 105

Rousseau, J.-J. 19, 35, 61, 62, 83; Comenius's influence on 22; committed to child's nature 27, 64, 88; Emile: or on Education 27, 29, 30; influence of [on Froebel 44; on Isaacs 105; on McMillan sisters 59; on Montessori 80, 90; on Owen 38; on women pioneers 5]; influenced by [Locke, 25; Plato 12]; key ideas 29; life and work 27–9; and progressive education 102; three principles of contemporary education 28–30; time and space 28

Royal Society for the Prevention of Cruelty to Animals (RSPCA) 107

RSPCA, *see* Royal Society for the Prevention of Cruelty to Animals

Ruggles Street Nursery School, Roxbury, MA, USA 132

Ruskin, J. 64

Russell, B. 102

Rutherford, E. 104

Sageie, J. 66

Sanitary Institute 58

Sayle, A. 69

Schmidt, V. 102

school meals 59, 60, 73

school medical inspections 59, 73

School of Infancy (Comenius) 20, 22, 23

schooling: half-time system 58; regulation
    of (Luther) 18; universal 31, 71
science 13, 38, 43, 57, 71, 83
scientific attitude to life 110
Scuola Magistrale Ortofrenica 80
SEAL 131
Seguin, E. 59, 83
self-activity through apperception 31
sensory learning, materials for
    (Montessori) 83
sensory training 28, 29, 59, 129
sex education 108
sex and relationship education (SRE) 108
Shaw, G.B. 54
singing 36, 38
Smith, A. 56
Smith, R. 11
Smith Hill, P. 132
social deprivation 67, 73
social exclusion 74, 75, 76
Social Party of the Child 22, 90
social pedagogy, Pestalozzi's influence
    on 33
social reform, constructive 91
social science of poverty measurement 57
socialisation, anticipatory (or proactive),
    pedagogy as (Plato) 12
Socrates, formative influence of, on
    Plato 11
Soëtard, M. 30, 31, 32
sound mind in sound body 29; Locke 26
Spielrein, S. 102
Spitalfields, galleried infant schoolroom at
    (Wilderspin) 39
SRE, see sex and relationship education
Standish, P. 28
state as educator (Plato) 12–13
Stead, W.T. 53
Steedman, C. 53, 68, 78
Stellway, H. 91
storytelling 12
subject-by-subject-based learning 73
Summerhill School 102
Swedish curriculum 127
Sylva, K. 37, 46, 75, 123

tabula rasa, child's mind as, at time of birth
    25, 96
Talamo, E. 81
teacher as facilitator 84–5
Theosophical Society 88
Te Whāriki 134–5
Third Lateran Council (1179) 16
Thirty Years' War 21

Thomson, J. 56, 77
Tickell, C. 3, 4
Tickell Report 3
truancy 62
tuberculosis 62

UK Sure Start Children's Centres 40, 69,
    74, 75, 123, 130, 133
unconscious phantasy, concept of 103
UNCRC, see United Nations Convention
    on the Rights of the Child (UNCRC)
UNESCO, see United Nations Education,
    Scientific and Cultural Organization
United Nations Convention on the Rights
    of the Child (UNCRC) 22, 66, 118,
    125, 130
United Nations Educational, Scientific and
    Cultural Organization (UNESCO) 90,
    91, 125, 133
Unity of Brethren 20, 49
Universal Education (Comenius) 21
universal nursery education 68, 73
universal schooling 31, 71
Universal Wisdom (Comenius) 21
University College, London 99

Vygotsky, L. 102, 115, 120

wartime evacuation, effects of, on
    children 119
Watson, J. 104
welfare state 61
Welsh Foundation Phase 67
Whitehead, A.N. 11
whole-group learning 85
Wilderspin, S. 37, 38–41, 42, 44, 60;
    galleried infant schoolroom at Spitalfields
    38, 39; On the Importance of Educating the
    Infant Poor from the Ages of Eighteen
    Months to Seven Years 38, 41; key ideas
    40; Object Lessons 38, 41; school
    playground 39; use of outdoor space 70
Williams, L.R. 136
Wilson, E.O. 67
Wise, U., see Isaacs, S.
Women Sanitary Inspectors' and Health
    Visitors' Association 69
Women's Industrial Council, Liverpool 59
Workers' Educational Association 99, 100
working-class children 34, 37, 60, 61, 63,
    64, 76
working-class housing conditions, London,
    in late-nineteenth to early twentieth
    centuries 55

workplace nursery, first (Owen) 35–6
World War I 1, 68, 85, 99, 134
World War II 56, 88, 119
Wright, F.L. 45, 46
writing 40, 41

Zone of Proximal Development (Vygotsky)
115
zoology 21, 34